GOD BLESS THE GRASS:
Studies in Helping Children Grow in Self-Esteem

By Robert E. Newman

PALO ALTO, CALIFORNIA

Published By

R & E RESEARCH ASSOCIATES, INC.

936 Industrial Avenue

Palo Alto, California 94303

Library of Congress Card Catalog Number

81-51213

I. S. B. N.

0-88247-601-7

To my father in remembrance of
those times when he showed me
how the grass was growing through,
in his life.

Syracuse University

God bless the grass*
that grows through the crack.

They roll the concrete over it
and try to keep it back.

The concrete gets tired
of what it has to do,

It breaks and it buckles
and the grass grows through,

God bless the grass.

  ... ...

God bless the grass
that grows through cement.

It's green and it's tender
and it's easily bent,

But after a while
it lifts up its head,

For the grass is living
and the stone is dead,

And God bless the grass.

*by Malvina Reynolds, with permission.
(From the lyrics of "God Bless the Grass"
sung by Pete Seeger in the album, Banks
of Marble... (Folkways Records FTS 31040).

INTRODUCTION

I first heard Malvina Reynolds' song <u>God Bless the Grass</u> when Pete Seeger sang it. There was something there that seemed to express my experience so well - the recognition that the naturally loving, capable and keenly expressive self which each of us is at birth is soon covered over and neutralized as the dominant force in our growth. This covering of this real-from-birth self is done particularly well in our elementary schools in spite of many parents and school people who want it otherwise but who unwittingly participate in what the schools are doing. The song's lyrics also express what I have learned - that this essential reality in each of us at birth is a tough as well as a lovely and capable persisting power that can't be denied; with sensitively aware schooling and parenting it can be one's dominant life guide and thus the basis for the deepest kind of self-esteem. This is a self-esteem derived from appreciating how one's life is in tune with one's strong and beautiful essences.

These realizations first came to me when I began teaching in my one-room country school and then in a graded school. I began to sense the natural me as the children in my classes let me know what they enjoyed and respected in me. Then when my daugthers came into my life this natural self came through to me with vividness.

I could not have written this book before my daughters, Dusty and Robin, were born. Through Dusty and Robin I saw the neat me that was born with all sorts of inventiveness, sensitivity, lovableness, with a wonder and delight about the crinkly shape of the leaf that the three of us might enjoy on the way to the library on Saturday morning. It was as if the neat me had been under wraps before I sensed how Robin and Dusty were in touch with it - even though it sometimes broke out with the persistence of grass making and finding cracks in the concrete. And largely because of our easy love - Robin's, Dusty's, and mine, - I had the courage to begin work with others to establish the small elementary school where most of the action in this book takes place; where I've learned so much that is presented in these pages.

Dusty and Robin were (and are) on such a satisfying two-way street for me. They gave (and give) so much, so easily, to me; I find myself smiling warmly when I think of how much I have been enjoying what I gave (and give) to them. I gave to Robin and Dusty the kind of nurturing that helped them stay in touch with that to which I was reawakening.

During the time when Robin, Dusty and I were growing up, I was moved to work with teachers and in schools to bring about the growing of children and teachers on this same two-way street. I found ways for teachers to come close to the lovely power in each child with whom they were working; I found ways to help teachers share their own real-from-birth selves with each child. I showed teachers and children by my example what it might be like if they all could grow in tune with their natural birthrights - what it might be like to feel self esteem built solidly on this awareness.

This book is my attempt to present all this to parents and to their children's teachers. To make the book useful and clear I have chosen to address most of it to elementary school teachers - the people with whom I work. I hope, in this way to make my points for parents and at the same time provide a practical way for parents and teachers to influence schooling.

Robert E. Newman

Syracuse, N.Y. 1978

TABLE OF CONTENTS

Author's note about the identity of the
people you will read about in this book:

I speak of many people in this book. It's all true. In giving
their permissions the major characters (like Rob, in Chapter V)
and/or their parents told me that I need not change anything.
I felt more comfortable with changing all the children's names,
however. To protect the identity of some people when I speak
of their distress, I've often drawn one person, like Sean in
Chapter III or Rocky in Chapter VII, as a composite of the behavior of several people and changed the non-essentials of the
settings.

                    R.E.N.

PROLOGUE: HOW, WHERE, AND WHY THIS ALL CAME ABOUT

I was just finishing breakfast on a summer Wednesday morning. The phone rang. Dusty, my eight-year-old daughter, told me it was Susan Manes wanting to talk with me.

"Hello, Bob, I just had to call you before I got cold feet. You know, Sidney (Susan's husband and a lawyer) read in the paper that the City wants to sell a firehouse on the North Side. What about starting our school there? Sidney could check it out today."

I remember my uneasy reaction. It was one of feeling all sorts of doubt. ...feelings of how I might let down my friends who looked to me to lead them in setting up a schooling that we all had spent hours talking about. And feelings of not wanting to add all that work and hassle... On the other hand I felt myself smiling as I was in touch with Susan Manes' easy courage and enthusiasm. Then, as I turned over the idea later that day, a kind of measured excitement began to replace fear as I thought about Dusty and Robin - my eight- and six-year-old children. I wanted for them the kind of elementary schooling that Susan and I had been talking about. Dusty, in her present inner-city elementary school, seemed to be withdrawing, feeling intimidated by children trying to act super-adequate - big and tough; Robin appeared to be bored in the same school as she was trying to please the first grade teacher in a "hurry up and wait" kind of scene for her, where she was catching on to reading faster than the others. As I called Susan back and told her to go ahead with finding out about the firehouse, my thoughts began to turn more and more to our vision of what elementary schooling just might be in America today. Yes, doing this - setting up our own school - was something that I could commit myself to. Doing something tangible, as opposed to just talking about what should be, was an important next step for me - important enough so that I could take the fearful-for-me risk of failing right out in front of my colleagues in the University's School of Education where I was a professor; ...right in front of parents and teacher friends who felt that my ideas made sense to them. Yes, it was worth it.

What was worth it? What was the vision we had? We had a vision of a schooling where we would set right what was wrong. We wanted a school where teachers listened sensitively to each child as a matter of course - as the basic fabric from which teachers' actions grew. We wanted teachers and children to enjoy keenly the unique ways that each was living out her or his inborn warmth, inventiveness, curiosity, fascinations and sense of humor. And we wanted to help children who were frustrating the assertion of some of their delightful humanness - help them help themselves get around these self-imposed roadblocks.

I had some practical ideas about organizing for learning and individualizing that would allow this to get underway in the right directions. Susan had tried these out in her two-and-one half years in the field-based Enabling Teacher Education Program I directed. Our vision and commitment grew from Susan's and my years as parents, my beginning teaching in that one-room school in the California back country, my experience teaching second and sixth grades in a suburban school; Susan's experience teaching fourth grade in an inner city city school; my growth as elementary school principal at the University of Chicago Laboratory Schools.

I was committed to a public education acting on the charge of making respect for the individual person its distinguishing characteristic; public education which then would be the wellspring for a society that could be responsive to each citizen who was educated in its schools. I didn't see the public schools doing that. I didn't see this happening to my own children or to others' children. Instead I saw a public education paying lip service to helping each child to be the uniquely splendid person he or she could be. In reality I had found that public school leaders were forced to do the best that they could do to try to make a hodgepodge organization work efficiently - an organization that had grown from long forgotten happenstances and expediencies. I saw educational leaders working long hours with no significant time or energy even to begin to consider what it might mean to have schooling which might help my children draw increasingly from their loving warmth, their magnificent intouchness with the lovely sound of a raindrop, their easy chuckle, the intricate thinking and inventiveness I saw in their art work, in their fresh-thinking intelligent questioning. I felt and saw all this come into the world when my children were born. I knew it was there in my children and in all our children.

I had learned that in reality public schools were bureaucracies where the needs of the "system," as opposed to needs of each child, dictated action; where good thoughts and well-intentioned workers were frustrated.

I knew I wanted a place where children would learn without being managed by the threat of restimulating deep-down old fears of "I'm not all right" anxiety - the fears that each child had tried to protect herself or himself from since infancy; the fears that frustrated the healthy natural assertation of one's unique real self. I didn't, however, know and understand the dynamics of this as I do today. Much of what I learned, I learned as Susan and I carried out the schooling that came to be known as the SIEE School (the Syracuse Institute for Enabling Education School).

We began the school in the basement of the Syracuse YWCA, downtown, with eighteen children. The school now enrolls fifty-five children, and is housed in a large center-city church building.

The school became the setting for the studies of children we shall be discussing in this book. We organized so that the school would revolve around what teachers heard as they listened to children with heightened sensitivity and as they helped children to understand and "hear" the teachers' needs. I had learned that if children were learning in a way that reinforced their feelings of being adequate people, that involved their growing feelings of humanness, they could learn faster and with far less mindless routine drill. This knowledge, translated into practical day-to-day school atmosphere, gave us more time - time for children to express their feelings in the visual as well as the language arts, for example. This, in turn, gave us time to listen to children as we helped them explore the exciting and taboo-filled adult world. Then, too, we began a schooling that introduced books and reading to children as something that gave them feelings of capability and enjoyment as opposed to exercises to be done for teacher's approval. We began using ways I had worked out to teach writing and reading so that children could approach it as an expression of their feelings and others' feelings; so that children could learn the beginning reading fundamentals through games that would help them to be on their own in reading in a relatively short time.

As we began I was growing fast in my understanding of how to put all of this together so that children would sense clear boundaries that would help them make predictions about what will happen when and if... I felt I had learned how to guide such a school smoothly as I kept a close one-to-one relationship with each staff person - listening to him or her and helping him or her to listen to me.

In this school I wanted each staff person to be there because she or he felt this to be a place where he or she was getting an education as well as giving one. This was the theme of the Enabling Teacher Education Program where Susan and I had come to know each other a few years before, working in suburban and inner city schools. I wanted each teacher-to-be, in that program, to try out for herself or himself an education that was individualized around each person's uniquenesses. We exchanged our feelings and thoughts in weekly journals which I kept with each student in the program, and in bi-weekly one-to-one conferences. These people tried out for themselves an education which was designed to help them learn to manage their own time, to make their own contacts with principals in the field, to find out for themselves what a particular child needed, to move ahead in reading, to... My role was to support people in doing this.

I felt sure that if I listened to each person in the Program with the sensitivity that brought me close to the enjoyableness and strength in each person, and if I helped each of them to listen to herself or himself, then my decisions and leadership would take us in the right directions.

I found myself doing far more than "listening." I found myself helping people in a great many ways to accept and deal with their fears. ...the fear of listening to each child in those threatening groups of children in an inner city school - those groups that the teacher was supposed to manage; ...the fear of thinking for themselves and defining problems for themselves, instead of following their ingrained tendency to want to know what I, their teacher, wanted them to go out and do and how they could please me; ...the fear of getting in touch with the hurting under their angry and defeated feelings; in short, the fears they felt whenever they got close to those old uneasy "I'm not all right" feelings that had been laid down in them by well-meaning adults when they were children.

I found myself doing much of this support while being supported myself in handling the fear that I felt - the same kind of fear that I sensed in the teacher-to-be - fear of fear itself. Someone was listening to me as I was listening to the students - helping me to "hear" the "I'm just fine" real me that was there at my birth and had persistently asserted itself all through my life even though my own self image was well conditioned by the fearful "I'm not adequate" theme playing deep down below my level of consciousness.

As I look back at my own life and the lives of others, like those in our Enabling Teacher Education Program, I realize two things. First, how much of my life was oriented so that I could avoid feeling that load of fearful "I'm not all right" music that was playing down deep inside; and second that all this time the real me, the adequate, loving and capable me, was acting on my life - like grass persistently growing through cracks in the concrete pavement (in this case the concrete pavement of behavior patterns I had adopted to avoid coming close to that fear down there).

Much of this book is about helping children to move out, in touch with guidance from the lovely, completely adequate, and capable real person that we parents can see so clearly when we experience our newborn children. Much of the book is about supporting children so they can handle their fear of fear itself. But this book might be sobering as it shows how long it takes, usually, to help people change ingrained ways - habitual behavior patterns that at one time (usually when we were small children) helped us to avoid the hurt of experiencing fear but later just got in the way of acting on our real-self direction. I hope that this book, at the same time, will celebrate the persistent energy of the natural, strong but tender real self "grass" inside as it seeks to guide our behavior.

> "God bless the grass that grows
> through the cracks..."

CHAPTER 1

JIM, PINA, PEDRO, AND MARIAN

How the naturally lovely and capable self comes through when we
listen and come close to children and their parents in the
intervue.

I hope that your reading of the prologue has given you a feel for the SIEE
School where so much of the action that you will participate in takes place.
But this is not a book about the school, as interesting as that might be. It
is a book about how parents and teachers can help children build their self
esteem as they appreciate and develop the natural capability and lovliness with
which they were born.

I hope that when you read the prologue, you felt introduced to me. I'll
be leading you through this book as we come close to the natural essences in
child after child, in some of their parents, in me.

So let's begin now by discussing our natural capability and lovliness -
our real selves. Think of a child shortly after birth. (I'm thinking of one
of my daughters.) My first picture is of my child when she was just a few
weeks old. Here is a tiny person who hasn't learned to deny any of her real
self. I can marvel at this person's sensitive awareness of a branch outside
her window as the slight breeze moves it one way and its inner strength always
seems to bring it back to just where it was. I can feel her trusting and loving
warmth when she sleeps in my arms as I rock back and forth; and I can feel my
own warmth and loving so easily and so undiluted as I gently support her head
on my chest. I sense how this child seems to know that she is just fine -
enjoys knowing easily how much you like her; she doesn't feel inadequate, doesn't
seem to have a residual of angry fearful feelings from old frustrations, old
hurts. Why? Well, for one thing, she spontaneously lets out that anger, the
fear, those hurting feelings as they come to her awareness. She crys, when
she feels the hurt; she shakes when she feels the cold tension of fear; she
sweats and spontaneously moves as she reacts to her increased metabolic rate
that is helping her to "get it out." And we can delight with this child as
she laughs, smiles - lets out her happiness in being - in feeling the love and
warmth around her, of enjoying her sensitive awareness, her playful quirky self,
her acceptance of living in a world where she can let her needs be known and
where there are people who will respond; in living in a world where she can
enjoy the ways she can meet others' needs for love and warmth by just being her
loving self.

Then as she grows up we can see and celebrate how capable this child is;
how, for instance, she learns the tens of thousands of sounds and subtle ges-
tures that make up communicating and does much of it in just a few months. We
marvel at her inventiveness as she puts the elements of her world together in
ways that just never occurred to us - fun, quirky, but logical and sensible.
"Look what I can do...!" as she so easily and openly enjoys herself, is proud
of herself. And her putting-things-together for herself curiosity - that clear
desire to <u>know</u> that is tied to her fascination and enjoyment of her world.

The lovely and capable <u>real-from-birth self</u> - yes it's really not all that
difficult to understand and to know when we see it in young children. But is
this an over idealized picture? What about the "Terrible Twos," infant ornry-
ness, and all the other distress, fear and interpersonal conflict that we see
so often between adults and children, between children and children, apparently

within children themselves? We can't deny this. We see it all around us. We feel the residual effects of sometimes intense anguish - distress - as it is restimulated in our adult lives.

I hope that I can be quite direct here, about my assumption. I am intentionally trying to draw a clear cut distinction for you between the real-from-birth self and what becomes not the real self but a chronic frustration of the real-from-birth self to one extent or another in all our lives. This book is about helping children (and ourselves?) to affirm their real selves, to draw self-esteem from the sense of how their real-from-birth selves are coming through in their day-to-day lives. This book is about helping children to help themselves take continuing direction from this perfect core in them. First we are going to enjoy the real selves in several children and a parent; then, by contrast we shall discuss examples in children's lives of how some of the behavior guided by the real self can be frustrated and some of the effects of this damage. These examples and others in this book will illustrate, also, how this thwarting of the real self never seems to be complete - the real self "grass" always seems to grow through the "cracks in the concrete" of real-self defeating behavior. Then, further in the book, I shall enjoy telling you about how my real self has manifested itself in my life despite the roadblocks; next I'll try to develop a theoretical frame-of-reference about how so much of this frustration of the real self comes about. All through the book I'll show you how I find myself coming close to the real-from-birth selves in children and adults as we share in what I call the intervue. I'm spelling it "intervue" to emphasize that we are not talking of the usual "interview." The intervue I'm speaking of is a special time when both the teacher and the child can share and enjoy their real-from-birth selves. This is at the other side of the world from the usual interview which puts the interviewer in a superior position with the interviewee who is trying to appear adequate and full of self-confidence. "How did I do?" is the interviewee's usual feeling at the end. I have developed the intervue over the years and use it with each child in our SIEE School as an integral part of our child-study program. You will be reading writeups from many of my intervues. All through the book I'll attempt to explain why I am doing what you will be reading about in these intervues. When you get toward the end of the book perhaps you will want to try the intervue with children yourself. I'll give you specific suggestions for doing this in Chapter VIII.

Now I want to try to help us both share a sense of being close to that real-person center in a few of the children I intervue with at our school. You will be reading in this chapter about children who were feeling the clear guidance from their real-from-birth selves in much of their lives. You will be reading about what this felt like to me as I intervued with them and one of their parents. You will also be involved with us at school as we moved to support these children in taking guidance from their real-person centers. You will not be reading about children who were far out of touch with guidance from their just-fine real selves. You will be reading about children whom I find in abundance in our schools; children whose lives are not far out of line with the clear right direction from their real-from-birth selves; children who, like ourselves, can benefit so much from a nurturing that helps us control the habits that have grown to prevent us from taking guidance from our real-from-birth selves.

In this chapter I'll try to bring you with me as I intervue with these people; as I try to move each of us close to our real-from-birth selves and to the real self center in the other person.

Come with me, then, when I intervue with people from our school community. First, let me introduce you to Jim. He entered at the beginning of our school's third year. Jim was the oldest boy in his group. He was ten at the time. My first intervue with Jim was after he was in the school for two months. He talked about his wanting to leave his former school which some people described as a place where children decide what to do and when to do it. Jim described his reasons for wanting to come to our school in quite pragmatic terms:

Jim: I came to SIEE* because I didn't do any work at the Syracuse Free School. We have a regular schedule here at SIEE. At the Free School kids play all day. If you didn't do any work nothing happened. Nobody has to do things. But on Mondays we had creative writing. That you HAVE to do but only if you signed up. So really it's if you want to. Math is every day if you want to.

REN**:You mean to say that you didn't have to do ANYTHING you didn't want to?

Jim: Well, yes, I didn't have to do anything but sometimes a teacher would say, "How about if you and I do some math today." I always did this with a teacher when she said this.

I kept telling my mom during the year that all I did was play - not much work, so we decided to come here.

REN: Why didn't you just ask the teachers at the Free School for more work to do?

Jim: Because other kids are playing and you... they distract you. Like when kids are lassoing each other you say, "I'm going to do this work later" and you join them. Then later you don't get around to it.

REN: Well, then, why didn't you go to Ed Smith School (the neighborhood public school)?

Jim: I feel that Ed Smith is too hard for me. Also there is not as nice a teacher there and I wouldn't do as much creative things.

From the beginning, as you just read. Jim seemed to know what he needed and what he wanted - that he was, at the core, just fine. He seemed to let other people know where he was and yet his needs for attention apparently were well enough satisfied so that others felt comfortable - didn't seem to feel that he was asking for too much. He fitted in easily, with others understanding him and letting him know their needs.

During his first year, Susan Manes, his teacher, had worked to help him accept that he had normal aptitude for learning to read and write as well as for other academics. He came to our school feeling "behind" in these skills and apparently had some surface doubts about his adequacy, academically, as he became aware of being behind schedule. With his characteristic straightforward-ness, he asked for reassurance often as he did his academics. For example, in a complicated math problem he would often check with the teacher each step of the way.

During his second year at our school, staff people seemed to sense that much of his real-self confidence in his adequacy - his academic ability in this case - had reasserted itself but he continued to need step-by-step reassurance

---

*Syracuse Institute for Enabling Education School - the small elementary school Susan Manes and I started.
**Robert E. Newman

from teachers. So we found ourselves shifting from helping him deal with a major roadblock to taking direction from his real-self (not feeling clearly his just-fine capability) to wanting to help him by keeping in tune with him as he moved to assert the intensive inquiring sensitivity that welled up from the real-person center of his being. Here's the writeup of my second intervue with Jim, in October of his second year at our school:

Intervue with Jim Haroldson

I contacted Jim in his room and we went upstairs into the sanctuary* on our way to the foyer. As soon as we opened the door to the sanctuary, Jim said something like "WOW, hey I really like this!!" He said it in kind of a hushed voice. I asked him more about his feelings and he said that this was like some of the churches that they had visited in England.

Jim: Those are neat boots. (as he points to my sheepskin-lined snow boots. We both were seated on the rug. I had taken off my boots.)

REN: I'm having a hard time switching gears. I just had a super talk with Mio about making the art room into an "awareness workshop" which she would have. This would be place where people really feel like getting in touch with feelings and expressing them with some art materials, tools, color or in writing or enjoy the feelings of others through books, visiting people who are good at expressing themselves a certain way... Wow. It really excites me.

Jim: I haven't been doing much art lately because I've been doing so much work - I feel bad about that. I like doing drawing - three dimensional things - things that I can see, feel, and... Things with shape. Pottery, triangles, sculptures. I paint a little; draw.

REN: What does "academic work" mean?

Jim: It means math workbooks, writing projects, etc.

If there was more time to school - like if we went until 5:00 in the afternoon, then I could do art for about three hours. Not three hours, maybe, but for quite a long time.

Others play and things like that but when there's nothing much to do I like to do art.

(He kept sitting up as he was sitting on the rug, turning and looking into the sanctuary).

You know, I like the way that everything is so sort of neat there in the sanctuary. Sort of prim. What does "prim" mean anyway?

REN: Well, it means that everything is kind of stiffly in it's place; the expression is that things are "prim and proper."

---

*The school now was renting space in a large urban church.

4

Jim: No, that's not what I mean. I mean it's just like everything is in rhythm
      in that room. If a squizzle is on top of one piece, a squazzle will be on
      top of the next, and so on.

REN: Jim, will you go in that room, look around, then close your eyes and see
      what else comes to you about why you like that room?

      (he did that and came back)

Jim: I don't know - I really like it. Well, there is something about vastness
      - bigness. It's a place for very elegant people but it doesn't seem like
      it can be for elegant people because everybody goes to church.

REN: Wow. That's really a profound thing that you just said.

Jim: What does "profound" mean?

REN: Well, "profound" means what you say cuts right through to wisdom. You
      are saying something that others could do well to think about.

      Yes, all of that in there makes people feel in the presence of elegance -
      special, bigger and more important than they were before they came in.
      Huh...?

Jim: Yes, fit for a god.

      (Jim was whistling now picking up his coat sleeve and twisting it.)

REN: Well, let's see. Oh yes we haven't gotten to the Giant Memory Machine
      question yet - the machine that needs to know the specific memories that
      you don't want it to take away?

Jim: Yes. I don't want to forget the time my brother and father had a water
      fight and I was in it. Somehow me and my brother got into a water fight.
      The tub had old bathwater in it. There was a pail near the tub. Bill my
      brother, lifts me into the tub with all my clothes on. I pull him into
      the water too - he had his clothes on too. My father dumped a pail of
      water on us both and then he got all wet too.

      Oh sure, sometimes the water in the bathtub stays for quite a while. Some-
      times we use the bath water and really don't get it very dirty. We leave
      it for someone else and then we forget it. It gets cold then.

      I really love Bill. He's sixteen. I like to play around with him and he
      likes to play around with me. He'll teach me. We'll play games (checkers,
      and things like that). He'll wrestle with me. He's altogether very nice.

      Do I argue? Well, Patty my sister, and Bill sometimes argue against me
      and my father and then my mother comes in on my side.

REN: What do you need in this world, Jim? Something like money?

Jim: I tell you what I'd like to be - sort of like a wild man who lives in a
      tree. Like if a human starts hunting a deer with a gun I'd jump on him
      and eat him - stamp on his head and pull out his eyes - I'd be so angry

5

because a deer is really a nice thing. It's so stupid to fight with a gun; not fair to kill a nice pleasant deer.

Well, I wouldn't kill the hunters. I'd really beat them up.

I'd live there in the wild all my life - like a squirrel or a monkey.

REN: Wouldn't that be lonely - without your friends?

Jim: Friends? I wonder. I don't like the idea of killing people. Today I saw a dead cat. I told Karl about the cat because it looked to me just like his cat and he had been missing his cat. I told Karl about the cat but you know, when I did I smiled!! And because of that he didn't believe me. The cat had white paws and blackish ears. Well, me and Sam took it out of the street. We picked it up with twigs.

Like if those wolf hunters are up in a helicopter shooting the poor wolves down there. I'd really get even with them. That's how I feel.

REN: How would you eat, out there in the wild?

Jim: I'd eat the person I killed just for the meat.

REN: Would you miss Hanukkah?

Jim: Why I'm doing this, is that wild life needs to grow. Later there won't be any. There are too many humans. It's violent - all this I've been saying, I know, but I think it should be done once in a while.

REN: Are you angry about another thing?

Jim: Yes, at my sister once in a while because like in the night she stays up until 1:00 doing homework and the light shows over the partition into my room. She'll never turn it off.

REN: Can you tell me more about that?

Jim: Well, why can't she read in the living room? There is a whole living room there with no one in it - so I can sleep.

Mr. Newman, do you think humans are overpowering animals?

REN: Wow, Jim, I think of that book JULIE AND THE WOLVES - where the hunters shot the wolves from the airplane. Robin (my ten-year-old daughter) and I just finished it.

REN NOTE: I began to cry with the feelings from the book, Robin, and with my special feelings about Jim. The book had a sequence in it where these ex-jocks were flying around in an airplane killing wolves - wolves who had accepted the girl Julie into their way of life and helped her to survive and experience love among them. I didn't quite get to the point where tears were coming down my cheeks. I found myself holding back - wondering about the effect this would have on Jim.

Jim: What time is it?

REN: Jim, how did you feel about my almost crying - starting to cry?

Jim: I was a little shocked. I've never seen my father cry. He almost crys
      when he gets really angry, though.

      Sometimes I really feel like crying - like when things are mean to animals.
      Like some stupid guy comes in with a machine gun... Like when someone
      starts shooting...

      Wow. You've written eleven pages (on my notepad).

REN: Yes, eleven pages and it was really worth it. Now would you tell me one
      thing about Jim Haroldson that is special?

Jim: One thing about Jim Haroldson that's special is that I know quite a bit
      about birds and wild things - like I was walking on a path and I can spot
      things to eat and I know and can see them.

REN: Yes, and what pops into my mind is a beautiful sensitive intensity about
      you and in what you say. I find myself completely attentive to what you
      are saying and feeling. You provide all I need, to give you my complete
      attention. It pulls me right to you.

      REN NOTE: I jotted down something like this when I left: Jim seems
      to be so beautifully sensitive and aware. I wonder where can he
      feel safe enough and supported enough to express all this intensity
      that he apparently felt safe enough to express during our intervue.
      I wonder how much he yearns for the kind of safety that will let
      him let it out - let out all that aesthetic turned-on hooked-up
      aliveness and caring and concern and fun. ...the angry feelings
      too. I remember his being irritated at people at the Free School
      for not supporting him in doing things he wanted to address him-
      self to. I think of his talking about his sister. I think of Karl
      who didn't listen about the cat because he didn't take Jim seriously
      - Jim who was so full of feelings he couldn't deal with, that he
      smiled and sort of blew it. Wow. Can we help him feel safe enough,
      free enough, supported enough to express and use his power?

    Often, children like Jim, will tell us what they need if we listen to them
and if they are helped - helped by feeling "safe" and by being intervued by a
person who takes them seriously and knows how to ask the questions that draw
from their real-from-birth selves. Yes, what about our listening seriously to
children like Jim, and then having a non-rigid school setting where we can be
responsive to the needs that we find out by listening to children?
    I think Jim's intervue is a particularly good example of this point because
here he's telling us about this "free school" which, as he sees it, is a very
rigid place - everyone has to learn in a certain way regardless whether it would
be better for a particular child to learn, at least partly, in another way. I
infer, from Jim's experience, that this is just one more example of school
people following some doctrine rather than thinking for themselves.
    The next intervue I'd like to share with you is with a parent who seems to
be thinking for herself and drawing much from her real-from-birth self. I guess
one reason I'm drawn to this person is because I see how she protected and

nurtured her own real self as she grew up despite adult pressures. (I suspect many of us end up following one doctrine or another as adults, just as we followed adult pressures when we were little.) I find myself enjoying her being in tune with her child's real-from-birth self, fascinated with the wonderment and loveliness of his unfolding from that center but at the same time very practical when it comes to helping him take step after step. Along with this I hope you can sense what I sensed as I was intervueing with her - how she is not very afraid of fear; how she seems to be able to accept and deal with the uneasiness or "shyness" of fear. Another way of saying this is that I sensed a great deal of courage in this person's living of her life - courage to be open and trusting in this intervue, for example. (This was the first time we had talked together seriously.)

> Pina and I met at the Treadway Motel restaurant, across from the School, in mid-morning. She had just been to the garage and found out that the alternator, voltage regulator and gas-filter on her car were in bad shape. We both had Dodge Darts. I told her how the alternator and voltage regulator both went out on my present Dart and my previous Dart. We were sitting at the round table in front of the west window.

Pina: No, I don't have anything particularly on my mind for us to start with. Why don't you begin.

REN: OK. Let's see... How to get started...? Can't seem to get in touch with the right thing to begin with. Hard...How did you hear about the SIEE School in the first place?

Pina: Pedro (age four-years) was at Harrison nursery school. Some people there were talking about the SIEE school. Sounded good but expensive. I observed in several schools: The Free School, Stonyknoll Day School, and local public schools. I was disappointed in the public school program. For example at our neighborhood school all they expected out of the kindergarten children was counting to 10, learning shapes, etc. Pedro was a curious child and ready to move out. Sampson Street School was different - depending on the teacher. I've been told they get into reading in March or so - they start with a sentence and then add more sentences and words. The children memorize these.

REN: It's practically never that I hear of parent who will systematically study the alternatives for schooling with the closeness that you did. How do you account... What's one reason that you found yourself doing that?

Pina: I want the best for my child. When I go to observe I don't find what others have been saying about the school. I just can't talk with other parents and make up my mind. I've always worked hard with Pedro since he was born. For example, perceptually. I'm a painter and this is one of the things that's important to me.

REN: A Painter?

Pina: Yes, I used to teach art...

REN: My question, in other words, is that it seems to me that it takes the best kind of assertiveness, courage, to take the risks of walking in that room for observing, and all the rest. Where did that sort of strength come from?

Pina: As a little girl I was super shy and super sensitive. I was in a cast from eight months to three years. The cast was from the waist down. I was born with congenital hips (that is, no hip sockets).

REN: Super shy?

Pina: I don't know an illustration that I can give you. You try to forget about those things. You know, you overcompensate for your shyness as you get older. A lot of people would.

REN: You were an art teacher...?

Pina: Yes, I have my masters in education after my BFA (Bachelor of Fine Arts). When I was getting my masters in ed. I observed about ten teachers. I developed what I thought were good teaching methods from this observation and what I put together. Then I taught as an elementary art teacher. After a year and a half I wanted to have more time to paint. So I taught at places like the YWCA - adults and children.

REN: How did you get the job at the Y?

Pine: Let me think... I just walked down. They didn't have anything like it so I just developed a few courses.

I don't know... It was unique, not a regular art class. It combined different things - drama, music, as well as art. We had field trips but I always brought it back to art - always tied in the art. Like I'd show a film and I would have them make their own films. We used magic markers on Kodak tape and then I showed it on a 16mm projector. That was a good thing for pre-schoolers. I'd do things with pre-schoolers that I'd do with sixth graders. Children are the best artists around. Less inhibited.

REN: Painting now?

Pina: I'm going to have a one person show in Toronto in March.

REN: Was painting a serious thing when you were a little girl?

Pina: Uh huh - but I didn't want my parents to see it. I didn't paint for a couple of years because I didn't want comments - actually it was more than two years, from the fifth to the eighth grade. Teachers got me back into painting. Instead of study hall I'd go into the art room. They just let me alone. Didn't have to work at home that way. I'd stay after school and work in the art room.

REN: Do you have space and privacy now for your painting?

Pina: Painting is very personal for me. I could never paint in front of a group. What I like about what I'm doing is now is that children can really relate to my work. You know... I'll finish with painting and put it on the floor. Frankie Singleton and other kids who are over at the house will start commenting, "The monsters are eating the egg..."

REN: Pedro?

Pina: He loves it. As I work, the kids come over and talk with me. Children's pressures don't bother me.

REN: I realize that I don't know Pedro all that much. I haven't intervued with him yet.

Pina: You might not find out about Pedro in your intervue. Up until this year he's been shy and sensitive also. But in this year and at SIEE he's really opened up. He's become more assertive toward other people.

REN: Do you have a message to the teachers about Pedro?

Pina: I think they're fulfilling my goals. I haven't had a conference, but don't know if it's all that necessary as they are fulfilling his needs. It would be nice to hear some of their impressions. I've always had con- ferences. At the nursery school I had two conferences a year and feedback is important.

REN: What was summer like for you when you were a child?

Pina: Don't remember - go on vacations, I guess. Went to Mesa Verde one year. I have an older brother and sister. We moved in ten different places until I was in the fifth grade. My father was a railroad bridge consult- ant...Mojave, California; Grand Junction, Colorado; Chicago and Harmon, New York. That's where my parents live now - Harmon. Yes, I'm very close with my father. He's a strong moral person, eager to learn. Has an open mind.

REN: Like one warm and special time?

Pina: Ummm... I don't know... I know he liked my art. When he was operated on he was in the hospital for four weeks, I sent him a lot of art. He told me it made him happy. I think he wrote me a letter about his feelings about my sending him those pieces. And he's not one for words. When he does say something you know he believes it.

REN: What probably was one thing he really liked about you?

Pina: I think he saw a lot of himself in me. Always was watching out for me. Hard to make him and my brother realize that I didn't need it. Do you really want to talk about me or Pedro?

REN: Do you want me to say at this point what you want for Pedro as I am coming to understand some of the things that are important to you - as you are illustrating them from your own childhood?

Pina: I think I could too.

REN: But let's talk about Pedro more directly now. What's one thing you like about him?

Pina: He likes to learn. He wants to know about life. You don't have to write this down...*
_____
*I was writing notes of what we both said, as we talked.

REN: Could I?

Pina: Well, OK,...I have this book and write down a lot of what the boys
      (Pedro and his brother Ramon who is 20 months younger) say during these
      years. You can really tell a lot about them. Pedro's super scientific
      and logical and Ramon - everything that comes out of his mouth is extremely
      funny. And it was, right from the beginning. When something strikes me
      - exactly what they say - like every six months or so I find myself writing
      in this book what they say. Lately Ramon... he's been saying things that
      are hysterical. Pedro will do a lot of deduction from what's said... For
      example, like once he was concerned about robbers coming into the house.
      So he hid things under his bed. "You know if there was a wheelchair robber
      he couldn't get under my bed." I can't remember his exact words and what
      I just said doesn't really sound like him. It was better than that. I
      was reading him a planned parenthood book on reproduction and he said:

      Pina: "Every mommy has eggs and some become babies when sperm
              meet them in her uterus."
      Pedro: "Who was the first mommy who had the eggs before all the
              rest of the people in the world were born - some mommy
              had to have it before more and more people had eggs!"*

REN: What's one thing that Pedro likes about you, probably?

Pina: I listen to him.

REN: Are there very many feelings in you about how "I should listen to my sons...?"

Pina: I'm just really interested in whatever he has to say. I want him to
      feel he's a valuable person.

REN: Does he feel that way?

Pina: I think he feels good about himself. Hope so.

REN: What's an example?

Pina: I don't know... The fact that he continues to be eager about everything...

      Except... he's not a physical person at this point. He often feels that
      he's overpowered physically by his peers. Like he says that a child
      "pushed me off the merry-go-round." He remembers that time for a long
      time. Like in the fall he told me how it felt - people were going over
      him and he was coughing and crying and Susan Mock carried him back.

      By the way, he's very close to Susan. He talks about her a lot. When I
      talked to Susan, she was amazed that Pedro keeps referring to her as "his
      teacher" because of that time after the merry-go-round incident and other
      times when Pedro has talked with her. A week ago, someone punched him in
      the stomach. "I felt I couldn't breathe - like the time I was pushed under
      the merry-go-round."

----

 * Pina gave me this quote later.

The other day he woke up with a nightmare at 4:00 in the morning. "I had a bad dream about a whole bunch of big kids beating me up. I couldn't do anything about it."

I guess he's just started to realize it on his own that he's physically small. I haven't ever made a point of it.

REN: As you were telling about his dream I found myself being restimulated about some of the ways that I felt fear when I was little. To what extent does this restimulate old feelings in you - when you were a little girl?

Pina: I listen, compassionately. "It's a dream, Pedro, not real." No it didn't scare me. 'Cause I never really had those feelings when I was little. As a little girl I never felt powerless - even though I couldn't do a lot of physical things. I couldn't take the ballerina classes or PE. Always had physical limitations because of my hips. ...just have to be strong and go beyond that... have to find out where your strengths are. That's why I guess I find myself being compassionate - but not more. He has to find out what he has in himself - other than a big muscle.

REN: Anything you think we should deal with now, other than what we've done?

Pina: I think we've covered basically what Pedro's all about...

He's really opened up this year. Whatever you're doing I think it's the right thing. I know that if he went to a public program... Like when Curt crashed down his leggo structure onto Pedro, Susan put her arm around Curt. She said to him, "Why did you do that?" He said something flip and she said, "Do you think you can both build something together." Curt said, "No." Susan countered with "I think Pedro can build a lot with the leggos." Well, it ended really great. Instead of siding one against the other... In a public school that kind of a problem wouldn't be worked out probably. Pedro never spoke badly about Curt after that.

REN: I enjoy what I hear... I like the feeling about how you're right there ... enjoying and appreciating and listening...but you're letting him work things out and you seem to enjoy what he's doing for himself.

Pina: It's important for parents to appreciate children. Time goes so fast. If you're not close in early years...very difficult to be close later. Family...really important to me. I really believe in it. It's just such a beautiful miracle to watch unfold. I didn't want to put our children in a day care center for others to watch...and not me.

REN: Funny. You labelled yourself as a shy little girl. But as I sit here and reflect on it, the story didn't come out that way. You found yourself asserting your needs for privacy and all with your art. Then at school you seemed to be aware of your needs and arranged things so that they could be met - like taking all that time for painting at school and not doing other things with your time. Being on the physical sidelines (like in PE) but having strength and using it - to make the most of what you had...??

Pina: Maybe I wasn't so shy.

Now here's my intervue with Pedro, Pina's son, about ten days after Pina's intervue with me:

Intervue with Pedro (five-years-old)

NOTE: Give a copy of this to Brian (a part-time teacher) because Pedro responded to my explanation of some of the reasons I intervue children by saying that Brian maybe doesn't know him all that well and could use a copy. I explained that one reason I do this is to help teachers get to know children.

We were sitting in the art room on the little rug under the windows and in the middle of the room.

REN: What's one of your favorate foods, Pedro?

Pedro: One of my favorite foods is apples. Then I like meat. Well... I like it not... without sauce - dry.

I was born in Michigan in a hospital - in upper Michigan.

REN: I call this next question the Giant Memory Question. Pretend that this big machine over there would take all your good memories for a bit unless you told it about some you wanted to keep. What's one good memory you'd like to keep?

Pedro: I remember my birthday. I got mostly models and that's what I like. I especially liked my space ship models. Don gave me the space ship model. I told him that I'd like a model or a Matchbox Car, when I invited him. A lot of kids came who aren't in this school.

That model broke and me and my father will fix it. We have this glue at home...

Another thing I want to remember and not have that machine take is when Frankie came to my house (Frankie Singleton). Like the time when he brang his guns and one of the fur things and us going around pretending we shot ourselves (smile).

REN: Pedro this is another question that I invented. I call it the "Magic Shoes" question. Pretend that there were a pair of magic shoes here and you could tell them what you wanted so that you could have and do anything, be anything - but just for a half hour.

Pedro: Take me to Frankie's house. I've been there but I like him a lot. He's one of my best friends. One reason I like Frankie is that sometimes I get to sleep over at his house. Like the time we both slept in my sleeping bag. It's very fat. Whenever we got scared we crawled under it - we could go very far down. He also comes to my house. I let him sleep in my bed. I get in my sleeping bag and when I get scared I go crawling down and I have my stuffed dog holding up the hole at the top.

REN: What's it like for you when you feel scared?

Pedro: When a a aaa... When my door's closed, cause it gets very dark. A night lite doesn't lite up very good.

REN: If you could tell the Magic Shoes something that would happen so that you wouldn't get scared, what might you tell the shoes?

Pedro: Turn on my closet light. The closet lite really shows.

REN: What's one thing you like about yourself?

Pedro: My vest - my down vest (He appeared to be restless at this point.)

REN: Wanta ask me a question?

Pedro: Well - OK - what's what you like about yourself?

REN: Myself? OK, I take good movies. That's one thing I like about myself.

Pedro: I can count to 100.

REN: Can you do any reading?

Pedro: Yea. My brother's Raggedy Ann book. My brother's name is Ramon.

REN: Like school?

Pedro: Yup. I get to come in here (the art room) when Beth is here. She lets me be in here to do some stuff - all sorts of stuff. I like her... She lets me come in here. Tye dying I like the most.

REN: One person here who knows you're good at doing things in the art room?

Pedro: Sue does. I like... She lets me come in to the other art room. She works in the other room. She lets me make cutouts. She also lets me use clay.

REN: How about the summer?

Pedro: We swim at the beach. We'll go to the new park near us. Just have to walk about ten minutes. Just like walking around the block. I'm very good at walking around the block. I go with my father 'cause he mostly likes to go there too.

I like how my father helps me make models. I help him too. If he needs glue I tell my mother and get it for my Daddy.

REN: What's different about you? Like me, I cut my own hair and I'm proud of it. I don't know any man I know who cuts his hair himself.

Pedro: I do lots of experiments with my grandfather. I find lots of ways to make these small lights go on and I make the alarm go on. I do this in the summer mostly when he comes. He comes over for a week mostly.

REN: He likes you?

Pedro: Yea

14

REN: What's one reason, probably?

Pedro: Because I'm... (long pause - 1½ minutes)...because I'm good experiment person. I do experiments very good with him.

I like to make the alarm go on. We do it early in the morning when nobody's up. We make the alarm go on and it wakes everybody up.

I wake up, before then. I wake him up. He doesn't mind when someone wakes him. He lives by himself.

REN: Look at TV? OK, who's a TV person you'd like to be for a day - just for fun?

Pedro: I don't know. Most of 'em I like.

REN: Have a secret hiding place?

Pedro: Yeah. Under my desk. I goes into this place - see, only one person can be there. My brother doesn't know I'm there. He lies on the pillow in front and I bump on the pillow. He'll say, "What's that?"

I think something's in my eye. Like some fur sticking in it. (He tried to get at something that he thought was in his eye.) Know what was in my eye - two of them hard things. It'll stay there for the whole day.

REN: What's one thing you're looking forward to?

Pedro: Going to Harmon in a week. My cousins and grandfather and grandmother are there. He's a builder and scientist (my grandfather). I made a machine with lots of wires - brought out my gloves and touched the wires (didn't want to get shocked.) Never have gotten shocked. My father got one. It was like a cut. He got one when he was putting in the dishwasher. The old one couldn't be fixed.

REN: Pedro, one thing I like about you is that you think about things - and then when you answer, your answers are careful. That makes me think about my questions to you. Makes me listen to you carefully because I'm interested.

Pedro: Yeah, most people listen to me.

REN: Oh, that reminds me - listening - we're going to have a meeting about fighting in school. I want to make sure that all the kids feel safe here all the time; not worried about getting hit and stuff like that.

How about you?

Pedro: I do. My brother mostly hits me at home. I hit him back. It feels hard. I worry about that at school. I worry about Curt. I don't like Curt. He hits me mostly and he doesn't let me move anywhere.

REN: Now we both know that Curt isn't here now. What do you need to say to Curt?

Pedro: "Curt, don't hit me 'cause it's not nice picking on other kids who aren't your age."

REN: Stand up here and pretend that you are a lot bigger than Curt. Talk down to Curt down here.

Pedro: "Curt, don't hit me. Don't punch me either."

REN: If you were the biggest boy here???

Pedro: I would... If someone picked on me I would kick them or punch them.

REN: Anything that we - the teachers - can do to make it so Curt won't hit you?

Pedro: Tell him not to do it.

REN: How can we tell that he's mad?

Pedro: When he's fighting me. Usually a teacher does do something about it. Sue does usually, more than the others.

Any more questions? (He put his head back and rolled his eyes up to the ceiling as if to say, "Wow - we've done a lot!")
******

"Yeah, most people listen to me."... That made me feel so good as I tried to accept this matter-of-factly and write it in my intervue notes. This little five-year-old boy, so obviously to me, felt how his parents and those of us at the School were there to help him think for himself, in tune with his real self.

When I listened to Pedro talk I felt so good to sense how he accepts fear in his life; and I found myself feeling so good about how this young person just isn't being manipulated by fear - the fear of losing the support of the important-to-him big people in his life. But, on the other hand, at age five he's learning to sort out the world; he's learning to live with his heightened sensitivities and yet live with Curt, too.

Then what is he telling us that he needs from our school? He's saying that he needs the feeling of safety that he gets from the assurance that "Usually a teacher does something about it" if someone begins to push him around. He's saying that he expects and finds teachers listening to him - having the kind of awareness so that they can tune into his scene without making a conscious effort to do that. He's telling us that he needs an environment that will be full of things to explore and invent; an environment where teachers will enjoy, with Pedro, his fascination and wonderment with what's around him. Pina is saying how she can and will provide much of that during his home hours.

What seems to permeate all of this is how easily Pedro responds to the appreciation and awareness of those adults who care for him; how easily this supports him in staying in touch with the just-fine, capable, trusting and warm real-from-birth self that he's drawing on so much of the time for direction; how he needs this affirmation and expects it. He feels his capability but he is telling us that he needs us to help him appreciate it and exercise it. He is very responsive to feedback from others which affirms that he is capable, strong, and doing things that one can feel proud of. (Turn to chapter VII for more on how he seemed to soak up, thoughtfully, the admiration that other children gave him at a morning meeting one day when he talked about what he and his dad did on their camping trips.)

As I watched Dottie, Mary and Susan work with Pedro during the year, I noticed that often they would be right there to celebrate with him the things he made, the writing that he did, smile with him at his subtle humor, "be there" for him in ways that made him feel safe. I'd sense the warmth and trust that Pedro exchanged and enjoyed with them.

As I observed Pedro, I sensed a little boy who was perceiving reality as it was, moment-by-moment - in present-time - as opposed to filtering his perceptions through screens clouded by accumulated old distress that he had not let out when the hurtful event originally felt bad to him. Remember how Pina described Pedro's memory of the fearful distress of being under the merry-go-round as the children were running over him? Pedro remembered that feeling; he had had plenty of time to cry and express the hurtful feelings at the moment it happened and afterward; he still talks about it when those feelings get re-stimulated by similar feelings. But he clearly distinguishes, apparently, between that time and now. He uses that memory, vivid as it apparently is, as experience to help him describe, weigh, sort out other events. It seems that the feelings of panicky powerlessness, that he experienced then, do not rise up and distort other similar hurtful scenes in his life now. He's able to see the new situations for what they are and react to them in terms of the real danger he senses in the present-situation - be it more or less or of a different quality from the danger he felt as he was lying under the merry-go-round with the children's feet hitting the ground around him and some of their feet hitting him. Pedro seems to be able to "see" and react to emotional events in his life in terms of present-time reality.

Let's explore a bit further this aspect of the real self-living and reacting to events in terms of present-time reality. I'd like to take you, now, with me as I intervue with five-year-old Marian. I hope that you will feel, as I did, how much of Marian was responding to her world as each element presented itself - with fascination, curiosity, humor, warmth, openness. I hope that you will sense what I did - how she seemed to perceive her world just as it was and not clouded by undue fears or optimism. (She appears to see her world as safe for her, with people like me whom she can trust. She seems to see her mother and father loving her in a warm, easy, secure-for-her way. That squares with her reality as I judge it. And I can judge that pretty well as Marian's mother works at our school. I feel I know her parenting and the parenting of her husband, well.

So let's be off for my intervue with Marian over lunch at the restaurant, across the street from the school:

Intervue with Marian Summers (Five-year-old)

Marian and I were walking out the church's side door. As we got close to the doors she said, "Funny about these doors. When you go to try to go in the sign says 'Use other Door' and it doesn't open." When we got to the Treadway I had to stop at the desk to cash a check. I can't remember what the man said but I remember my feeling - I squirmed a little as the man did the best he could, I felt, but at that moment it came out as talking down to Marian and saying something like, "Yes, he brings lots of children here from across the street." This didn't seem to make Marian feel all that uncomfortable but I noticed that she just didn't respond but looked at the man in a way that many people would call "courteously." I just thought of what it must look like to someone Marian's size as she hears a voice from the other side of that desk. She might not have seen much of the man because of the giant desk looming between them. Funny how I ordinarily don't

think of her as being little or big but I do when I think of
of her there.   I remember one other time during lunch when I
thought of that. She was sitting across the table from me with
her coat off and in her tee shirt. She looked delicate and small.
I think that was just after she had told a joke to the waitress
who seemed to be enjoying it so much. I guess, too, that I remember my own children at five and six... So much clearness there.
They so helped me see the world and myself in a clear present-time
real way. Marian does that too, for me.

So we sat down at one of the window tables for two. I began
writing on my notes:

REN: HHhhh... Marian... (I was writing this at the top of the first sheet.)

Marian: Petesakes. For a minute I thought you'd spelled my name Mari_o_n.

REN: I need a chance to sort of let down and get into our lunch... (Jan, the
waitress came with the menus.)

Marian looked over the menu. My feeling was that this wasn't helping
her, even though she was able to read it, so I said "they have ham-
burgers, cheeseburgers, french fries and all that. Don't know if
that's on the menu or not."

Marian: I want a hamburger and fries and a coke.

REN: I'm beginning to feel better now. Just had to call a parent a few minutes
before I picked you up - about paying their school bill. Don't like that
kind of a telephone call. Being with you is making me feel better all the
time.

Marian: That's the same with me. I felt rotten at newstime. I can't... Too
hard for me to explain.

Maybe you forgot something? You need to put two little lines at the bottom
of that page you just wrote on to show it's on the next page.

REN: OK, you mean like this? (Here's what I put on the corner of my note
sheet. Marian nodded that this was what should be there. "=")

Marian: Bob, know what? My mother will be reading this at home and she'll
be laughing like crazy. I know it.

I have something that you probably don't know. Do you know what "shajune"
means?

REN: No.

Marian: It means "very boring." My Dad told me. He knows almost everything
I don't know.

REN: Shall I ask the next question or you ask me?

Marian: I don't have any questions right in my head.

18

REN: OK, where were you born?

Marian: That's easy. I'm going to tell you which part of it?

REN: Yeah

Marian: I was born in California and I was born in Los Angeles.

REN: What's the difference between California and Los Angeles?

Marian: Don't know.

REN: OK, the next question... Let's see... I know what I feel like asking
you - the Magic Shoes question. ...like there was this pair of pretend
magic shoes there on the floor. You could put them on and tell them to
do anything for you that you wanted and they would - take you anyplace,
with anyone, with...but only for a half hour. What's the first thought
that comes into your head?

Marian: (Just then our food came. Marian was holding the new ketchup bottle
up over her hamburger waiting for it to come out.) Slow poke (ketchup)...
terrible...new bottles of ketchup. (When the ketchup finally came out -
after she shook it and coaxed it out - she put the cap on and screwed it
down.) Bet all these seats here in the restaurant have been used more
than a hundred times.

REN NOTE: I wrote "delicate - beautiful" in my notes as I found
myself responding to Marian. Something about the way that she put
the cap back on the ketchup that brought those words up: Don't want
to analyze it here.

REN: So. What would you want the Magic Shoes to do for you?

Marian: Start all over being a baby in California. One thing - if I ended up
and was a baby... Know what? The shoes would be too big, wouldn't they?

REN: You know, when you were eating and talking there I was feeling how delicately beautiful you were. Made me feel good - like I was walking through
an art museum and suddenly saw a nice picture and stopped and looked at it.

Marian: I'd be riding a motorcycle (with the help of the magic shoes). No,
there wouldn't be anyone else with me. I'd be taking the quick way back
here on the motorcycle. I'd go to the museum and look at dinasaur bones.

REN: Wanta ask me the next question?

Marian: I got one. How did you get the job?

REN: What job?

Marian: One you have right now - at our school.

REN: Let me think. Well... it always was that way - from the very beginning.

Marian: Always what way?

19

REN: Well, Susan Manes and I decided we'd have a school...

Marian: A church with a school in it.

REN: It always was that Susan Manes would teach in it and I'd be what we call the director.

Marian: You forgot those two lines again. (Marian mentioned this at the end of each of my note sheets when I forgot to put "=" there.)

REN: All right, my next question is, "What's one thing you like about yourself?" I'll go first and answer it about me if you'd rather...?

Marian: You go ahead first. I know one thing I hate about myself. I hate these snarls that always get in my hair (she ran her fingers through her hair)...a rat's nest. Hope they don't lay their eggs.

REN: (laugh) It's neat being out to lunch with you, 'cause I laugh a lot.

OK, one thing I like about me... Oh, I know one thing - just thought of it - how easy it is for me to laugh when I'm with a person like you. And another thing. The laugh comes from way down inside.

Marian: Yeah. The laugh is taking a elevator up.

REN: So, what's one thing that you like about <u>yourself</u>? (Marian paused reflectively.) ...like maybe you'll come up with something like I feel right now as I find myself thinking how I like your beautiful eyes and like just being here with you - how nice it feels for me.

Marian: That ummm... I'm glad my mother picked me to go into the school that she's working at.

REN: OK. Now what's one thing you like about <u>Marian</u>?

Marian: I like how I can be a friend with old persons. Like one time I was walking down the street and I met this old person. We just were friends.

Know what? I've got a joke for you. You'll have to say things I tell you or the joke won't work. First thing you say is "I'd like some split pea soup." Then I'll (pretend to) give it to you. Then you say "Where are the peas?" Got that?

REN: OK, I'd like some split pea soup.

(Marian gestured as if she were giving me my bowl.)
Where are the peas?

Marian: I guess the peas musta split.

REN: (laugh) (I couldn't seem to stop laughing. Just then Jan, our waitress looked over. I asked her to come over and hear this joke. Marian told it to her and she started laughing and laughing. Then I heard her tell it to Carol - another waitress - around the corner and they both were laughing.)

What do you say <u>we</u> split - back to the school now?

Marian: Bob, did you know that this is my first intervue in my whole life - even last year I didn't have one?

REN: Yes. I know that.

ON THE WAY BACK TO SCHOOL:

Marian: I knew that I'd get an intervue. It always happens that big people do things.

REN: Yeah. That's one thing I like about our school, too. Big people do those kinds of things with children. Each child can expect that big people will come through for her or him. But it doesn't happen that way in all schools. That's one reason we started this school.

Marian: I'm sure glad you made the school that way.

REN: Hey, that makes me feel good.

BACK IN MY CAR JUST AFTER I LEFT MARIAN OFF:

I was just walking in front of the church with Marian's hand in mine. What was my feeling? ...yes... The world is simpler and lovely ...yes...present-time...yes...Present-time is a smaller part of the world. Doesn't have all the old stuff, the old doubts and uneasinesses - not all the worries about <u>if</u> this and <u>if</u> that (the future). So easy for <u>me</u> to get into present-time with Marian.

REFLECTIONS AT THE END OF THIS TYPING: Marian seems to be hooked up with that real self that she was born with. Her mind is seemingly effortless in the way it functions with clear logic, in touch with the poetic beauty all around her, full of humorous wonderment easy to be warm and will take warmth, has the fine-tuned sensitivity of a spontaneous performer and yet she apparently doesn't insulate herself by her ability to dominate a verbal scene.

Don't know whether I will, but I'd like to intervue her mother and her father at this point. I'd like to let them read this and then right away ask them what's the first thing that comes to their minds in answer to this:

> What's one of the things you like about yourself,
> that has helped Marian be as she is?

I didn't intervue Marian's parents. I didn't need to. It was so apparent to me how they were living their lives in tune with their real-from-birth selves - staying in present-time themselves.

They are helping Marian to be in touch with commonplace-loveliness, fascination, humor, that's all around her. Marian's just not full of old fear. She can and does stay in touch with her real-from-birth self - that just-fine feeling lovable and capable self that she was born with.

But it's not all that easy - for big people or children to stay in tune with their real-from-birth selves in present-time reality, not all that easy as children grow up in a world full of parenting and teaching persons harboring so many pockets of accumulated distress from old hurts that they weren't helped to "let out" in safe-for-them situations. There is too much parenting and teaching by well-meaning adults who have learned to manage children by playing on the children's fear of feeling "I'm not all right" - distress that adults have allowed to be laid into children (as it was laid into them) from an early age and in school.

We're moving now to examine this in the lives of Carrie, Sean and me in Chapters Two, Three, and Four.

CHAPTER 2

CARRIE

How behavior rooted in Carrie's real-from-birth self was blocked
by patterns of behavior that she originally had learned in order
to survive in distressful situations but which increasingly got
in the way of her living with confidence and meaning. How teachers
loosened the hold of her self-defeating habits and nurtured behavior which was drawing from the essences of her being.

Carrie entered our school when she was nine. She had just finished the
fourth grade in a suburban school. Her parents told us that the school people
told them that she was about two years "behind," in reading and about three
years "behind" in ability to express herself in writing. She was polite and
"sweet" at school but teachers said that she daydreamed a lot, in class. Out
on the playground, on the contrary, she seemed to be able to have fun with
other children and would often be the close buddy of some child who did adventurous things.

From her teachers, parents, and Carrie herself I pieced together the following story: Carrie had a good kindergarten year. She painted with vivid
yellows and reds; with broad spontaneous brush strokes. There usually was a
lot of action in her pictures. She led others in fantasy "dress up" play, like
the time when she dressed as the fairy waitress who could grant you one wish -
so long as you paid your bill. Her teacher enjoyed Carrie's warmth, and spontaneity at circle time. Carrie would raise her hand vigorously with contribu-
tions to "show and tell." She'd beam when the teacher gave her approving
attention. The teacher liked how Carrie would seem to know the limits and
follow the rules easily. Carrie enjoyed moving in and out of closeness with
various children. It was easy for her, apparently, to reach out to others and
feel liked by others.

Carrie came into first grade full of expectation. "Now I'm going to learn
to read," she told her father one September night as he finished a book he was
reading to her. He read to her each night. She'd usually drop off to sleep
as he was reading. That was a special time for him as he sensed her security
and what he felt as complete trust in him.

Carrie had learned what seemed to her to be the basic rule at school: get
the approval of the teacher and you are OK.

But it didn't work out that way for her when it came to learning to read
and to write. Carrie filled out the dittoed sheets with the colors that the
teacher told her to put in the spaces. She did the workbook pages according to
the teacher's direction. She made the marks in the little boxes on those leaf-
lets that the teacher called "tests." But Carrie ended up in the low reading
group. She was one of seven children in that class of thirty-one whom the
teacher found were not learning up to schedule. So, as the school procedures
instructed and as the teacher had learned at training college, she put Carrie
in the "Sailboat" group. The teacher had a little rubber stamp with a bouncy
sailboat on it and the word "good" written below, with which she'd stamp perfect
pages for children in Carrie's group. "Happy Days" was the name of the middle
group. (They were beginning a reader titled "Happy Days.") "The Hummingbirds"
- the top group - had book marks with blue hummingbirds on them.

At first Carrie saw this grouping as just another thing to adjust to at
school. School was like that. But toward the end of the first grade year she

began to get a message from other children that being in the Sailboats was because you're not so smart. One afternoon, for example, when she was at her neighbor Sandy's house, Sandy said "How can you stand it down in the Sailboats with that wierdo Sammy Stonely?" One thing that got to Carrie was how this question seemed to perk up Sandy's mother who was working at the sink nearby. Carrie noticed that Sandy's mother had stopped washing the strawberries and was looking at her (Carrie) as she paused before responding. But Carrie didn't answer, she just shrugged the question off. She never did feel that Sandy's mother liked her a lot. Later Carrie overheard Sandy's mother talking with her mother about The Hummingbirds and The Sailboats. Somehow that made Carrie uneasy.

Toward the end of the first grade year Carrie was sent to "The Reading Teacher's Room" for a half hour each day and did more dittoed sheets and had more flashcard drill, learning the new words in her reading textbook. She went with Sammy Stonely and the others in the Sailboats. She liked Mr. Harris, the reading teacher. They sometimes played word games like consonant-bingo, in his room.

Carrie told her mother, one day in the car, that school was no fun anymore. Her mother said something about how, "Well, now is the time for you to work hard, dear. If you work hard you'll learn. The fun time was in the kindergarten."

But you know, that wasn't the way it was. Carrie <u>did</u> work hard. She <u>did</u> try hard to do what the teacher wanted her to do. But, unbeknown to her at first, she wasn't learning the words and sounds on the same time schedule as the others. No one told her but the rule that she had learned wasn't <u>the</u> key to success - it wasn't enough that you did what the teacher wanted you to do and got her approval. Carrie had to learn up to a certain schedule that she knew nothing about and if she didn't, all of a sudden she would find herself in the low group and with feelings of being inadequate. And, furthermore, she didn't know how to improve. Just "working hard" didn't seem to be enough. The most that you could do would be to try to do tomorrow's exercises so that you got a sailboat on each paper. "But you stayed in the Sailboats even though you got your papers right," Carrie told me one day in an intervue, four years later.

One thing led to another. In the second grade, for example, Carrie found herself looking out the window a lot when it came to "reading time." It just happened. She didn't plan or intend, consciously, to avoid what was going on in the group. Then the dittoed sheets began to come back without sailboats stamped on them, but with "Try Harder" written on top in red. Carrie's mother was "called in" to see the teacher. At first, Carrie's mother felt irritated at the teacher whom she felt didn't like Carrie. But she found herself uneasy about complaining to the principal because how could she get around the fact that Carrie didn't do well in reading in the first grade and now again wasn't doing well in the second grade? Maybe it wasn't the teacher? Must be something wrong with Carrie? ...something wrong with the way that Carrie was being raised at home?

There was another thing that Carrie's mother felt was not right for Carrie at school, but at the time she just couldn't seem to put this into words. As I talked with Carrie's mother, several years later, I put this together: Carrie's mother sensed that at school, children felt all right when they were up to learning schedule and doing what the teachers wanted. But this affirmation didn't come often. What did come often were reminders of not measuring up in different ways. But, as Carrie's mother was finally able to express it as we talked: wasn't that the way that school was supposed to be? That was the way it used to be for her; school was a place where alert teachers would catch your deficiencies and press you to correct them. Teachers were supposed to be pleasant but not self-revealing in ways that might lessen their authority-to-see-to-it-that-children-got-their-work-done role. It was unnatural, out-of-place, for

24

teachers to say things like "Hey Carrie that smile you just gave me felt nifty. I need that this morning." Carrie's mother expressed this to me in an intervue when she was reflecting on how Carrie seemed to have doubts about herself - especially when it came to anything connected to schoolwork.

But back to Carrie. In the third grade her daydreaming in class had become chronic. She still was compliant and followed the rules - lined up right away and didn't talk, for instance. And she seemed to be accepting her lot at school - according to the school psychologist who had been called in by the second grade teacher after the parent teacher conferences with Carrie's mother. The psychologist, Mr. James, reported this "encouraging trend." Even her walk had subtly changed, in school. She moved with a lazy gait - relaxed but lazy. That was the image of herself that Carrie found herself with apparently, more and more. It was an image that her parents also picked up and seemed, to Carrie, to like. What came across to Carrie was that they liked how sweet she was. A bit lazy, perhaps, but so were a lot of others in this world. She felt that her parents and teachers liked her when she put on an apparently accepting come-what-may relaxed attitude.

Her mother called me in late May of Carrie's fourth grade year. A neighbor of hers had a girl in our school who seemed to be enjoying books and reading and liked our school. Carrie's mother said that she and her husband had begun to feel that what Carried needed was more teacher attention. "She's behind academically and needs individual help." They didn't see her with any basic problem other than being a bit happy-go-lucky and she was "such a sweet little girl - but not too perfect." Her mother was worried, however, that Carrie didn't seem to have self confidence when it came to doing her schoolwork; it was getting close to the time when Carrie would be in junior high with the demands of homework and all. They just felt that she should have some close teacher attention and learn better work habits, as well as be helped to "come up to grade level."

They came, observed and liked our school. Carrie came to our school for a week in early June. She liked the school. She said that "kids don't have so much work at SIEE," when asked why she liked it. She hadn't seen any reading groups. There seemed, to her, to be more of what she liked in Mr. Harris' room and less of the hurry-up-and-wait kind of filling out dittoed sheets that she had felt characterized her classroom. And nowhere were there any basal reading books - the textbooks that were in her hands so much of the time when she found herself daydreaming.

So Carrie started at our school in September - the beginning of her fifth grade year. We found a girl who on the surface was sweet and acquiesant to adults. She never seemed to be all that "alive" when it came to schoolwork. Her self-image apparently was that she was lazy and not-too-smart. But with the children, when the scene wasn't to do with schoolwork, she was almost always in the thick of adventures. Children liked her. For example she and a little boy who enjoyed action were found climbing up behind the old unused organ at the front of the church sanctuary. There was a dark attic space there that we didn't even know about. They got in through a service hole at the side of an adjoining room. All of that territory was "off limits" but she was doing things like this with the finesse of a pro. She was the leader of the two of them. We just didn't suspect this kind of behavior, at first from this "sweet little girl."

We also found a little girl who was scared to death, apparently, about doing academic exercises. We found, for example, that unless she felt super-secure her mind would just blank when it came to writing and spelling - she'd spell "motor" m-p-l-r or some such mindless way. She began to find in Leah (our part-time math person and self-styled grandmother at school) someone with whom she apparently felt safe. We noticed this one day when Carrie was sitting next to Leah and actually touching Leah, person-to-person, then usually Carrie could write down words in an order that made some sense and spell with some semblance of patterned consonant-vowel-consonant phonics logic. Writing and spelling were so often mindless during that first year. We were often at a loss to figure out some way to get her mentally engaged when she was faced with traditional exercise papers. Doing her textbook work was also, it seemed, something that she would withdraw from. She would apparently learn an arithmetic process - even some sort of a math recipe - and then the next day apparently it just wouldn't be there in her memory. However, she seemed to take to our way of teaching reading. My hunch here is that it was so different in format that it just didn't contain the triggers of anxiety that the ways that we were trying to teach her in writing, spelling, and arithmetic did. (It didn't trigger "I'm not all right" fear.) In learning to read she didn't use any textbooks, didn't daily fill out dittoed sheets, didn't read and often fail in the daily oral reading group, didn't use graded materials that showed where she "was" in comparison with the other children. On the contrary, when it came time to read at our school, most children would select their own high-interest but low vocabulary level books (children who were at the fledgling-stage as she was). They would read quietly and would read a bit individually to the teacher when she came around during that half hour of silent sustained reading. Then, too, some of them would play games to become better at using the consonant-vowel-consonant logic of phonics. This she found herself able to do rather easily and retain what she learned. At the end of the fifth grade year her reading achievement test score was in the beginning fifth grade range. (When she had started as a 5th grader she scored mid-3rd grade.) But she still was fighting learning in the arithmetic book. Expressing herself in writing was coming along but often she would lapse into the mindless no-logic way of writing. It was as if she were saying "You can lead me to water but you can't make me drink." This was a self-defeating behavior pattern that we often saw in children who have experienced feelings of fear around failure at school. It's as if we had tapped a deep down recording that was made back in the first grade; a recording that was saying subconsciously, to Carrie: "Quit trying to write things down that just show everyone how dumb you are. Don't finish that dittoed sheet just so it will come back full of red marks. Protect yourself from those lousy feelings of being a disappointment to your parents. You can't decide not to come to school, (but try - exaggerate those sick feelings when they come up in the morning);...no, you can't quit school but you can quit psychologically. Protect yourself! Protect yours... Protect you... Protect... Prot..."

But NOW she was in a school - our school - where she wouldn't be shown to be deficient all the time, especially as contrasted to the other children. Now if necessary, we could take plenty of time rather than be so uptight about Carrie learning On Schedule. Now she got plenty of feedback about what she could do - honest reflections of accomplishment and self-value that she deserved for what she was doing and because of the person she was - her special real self, full of fascinating uniqueness that was there in bud from the beginning.

But despite the fact that she no longer needed the protection of daydreaming, other forms of withdrawal, her facade of "sweetness," and the "relaxed but lazy" image..., despite the fact that she no longer needed this protection for her self esteem, the defensive behavior went on in our school in its habitual and now clearly self-defeating ways. It was self-defeating because it was not behavior which was consistent with present-time reality, consistent with that real-from-birth self which felt adequate and was hooked up with her world with sensitive awareness and inventiveness. But what could we do to help her take direction from her real self - to change this? It wasn't simply a matter of calling her on it, (Hey, Carrie, stop daydreaming!) although that helped sometimes.

The danger was that if we were to call her on it, she would feel, once again, that she was not "measuring up" and really not understand what it was that we were trying to get her to change. Change her being acquiescent, "sweet?" What most likely would come across to her would be that we didn't like how she was. ...just the reverse message from what we wanted her to feel. We wanted to get across to her, "Hey Carrie, we know you are just fine as a person, you are warm, capable, trusting, inventive... We want you to know that too. We want to tell you about the ways that you are your real self."

So the manner in which we moved ahead with Carrie was not to nag her with how she was getting in her own way, except when this could be done lightly in a context where she felt safe and could feel safe and could feel good about herself. On the other hand we often could and did let her know about aspects of her real-from-birth self that we enjoyed - "You know, Carrie, it's so easy for me to smile when you walk in, in the morning. Like just now. ...how I felt an 'I trust you' steadiness in your eyes."

All this understanding didn't happen right away. It took time for us to confirm, at a high probability level, how Carrie seemed to see herself in her world. It really took most of that first year to feel for sure what some of the deeper enjoyable aspects of Carrie were; what some of the basic fears were that she might have and how these colored her perception of the threats to her world. By the middle of her second year at our school (she was officially in the sixth grade then) we had studied Carrie twice during our regular child-study program.* Her image of herself began to come out clearly to us. As I said above, she apparently saw herself as a "nice" little girl in the adult world but also a "dumb kid." She also seemed to have a kind of secret world in which she found excitement and where she felt alive, but we had a hunch that she tended to discount herself in this secret world. She felt that she did "bad" things like buy candy at the store down the block even though she promised her mother she wouldn't because her mother said it was bad for one's teeth.

Then when I intervued with her mother I found that she gave a kind of tacit acceptance to Carrie's apparent view of herself. She too, had "bought" part of the protective self-perception that once had helped Carrie dull the sting and fear of not being all right as a student. "Well Carrie's just not an egghead. She's basically a nice polite little girl with a kind of impish strain in her."

The words "nice" and "polite" came out in both my intervue with Carrie and with her mother. Carrie used "polite" when she said that was one thing that she liked about herself, but when she answered my question about what she'd tell the magic shoes (that could take her anywhere or let her by anyone for a half hour) she said "I'd tell the magic shoes to make me a crime reporter for a big newspaper."

In the summary that I added to the end of my intervue with Carrie and her mother, I found myself saying that my hunch (for discussion at our child-study meeting) was that the deep-down Carrie had learned somewhere along the way at school - the first grade probably - that the way to protect herself from anxious feelings of being a failure was first to concentrate on pleasing the teacher and then adopt the stance that Carrie somehow had sensed was readymade for her- self out there in the adult world - that of the nice, polite, easy-going but not academically talented girl. I can just see how this gave her mother and father an "out" too, when the bad marks came in on the report card. "Well, she's like a lot of girls - just not an egghead." That's what happens so often with children's budding self-defeating protective behavior patterns; both the children and their parents and teachers rationalize them into somehow seeming not just all right - but good. That, for the moment, cuts down everyone's

*The child-study program is described in Chapter Five.

distress but just makes it harder to change, later. ...later when the habitually patterned behavior begins to get in the child's way more and more. Later, too, the patterned behavior becomes an overlay tending to supress the real-from-birth self underneath as behavior guided from the real self struggles to assert itself - like grass growing through cracks in the concrete. Then the inevitable "personality conflicts" become visible. In Carrie's case we see an apparently "well adjusted" little girl with self-doubts about herself as a student, and not measuring up in her corner of the work-a-day world. We see a little girl so apparently "bright" not being able to learn at the pace of other children.

Now back to Carrie at the SIEE School at the middle of her second year (officially mid-way through her sixth grade year). It was important, for Carrie's growth, that all the staff people got a chance to consider how Carrie's fearful old recordings were probably instructing her unconscious. Then, too, at the child-study meetings and at other times people began to share their stories of how they were enjoying Carrie. Staff people were heightening their awareness of Carrie's real self. Much of the resultant teacher behavior seemed to be getting to Carrie.

For example, at the farm (where our children go for "art camps" for five or six days and nights during the fall and spring) teachers found so much of Carrie's real-from-birth behavior to enjoy. On the trip to the beaver pond to cut reeds for furniture-making her zest for the beauty of flowers, and the fun she had building a new trail section were contagious. Children wanted to sleep next to Carrie. Carrie and Joyce, our art teacher and owner of the farm, made a beautiful breakfast of French toast together. Carrie seemed to feel so neat about herself as she called out "Who's ready for more?" Yes, Carrie really felt, apparently, all sorts of feedback from teachers and children about her being both capable and enjoyable. Her "hearing" this feedback also suggested that the fearful message of the old recordings was much weaker now. One thing that helped was that her teachers seemed to her to be people first and teachers, in task-oriented roles, second. Out at the farm there just wasn't the need for pretense.

I think of the story Joyce told of the walk that the two of them took one afternoon at the farm. Joyce was sitting drinking coffee, talking with Mary. All of a sudden she felt a tug on her elbow. It was Carrie. "Hey Joyce, let's take Annie (Joyce's dog) for a walk." As they were coming back from that walk Joyce found herself giving Carrie a warm hug - something that Joyce does so naturally. She found herself saying to Carrie how, when she was Carrie's age, it would have been so great to have someone like Carrie for a friend - someone to show Joyce how so many of the little things in the world are really special.

Carrie began to act more and more from her present-time world at SIEE and less from the world of the fearful old recordings. Mary and David, her teachers, made a point of watching her academic work closely. They didn't give her big assignments to complete in several days' time as they did some children who had learned how to manage their own time and didn't have all the anxiety about producing written work Carrie did. David and Mary's routine, for Carrie, was to take seriously each little step before getting Carrie into the next step. "One little step at a time" became the increment and, more important, the teachers didn't let Carrie decide whether she'd finish or not. She had to finish each piece but often David or Mary was close by for support. At first the assignments were things that she could do and short in duration. Mary and David received her work with justly earned praise for Carrie - praise for doing something that was hard for her to do.

In writing, when she first came to our school we asked her to copy only six sentences each day for a week - a different six sentences the teacher would give her each day. Then next week it was eight and so on. After about eight weeks she would dictate sentences to Mary, her teacher, and would copy them. Then the number of sentences was increased, and so on. Then, too, Carrie would sit next to Mary when she did her writing whenever that was possible (this was during "power writing" time so it usually was possible as all the children were writing for a ten minute period of quietness. Mary was writing too.) In this way Carrie was, step-by-little-step, unlearning what she had learned about protecting herself from fearful hurt connected with writing and other forms of pencil-and-paper work. She was unlearning by moving out from one secure position in present-time to the next, all the time supported by the strength of teachers who made her feel that they were "right there" for her; but, at the same time, didn't give her the option of choosing to be "lazy" or to indulge in daydream behavior which NOW was no longer protective, but just got in her way.

I could go on and on, and tell how Carrie found in Bruce's creative dramatics classes another way for her to show the adults and children around her how inventive and just fine she was, how close her observation was of people and things. Carrie's hooked-up self had learned so much about how people act and feel that she could do character parts with compelling creative interpretation.

She became more and more proud of "kicking the habit" as she once told a child new to the school; ...kicking the habit of shutting down whenever written schoolwork was called for.

Carrie stayed at our school for the third year - her seventh grade. She took charge of her life increasingly so that direction from her real-from-birth self seemed to dominate much that she did. Even though the old habitual protective urges still made themselves felt, she usually took herself in hand, so-to-speak, and allowed herself to stay close to her real self. For example she helped herself to do things like pages in her arithmetic book with the attitude that "OK, I know that I'm liable to 'forget' to do this so I'll do these pages first." She had three years at our school of being with people who came to know her real self - helped her to renew contact with what was so everyday and natural when she was born.

The love of her father and mother was there for Carrie all the time too. But as I look back on it, it took longer for them to adjust their awareness to sensing Carrie's real self, than it took Carrie. At first Carrie's mother accepted my intervue writeups as something written by someone who liked Carrie, but wanted to minimize Carrie's "weaknesses." I sometimes wonder even now, if Carrie's parents ever have really shifted gears; ever have looked at what they saw as their "sweet but kind of happy-go-lucky impish little girl" as a protective image, distorting Carrie's from-birth reality. But we've been open about all of this in our discussions (Carrie's father and mother and I) - and now I can carry on these discussions with Carrie participating, too. It seems hard, also, for her parents to shift to my frame-of-reference from their lifetime of viewing people - themselves too - in terms of "strengths" and "weaknesses."

I tried to teach them and I'm trying to teach in this book that it's not a matter of being "strong" or "weak." It's a matter of helping each child to live out her or his just-fine, lovable and capable real self. "Weaknesses" almost always have grown originally from needs to protect one's self-esteem.

The key, then, as a teacher (or a parent or myself) is to be able to reach each child's real-from-birth self and enjoy the essence of this person with heightened sensitivity. ...support the child in drawing from this natural, strong essence while at the same time, bit by bit, sensitively interrupting behavior tuned to old protective "recordings." That's what this book is about.

But what if you can't seem to reach that lovely-from-birth real self in a child? In blunt terms, what if you find yourself just not liking a child in a basic kind of way? What about when the behavior of a child jars you to the point of your chronic fears, anger, or what-have-you? ...when the behavior of a child causes some of those old recordings in _you_ to urge you to protective, defensive, withdrawing, manipulative, or some other sort of behavior that you don't like but when you're honest with yourself you realize that you are doing?

Theoretically, you might accept that the child's real-from-birth self is out there (or in there) somewhere but _you_ just can't seem to feel it, reach it. As far as you are concerned the "grass just isn't growing through the cracks in the concrete" of the child's real-self defeating behavior. Maybe there are no cracks?

Let's consider the case of Sean and how this all happened to me, in the next chapter.

CHAPTER 3

SEAN AND I

How Sean's behavior rekindled uneasiness in me. I just couldn't
seem to reach and feel his real-from-birth self. What happened.

Let me tell you the story of Sean and I, from about four years ago when
we had our school in the basement of the YWCA. As I do now, I routinely studied
four or five of our children each month, with observations and always including
our intervue - which we often did over lunch at a restaurant.*
Actually I didn't set out to study Sean, a little boy who recently had been
transferred to our school from an affluent suburban school. I had planned to
study Pete and Bruce - two other six-year-olds. I began to observe Pete and
Bruce at our school. As I followed them I began to see Sean who was obviously
already the leader of the little "gang" in which Pete and Bruce were members.
I had my movie camera with me as I observed them and found myself taking shots
of Sean and what he was doing far more than I did the other two. So after I
got into the study I switched my focus to Sean, with a minor study of the two
boys I originally was following.
One of the reasons I wanted to do this was that I found myself completely
caught up in what came across to me as Sean managing the behavior of the other
children by playing on their fears. I was so full of angry feelings, so fascinated and yet wanting to withdraw, so wanting to step in and protect the other
children from Sean. Over and over I saw Sean doing a masterful job of manipulating the three boys and the girl in this "gang" by extending and withholding
approval. For example, Sean's radar could sense, apparently, the exact time to
intervene to his advantage in a fight between two of his gang members. The typical gang members' fight ranged from strong but sometimes subtle bickering to
shouts and shoves but almost always revolved around one child seeking to diminish the other's feelings of being "all right" with put-downs and threats.
Feelings were hurt but this also seemed to be an intense action "game" that the
children participated in with fascination. Sean was a master teacher, as I saw
it, in that kind of fighting. I wondered if the others had learned how to put
each other down by the fearful experience of being diminished by Sean when they
got out of line.
When two of the children were "at" each other this way there almost always
seemed to be a point at which both of them were most vulnerable to the fearful
questioning of their worth - when they both seemed to be "getting to" each
other. Then the always-cool Sean, would come in as he did one time when Pete
and Bruce were shouting angry put-down words at each other. At just the moment
when I sensed each boy was closest to those anxious, fearful "Am I all right?"
feelings, Sean deftly entered the confrontation. With precisely the right kind
of imperial pronouncement in his manner, he faced Pete with "Bruce is my buddy!"
Pete seemed to reel, inside, and just began to start hitting out at anyone near
him - including Ruth their teacher, who was on the scene by this time. I sensed
Pete's progressing from initially fighting with Bruce to trying to prove he was
really just-fine in that scene, to raging at the injustice he felt upon accepting
this final "You are not OK" judgment from Sean The Lawgiver. (I wondered if
the big hug that Pete and I exchanged a few minutes before helped him feel the
injustice and not to cave in completely - that hug was full of so much "You're

*See Chapter V, for a full discussion of this child study program.

31

just fine and I can feel it" kind of feeling for both of us; I know it had that kind of self-affirmation for me.)

Bruce? He was tapped by Sir Sean at the moment he needed his release from his fearful self doubts. As I watched Bruce for the rest of that afternoon I felt that he would just do anything Sean asked.

And Pete? The next morning I again saw Pete playing in the group, willingly allowing Sean to lead adventurous fighting action and directing it excitedly for the gang. (Much of the action was in a "lets-get-the-bad-guy" fantasy and would often revolve around children taking superhero roles, learned from their watching of Saturday morning children's cartoons.) Neither Bruce nor Pete apparently felt very warm towards Sean; they often seemed to feel not-so-OK when they were involved with him. For instance, Bruce asked me more than once in our intervue, "Who do you like better, Sean or me?" When I asked Bruce to tell me about a person he enjoyed playing with, he didn't pick Sean but another boy with whom he had a give-and-take relationship - they seemed trusting and accepting of each other.

I realized early in this study of Sean that his behavior was bringing up old fearful, angry, frustrated feelings in me. One of the tell-tale signs of this was how I felt as I was walking with Sean toward the Atomic Grill, where Sean and I were to have our intervue one morning in November. I remember clearly that I found myself noticing the fear that was "up" in me. This is my writeup which I scribbled in my intervue notes as we settled in at the restaurant:

As we were walking past the library on the way to the Atomic Grill, I seemed to be having a conversation with myself - as if I were the person up for child study, not Sean who was walking about four feet ahead of me. "Huh, why are you apparently playing it cool, Bob? ...kinda keeping a note of authority in your voice - sounds like you are afraid of this little boy; like you have to remind him that you are strong...?" "Yes I do feel that way. Don't want to. How can I have a decent intervue if I come into it this way?"

I was forty-seven years old and Sean was six-years-old, yet, I found myself reacting to him as if he were my peer - and a fearsome peer, at that. It was only much later - after this particular study was over - that I realized the probable nature of the "old material" in my past that this child's behavior could very well have restimulated. (How his actions in the gang resembled ways in which I had been manipulated, hurt, dominated...) But I didn't need to have a kind of in-depth view of cause-and-effect. I obviously felt the effect, that was enough to let me know I needed help.

So I ended up giving the write-up of my intervue with Sean the title: "Reflections from and on Bob Newman with perhaps some relevance to Sean." I felt that I could describe my feelings accurately. I didn't have to infer my fear, for example, I felt it. I did not want to lay on Sean my identification of his actions with things that had happened to me as a boy; things that had provoked in me feelings of fear, anger, and helpless-alone-frustration; feelings that were all restimulated in me now by Sean's presence.

What I did was to go to Ruth and Leah who were part-time teachers working with Sean and nine other five-, six-, and seven-year-olds. "Have you felt the real Sean? ...his warm, responsive, empathetic, trusting, relaxed just-fine self?" I knew that he was born that way. I knew that somewhere, someplace, this real-from-birth "grass" was poking through the "cracks." He was born just six years ago... What I found was that what I saw - his masterful manipulation of the rather guileless openness of most of the others in his gang - was seen clearly by the two staff people. They too saw how the cool, leather coated macho role had an almost unbelievable good fit in this six-year-old. They, too, often had to remind themselves that he was only six years old. They saw his apparent goal in a relationship was to win the upper hand in an exploiting managing-by-fear way as opposed to sharing his keen enjoyment and inventive self with others. But these two teachers weren't so full of restimulated fear and other emotions as I was, apparently, because they were able to give me what I was looking for.

Leah told me, "You know Ruth told me a story the other day about Sean that you ought to hear. I think Ruth is in touch with what you're looking for, in Sean - a glimmer of his real-from-birth self."

After talking with Ruth I realized that she, indeed, had been close to the warm, lovable, yearning-for-love-from-another Sean that I knew was there, some-place - that I couldn't "find" because the eyeglasses I was seeing Sean through were so colored by the fearful angry helpless feelings I had when I had been subjected to this kind of manipulation as a child; when I as a child felt I couldn't cry, rage, or fight back. "Letting it out" was a no-no in my upbringing.

I asked Ruth to write this story about Sean for the write-up I was preparing so that the reader and I would be reminded of the real-from-birth beautiful, loving, wanting-to-be-loved warmly self in Sean. Here's what she wrote:

Sean you are such a special individual. I want you to feel appreciated and loved and cared for. Gosh it seems like you're trying
so hard but you don't know how to let people love you. How can we
help you to get all those feelings out? How can we soothe the hurt
you seem to have inside? How can we let you know we appreciate you?
How can we make it safe to let you grow?

Last week I had a group of ten children for news time. Sean was
one of them. It started out with the usual testing of me. Sean
wandered about while the other children got their pillows and
chairs and settled down. Everyone was ready to start and Sean
wandered around picking up this and that and casting glances my
way to see if I was watching. I invited him three or four times
to join the group to which the response was "no" with a sheepish
grin. The next game usually begins on the "I'll come if you'll
catch me tone," which Sean seems both to like and dislike. He
likes being coaxed, chased after and picked up but he also dis-
likes the tussle, and fights like a mad man; usually ending with
tears and an affirmation of putdowns. This seems to be a repeti-
tive pattern. ("I want you to catch me but I don't want to admit
to you or anybody else that I enjoy being caught.")

So in tune to this, I just go on and start the group. Sean looked
a bit puzzled and tried one moretime by banging a few things on
the shelf and then he meandered over and sat right next to me.
I've noticed that Sean often likes to sit close to people - parts
of you just slightly touching. I smile, he smiles and by this
time we've gone through the date and day and it's time for news.

You, Sean, bop up all ecstatic, "Can I do news first?" I'm glad
you're eager and we all wait to listen to you. Your first bit
of news begins with, "My dad and I went to the store and he bought
me...(Isn't that funny, but writing this I can't remember what he
bought you. ...toys often but this time I think it was football
stars cards?) Your face was beaming. Boy you sure do love your

dad, he's a very special person to you. And then I ask "How
does that make you feel when your dad buys you things?" And you
say "It makes me feel so good - it just makes me feel great!!!"
While you're saying this you're slowly rising from the news chair
and at the words "great" you spring up in the air and throw your
arms wide and yell so loud. It makes me feel good that you can
express yourself like that with us. You just keep on yelling
GREAT and then stop to listen with a very thoughtful look and try
it again.

Well, this keyed up emotion is a bit too much for Stephen and he
immediately began shouting "great" and jumping up and down. I
like that about Stephen; he can tune in very well to people's
feelings.

Well, after everyone's quieted down I agree to let the group yell
"great" once all together and then again at the end of the group
if that's the way they feel at that moment.

Next Timmy gets up with his two teddy bears - one big and new,
and other little and old. Timmy: "I got a new teddy." Me:
"What's special about your teddy that you can share with us?"
Timmy: "I like him." Me: "What are some reasons why you like
him?" Timmy: "He's warm and cuddly and soft and fuzzy and he
keeps me company when I'm lonely." Timmy says this so sincerely
and seriously.

People in the group nod their heads - Bart adds "Like when you're
asleep at night in your bed and you're scared," and Tom says, "Yeah,
when you feel bad."

Timmy smiles, sits down and sits his two teddys right beside him
in the chair. Sean turns around and looks so intently at the
Teddys. Next thing he's up, with the two Teddys in his arms and
across the room he races. He stops in the corner with his back
to us and holds them tight to him with both arms. Gosh, he looks
so vulnerable yet so natural at that moment.

Timmy says: "I want my Teddys." I ask Sean to give them back, but
he shakes his head. I ask "Why not?" Sean says: "I need them."
Timmy replies, "But I need them Ruth, I want my teddys." And his
eyes begin to fill up.

Here I am caught - this is the first time I've truly seen Sean
really want something in a deep close-to-his-center way and not
as a tease or game. His face told me he was for-real and then
there was Timmy.

I suggested Timmy's sharing them as Sean really did seem to need
them now. Each could hold one. This wasn't agreeable to Timmy
- the pout only became larger. Then I said to Sean, "Timmy really
needs them too now and they are his - I know how you feel; they
are so warm and cuddly - how about if you come over here and sit
on my lap and I'll give you a big cuddly hug?" Sean said "no!"
But the next minute he was on my knee - nestling up close. We
finished news.

34

At the end of the group as everyone puts chairs and pillows away,
I heard a long slow sob coming from the library. There was Sean
sobbing, big tear-drops running down his face; he was shaking in
little quivers. I rocked him a while and then he headed in for
snacktime...

This story from Ruth was what I wanted and needed. Now I could move ahead
despite the restimulation of pent up distress feelings from my early years that
Sean's behavior had brought out in me. Now I could get in touch with the real
Sean - the real-from-birth self in this little boy. I needed this sensitive
awareness to help him draw from his loving real self in shaping his actions
and feelings.

Before I go on I want to pause for a minute and call your attention to
several things that are illustrated by this story of Sean and Bob Newman. First
how helpful it is to have more than one person know the children with whom you
are working and studying if you can work this out. In this case, it was relatively easy to turn to my colleagues to get a perspective on Sean - another view
from another person who knew him and whose restimulation did not get in the way
of her sensing the lovely center in Sean.

Then, too, note how our setting and priorities made it easy for Ruth to
come close to Sean's real-from-birth self. First, newstime was the occasion
each morning when each child was helped to sense and appreciate his or her real
self. (Newstime wasn't just a word study time although as Ruth wrote something
appreciative about each child on a large chart it became an excellent lesson.)
Ruth didn't consider what she allowed Sean to do a distraction. This was right
at the heart of what she was teaching. This was a time specially set up to
appreciate and face feelings about yourself - a key learning time. Second, ours
was a school where the teacher found herself <u>touching</u> children and affirming
them this way. (Would you ever touch someone warmly if you were afraid of that
person?) Third, notice how this group was small enough (ten children) so that
each child's needs - both physical and verbal - could be given significant play.
And, fourth, notice how much of what Sean had to "tell" Ruth came through his
actions - not his words. The children met in a small corner of the YWCA basement so that there was room for Ruth to let the children express themselves
through their physical actions. (Remember how Sean could play out his drama
by running to the other corner of the room, by retreating to the privacy of
the library alcove?)*

This story shows how valuable it is to <u>live</u> with children in a setting
where we see each other in a variety of activities, moods, kinds of relationships. This is quite a far cry from the usual classroom dominated by pencil-
and-paper routines, pupils taking dutiful submissive roles and other much-
narrower-than-life boundaries for expressing their real-from-birth selves.

And this brings up a further point - how important it is that people like
me (and every other sensitively aware person I know) get a chance both to acknowledge and explore how a child might bring up old hurts and fears from our
childhoods (or later) that cause us to miss being in touch with a child's beautiful-from-birth self. In this case I asked Ruth and Leah, two of our part-time
teachers, to help me as I realized that I was "stuck" - and couldn't get beyond
those old identifications when I was close to this little six-year-old.

I should spend more time here explaining what I mean by "those old identifications." This is an important assumption that I am making and I want you to

_____

*Teachers in conventional self-contained classrooms can do this in several ways.
One way is to train other school workers (the librarian, the nurse, the principal...)
to take one of your newstime groups each morning, thus freeing you, the regular
teacher, for working with a smaller group.

understand it clearly.

I am operating on the principle that when I find myself not able to enjoy the obviously enjoyable aspects of a child (like Sean's sharp, quick, logical, creative mind) there is something getting in my way. That "something" is almost always a restimulation of old hurtful pent up emotion from distress early in my life. At the time this happens I never know exactly what is being restimulated. I just feel the result: angry feelings, guilt that I dislike this little child so strongly at the moment, moody sleepyness or daydreaming, feelings of power-lessness, anger at the child's parents, or what-have-you.

When this happens I often turn to another whose past experience might not include the kind of unresolved hurting that this child's behavior restimulates in me. That's what I did in Sean's case and found Ruth able to reach and enjoy the real-from-birth self in Sean.

Often, even though I can't find someone else, like Ruth, to help me see the child's real self, just the knowledge that I'm probably getting in my own way helps me. It helps me not to act on my feelings toward the child because I realize that the intensity of my feelings is coming from old unresolved hurts and the "steam" just isn't justified by the child's behavior. The child's be-havior might be something that I can't allow the child to continue in my class-room, but that's where I need to stop. I don't need to inflict on the child - overtly or subtly - the wrath, tears and fear that I should have gotten out a long time ago.

So how did it all work out with Sean in our school? He stayed in our school for two more years. At our next child-study time, a year after the time I just recounted, it was obvious to us (not just a hunch) what probably was going on with Sean. The pattern became so clear as Sean was so blatant in his acting. He presented his unconsciously held pattern to us day after day through his actions. We "read it" like this: "I'm bad. I know it and you might as well believe it. With the teachers I'm going to create a fuss until you will give me the close attention and touching that I need; with the other kids in my gang I'm going to keep each one dependent on me for their feelings of being OK. But at the same time I'm going to keep my alone, tough-guy, 'I don't need anybody' facade so that no one will know where I'm vulnerable - where I can be hurt. No one will know that I really want very badly to have closeness from those around me."

Now we knew the basic script of Sean's constantly-repeated drama. We also felt in touch with the lovely-from-birth real Sean. I found that I could enjoy Sean now. I didn't enjoy his manipulative exploitive behavior and restrained him often. But I found myself interpreting this as the best that he could do, given the serious frustration of his real-from-birth self that must have taken place when he was younger (and perhaps was taking place still, outside the school).

Let me elaborate. I don't know what caused him to resort to this extreme to get what babies begin with in this world - the expectation of warmth and closeness from others. I don't need to know the "causes" of his behavior; and, as in most children's cases, I will never find out. But for the sake of explan-ation let's consider this scenario which fits Sean's behavior patterns as we experienced them at school.

The story might go like this: This little baby, Sean, entered the world full of trust and warmth toward those around him. This was his real-from-birth self. Let's say it was his mother who was hurting; who for instance found her-self resenting him in her life. When he would cry he would feel the response from his mother as a strong rejection - deeply held anger, primitive feelings of wanting to remove him from her life. (His mother valued what she saw as the "strong fearless woman" in herself. She had grown up feeling little warmth - feeling "I'm on my own" from an early age.) As an infant all of this came through to Sean as a denial of the "I am just fine" feeling with which he was born. The pressure was constant so as the infant Sean grew so did his perception of his world as confirming that he was not all right - a world peopled by persons important to him who wanted him to leave them alone.

As he grew, the kinds of behaviors that seemed to ease his hurting were these: He'd be accommodating to his mother at home; not cause her "trouble" so that he'd avoid some of the feelings of disapproval and being alone. And he had a model. This is what he saw his father doing - placating and accomodating his wife at home. But outside the home he sensed how his father seemed to act with bravado toward others. He saw more and more of this as he was out with his father increasingly. For example, his father would stand up in church discussions and dominate the scene fighting for his point. His father was a lawyer who, Sean began to sense, was well known in the community for his contentious arguments, for his ability to wither a witness's defense. He also sensed that his mother enjoyed the reflected light from her husband's "strength." Sean began to feel, at an early age, that if he behaved in ways that people saw as being "like your dad" his mother and father approved.

At school Ruth found much of this background suggested by a little scene that Sean used to play out almost every morning, in the early part of his second year at our school. This was during the beginning-of-school free play period. Sean would come in and stir what had been a play session between two boys into a fight or some other thing that the teachers had to stop. Then he would continue provoking the teachers until there was a "scene" and it was Ruth who usually took him from the room to "let it out." Pretty soon this became a kind of routine, with Sean hitting and crying as Ruth held him with firmness but nonpunitively. Then more and more often he would say to her, in words, how "I'm bad." He seemed to need to get this out each morning. Finally Ruth would just say to him, as he finished crying and thrashing, something like "I don't think you're bad. I just have to stop you stirring up that fighting. That fighting messes up our life here at school." In different ways, over and over again staff people seemed to begin to get this message across to Sean. Often the interaction would take place non-verbally. Often Ruth would hold Sean on her lap, bringing him close to her. He would push away; just enough so that he would not eject himself from Ruth's lap but enough so that he could go on with his facade of "not needing anyone."

It became more and more apparent to the teachers that Sean seemed to get the message from their touching and words: "You are not bad. You are all right. I enjoy having you close to me." Here was the message that confirmed his real-from-birth self expectations. He would respond by increasingly involving himself during the rest of the day without "stirring up trouble."

Sean left after his third year. His parents said that he needed to return to the suburban schools to prepare for junior high school there. They seemed to feel, in addition, that our school was too "soft."

"It was what Sean needed after his kindergarten year," his father told us, "but now that he likes school again he should be where his neighborhood friends are." His mother added that, "In order to be tops in junior high school you have to learn the ropes in the elementary schools out here."

I haven't seen Sean during this year since he has left our school but I have a reasonably good feeling that he's exercising his real-from-birth loving, trusting, self and getting much of what he really wants in closeness from others.

I'm inferring this from his behavior at our school during his third and last year. During this year in our school, university students who spent a few days working in the school often remarked that Sean brought out especially warm feelings in them. He often, for example, would conduct a visitor around the school for an hour or so in such a way that the visitor felt enjoyed while enjoying him.

He seemed to be learning that one could make expectations according to two different "worlds" in one's life - one world at home and one at school. One could turn to others at school for the natural closeness and accepting love that babies expect from birth. My hope was that he would come to generalize this further than just school, as he grew.

During Sean's third year at our school, in particular, Sean sought me out for time and attention. I found myself drawn to this boy whose real courage was so up-front. (From day-one in our school he was fighting for his self-esteem.) It was Sean who always encouraged me to continue with my weekly collecting forray around the garbage dumpsters behind the downtown stores. Other children came along and then dropped out but Sean always reminded me that "It's time to go." This developed into some nice acquaintanceships for us. Some merchants began to save their "junk" for us. We'd often come back from the camera shop on the next block with parts of projectors, lenses, and other fascinations. We always came back with interesting styrofoam shapes.

During these expeditions I found myself laughing easily with Sean yet almost always able to tell him how an action of his came across to me. One time I felt the tone of his voice saying, "How could you be so dumb" - and I was able to tell him how that didn't feel good to me.

I found it easy to share my strength with Sean, share my courage to nurture my self-esteem and deal with fear in my life, share with him how I could just be myself with him and liked that. And it felt so good to get a big hug from Sean the time when the woman who owned the stationery store gave us her old letter press that they used to use to print calling cards. That hug was such a neat warm celebration of our printing press...and us.

CHAPTER 4

ME

How my real-from-birth self prevailed - like grass growing
through the cracks in concrete

The real-from-birth me? In this chapter I'll sketch how the direction set
by my original self began to unfold and got nurtured despite my learning, as
Sean did, self-defeating ways to accommodate the pressures I felt as a child.
I hope that this chapter emphasizes a very important point: that the lovable,
capable, all-adequate real self so readily accessible at birth in normal babies
can be nurtured, can be reawakened without massive help from the outside. The
real-from-birth self has the basic drive within it to help its direction prevail, to help it re-awaken the dormancy of self denial.

Where shall I start? I find myself sitting here at my typewriter emotionally pulling away from trying to put it down on paper - put down some of the
ways my real-from-birth self has prevailed - ways that my behavior has taken
direction from the just-fine essence that was born me.

Today I seem to be moving out, as I understand and have learned how to deal
with my apprehensiveness - living life, taking charge of who I am and might be.
I suspect that I'm emotionally pulling away from trying to describe this, right
now, because for most of my life, up to this point, moving out this way meant
an upsurge of the fear of being alone, meant pitting the feelings of powerlessness I learned as a child against all the threatening and intimidating forces
I felt were around me. I learned, as a young child, to defend myself against
this anxious uneasiness by not moving out, or at least by avoiding clear straightforward expression of the real-from-birth me as I'm preparing to write here.
Where did I get those fears, anyway?

This fear and uneasiness grew from the "I'm not measuring up" distress I
felt as I tried so hard, as a small person in this world, to please the big
people whom I felt controlled by life; whose own lives were shot through with
conflicts and distressful needs of which they weren't consciously aware. It
would have been too restimulative of their own "I'm not all right" fearful uneasiness if they had allowed themselves consciously to feel the subtle conflicts
and ways they were blocking their own and others' potentialities. Then my fears
of "I'm not measuring up, I'm not as good as I should be, I'm not answering the
needs of these big people, I'm not..." settled into what I call recordings that
held and replayed constantly the "I'm not all right" theme with apprehensive
tone. (Remember Carrie's deep down, unconsciously-held "I'm not measuring up"
recording, Chapter II).

That was the uneasiness, laid in from infancy, that was reawakened easily
when I allowed myself to experience vividly my living. And that baggage is
still here as I travel along. Right now, my sitting here at my typewriter is
an act that stirs up my fears, that restimulates many of those distressful
uneasy-feeling old recordings that were laid in so innocently, in my childhood,
by well-meaning people who in many cases were acting out the distress that was
laid into them.

But today is different - quite different - in that I'm much more in touch
with the real-from-birth me. I feel a proudness and a vigor from those real
me feelings. I know how to let the real me direction prevail. I know how to
recognize, consciously, the old recordings for what they are - just old fearful recordings and not present-time reality. So I can write this. Here goes.

My feeling now, as I begin to write this, is that I really don't want to get you, the reader, involved with the details of how I learned to feel the not-adequate anxiety deep inside - how the old recordings were laid in. Suffice it to say that most of the big people in my life, acting out of the distress that was laid into them when they were little, laid-in my distressful recordings, always playing a compelling deep-down "I'm not all right" theme to me as a little boy. As I was going through elementary school responding to this self-image, I found myself having to earn vast amounts of approval ("You're just fine" message to me) from teachers, principal, my mother. I found that I would behave in the ways that they valued to get that approval. As I look back I see Bobby Newman trying so hard to do the "right thing." The "right thing" was determined by the reactions of my strong parent and authority figures; those same kinds of authority figures from whom I had accepted and internalized the "not all right" judgments. (These dynamics have struck me so very strongly as I see them at play in the lives of elementary school age children with whom I intervue and whom I get to know "inside" in other ways. Can you think of even one elementary school teacher you had or your children have had who didn't lead children primarily by giving and withholding the approval that children so want? I can think of a few teachers who, with love and sometimes firmness, lead children by sensitively helping them to assert their needs while the teachers are asserting their own but these are rare teachers.)

But back to my story. All this time, the real me seemed to pop up, to be there quietly, too, despite my strong needs to behave in approval-seeking ways. I remember the inner proudness I felt because I could build so many things with my hands - use tools deftly and with intuitive problem-solving skill. (I learned to use tools from my father.) I remember how our fifth grade study of ships started me on a life-long fascination that touched the inquiring, yearning, hope-filled real me. I remember how exciting it was for me to experience the sights, smells and sounds of ships; to go down to the docks with my father and visit the ocean-going liners and freighters, to go to the engine rooms down in their hulls where their life lay waiting for that engine-room telegraph bell, to be set into throbbing motion. I remember how other boys used to talk about doing adventurous things but didn't do them. But I did them - quietly and usually alone. I remember the delicious feelings of the smells on a summer morning as I wandered about, kicking stones and sensing the bits of loveliness all around me - but feeling alone, uneasy with my sheer enjoyment of myself, at the same time. (This real-from-birth me, that I was in touch with, conflicted with the fearful "I'm not all right" self-image.) I remember the warmth and love that I shared so easily with an aunt and uncle who I knew loved me just for myself - not for what I could do or should be. I didn't feel I had to earn love from my aunt and uncle.

As I scan those elementary school years I see Bobby Newman - a little boy who was trying so hard to be "all right" in the eyes of the strong parent and authority figures he felt in his life - adapting and conforming in ways that had no other basic goal than to please them. But at the same time I see the real me, who was there from birth, to be growing, too, but undercover. I see the inventive, sensitive-to-the-quirky-little-things in people, the fascinated-with-the-world, the easy-to-love-those-who-accept-me, the capable builder, the inquirer - I see this real Bobby Newman not being wholly denied. I see my life being influenced by the real me developing despite my consciously following largely real-self defeating goals - like looking to my teacher, my mother, or whom-have-you, for approval - that I too often substituted for the direction of the real me.

I see some valuable skills and awareness developing because of my need to adapt to the needs of those authority figures, that later could be used to help me move out under the direction of my real self - like my fast developing skill to know where the other person was "at," my skill in sensing the moods, the "inside" state of the other person whom I so wanted to please. I think of the good feelings about myself I'd get as I learned to be good at being "right there" for the other person who needed help in taking the difficult next step. Good feelings?...yes...But, again, there was this thing of my doing all this for some of the wrong reasons - to get my feelings of respect from the approval that I earned, that way, from others. Oh how I needed big doses of the kind of acceptance that I received from my aunt and uncle - "Hey, Bobby, we love you just as you are. Because you're you!" I needed help in learning to accept those anxious "I'm not all right" feelings implanted in me like recordings, in learning to accept these as "just that stuff that I learned; stuff that in most respects does not stack up with who I really am from birth but, nevertheless is like a recording that plays and plays." I needed help in learning, on the contrary, all the ways that I was just fine - and I needed to be supported not only to appreciate what I could do well, but to enjoy pleasure that I could get when others did things for me - just because I'm me, no strings attached, no due bill to be paid; just because they can get in touch with the beautiful me that has been there all the time, from birth; just because I'm me.

And a funny thing happened to me. The funny thing was that when I stumbled into teaching at age twenty-seven I began to find out that people didn't seem to be aware of all that "I'm not all right" feeling tone that the recordings seemed to keep sending up in me. They didn't seem to "find out" about it. Each year of my teaching I found that I relaxed more and more - didn't have to heed the dull fear that the children, my principal or some of the parents would "find out."

During this time I helped someone in my family who couldn't function in the work-a-day world because of what the baffled medical doctors labelled "nervous exhaustion." I got this person into a deep counseling relationship. The psychiatrist I found listened to this person twice a week - just listened, usually. I realized that I wanted this for myself, as I saw the self-awareness emerge in this other person, even though my desire conflicted with my fear of facing consciously the "I'm not all right" anxiety that I was trying to withdraw from - my fear that "they would find out," for example, but, as I just said, I was beginning to get the hazy understanding that at least in my teaching work, there just didn't seem much bad stuff that "they" ended up finding out anyway.

I remember how my fear of seeing this therapist was counterbalanced by my pride as I invented a way for me to see this busy man. I made a deal with him that I'd ride in his car once each week when he had to make a long trip as part of his work. Then I'd take the Greyhound bus home. This was the only way he could see me; his schedule was full. By doing it this way I found myself feeling strong. I was in charge. This felt good. This helped me savor the fully adequate, inventive, fascinated-with-the-quirky-and-different, real-from-birth me.

As I look back on this, I see how I was able to face consciously the fear of exposing the "I'm not all right" anxious me that the unconsciously-held recordings were supporting as my self image. I was able to face the prospect of this self-revelation partly because I helped myself to be in touch with the just fine real me - seeing a psychiatrist just wasn't too fearful because I was reminded of my capableness as I created the process of seeing him.

This allowed me to accept the help of a good listener. It opened the door, also, for me to secure the other thing I needed which was the assurance that if I faced these self-diminishing ("I'm not all right") feelings, he would somehow get me through. Yes, I was afraid of being afraid. It was scary for me to contemplate moving to give up the main barrier I had come to use in defending myself against the fear of the "badness" in me - my defense of consciously withdrawing from the awareness of the "I'm not all right" feelings. I didn't realize, then, how common this defense of conscious withdrawal is. I didn't realize how so many people adapt this way all through their lives - with the aid of the 5:00 pm "happy hour", the "keep the good thought" teachings, and dozens of other ways. (I'm not saying that a few drinks at 5:00 pm or at any other time, or "the power of positive thinking" is necessarily all that bad. I probably could make a pretty good argument for how these things help countless good people to survive and let some of their real-from-birth-selves emerge a bit. But at least I see this as just that - survival - as opposed to letting the real-self humanness dominate and lead one's life.)

So I found myself able to deal with the initial fear of facing the scary "I'm not all right" music that I felt inside. I found myself beginning to have some doubts as to the truth of the recordings' message - at least in my teaching life. I enjoyed the feeling of being in charge of the fearful process of "seeing a psychiatrist." I felt secure that this man would "get me through" my apprehensiveness over the spectre of self-revelation.

And, too, the skilled psychiatrist with whom I worked tended to support my feelings of being in charge in another way. He just listened, almost all the time. He almost never gave advice - just questions. His questions helped me to talk about myself, to come to enjoy the real me as well as bear to experience consciously the anxious messages from the recordings which seemed to go on and on in that dull barely consciously aware part of me. The messages were woven into what I was talking about - the endless monologue from me; about how I felt when this or that happened yesterday, and when... In effect, I was comparing the day-to-day real-from-birth me with the image of me sent up by the recordings. The process tended to bathe the uncovered and subjectively held old recording images with the light of present-time objectivity. As I remember it, neither the therapist nor I talked much of "recordings" or did much verbal analysis with other psychological jargon.

So, I progressively became more aware of the real me, and the fearful overtones from the old recordings seemed to have less and less hold on me - even though the recordings seemed to keep merrily on, down there. I was able to get myself a supportive listener and questioner who encouraged me to be in touch with the neat things I did and felt, along with the distress. I'd hear myself progressively more and more.

Thus the recordings went on but so, also, did the beautiful-from-birth real me increasingly make contact with my consciousness. But the real me behavior usually came out in spontaneous ways that happened without my consciously thinking and planning seriously for them.

An interesting thing here was how I began consciously to let those spontaneous moments have "space." I began to value the spontaneous side of me - "that feels good, like fun- I'll do it," or "I think I'll take a lark and try that." I was finding myself responding more to the spontaneous, zestful, fascinated, inventive feelings that so often came from the real-from-birth me, inside. Then, often, good things would flow.

During my teaching in my one room schoolhouse in the hills near Santa Rosa, California, I found myself reading books about ships to the children - just letting out much of the real me that grew in and around my interest in ships and in the sea. This led me to take thw whole school (twelve children from six- to thirteen-years old) on a field trip to the San Francisco harbor, about seventy miles away, to study a fireboat and the liner Lurline, then in the California-to-Hawaii service. When we got back we turned a quarter of our ninety-six-year-old school building into a replica of San Francisco harbor. Much of this came from the real me inside - the real-from-birth me who used to go to the Los Angeles

Harbor with my father; the real me who was encouraged by Mrs. Hendrickson, my fifth grade teacher, who accepted me as good; who somehow got through to me as we studied ships in her class; who appreciated my inquiring, fascinated-with-ships-and-the-sea bent; who didn't manipulate me by extending and withholding approval. She helped me to like the real-from-birth me who would often step out quietly and do things that others talked about but never got around to carrying out, (for example, how I got my father to explore the harbor with me).

So, let's pause for a moment to consider this important point here. The point is that the real-from-birth me was acting all the time but my own image tended not to include much of the real me. That self image was pretty well patterned by the anxious "I'm not all right" feelings and the resultant need to please whatever authority figures I sensed were in my life at the time. But the real-from-birth me often prevailed in subtle ways (long before I got the help of my skilled listener-psychiatrist).

Consider these illustrations from my early twenties: After I graduated from Antoich College I found myself allowing the real me to prevail simply by avoiding working for a highly manipulative and directive boss whom my "I'm not measuring up" anxious patterned self would strive so hard to please at too great a cost to the real me. I looked for a job where I could be my own boss. I found myself, also, drawn to the reality in nature. I sensed that somehow the elemental simplicity and magnificence of the Sierra Nevada foothills around Chico, California was akin to the loveliness-from-birth strength of the real me. I responded by getting my teacher training there, at Chico State College.

I found myself protecting that real me by removing myself from the omnipresent potential authority figures and seeking scenes which tended to nurture what was real at birth in me, like my being the teacher-principal in the one-room school where I had no boss but me. But, the other side of the coin was that I found myself alone a great deal, fearful of the kind of relationships which, in my childhood, had been dominated by my seeking to please the strong-appearing person I found myself seeking out, so often. It was as if I were still more comfortable with the authority-pleasing way that things were when I was a child but the real me inside was pushing me away from this self-defeating "comfort" all the time. The result was often an uneasy restlessness - a feeling of not being "in gear," of conflict.

There were times, though, when my need to please those I had chosen to seek approval from and my increasingly conscious responding to my nifty real-from-birth self didn't conflict. Take the way I found myself in graduate school pursuing a doctorate, for example. Word got to Paul Hanna, a senior professor in Stanford's School of Education, that there was a young man in a one-room school who seemed to be making learning real for children. (Hanna's specialty was social studies education.) He wrote, inviting me to come see him to discuss my becoming a leader in elementary education, with a doctorate. "Me? A doctorate in elementary education? Why, no one in my family had more than a high school education..." The "I'm not good enough" feelings quickly asserted themselves...but...but along with these came the thought (I remember it as if it just happened this morning) "Huh, my wife will be so pleased with me when she hears about this." So I went to see Paul Hanna and I'm now a professor in a School of Education with a doctorate writing a chapter in a book that might influence the education of quite a few people.

However, sometimes this would backfire. Often I adapted in approval-seeking ways that allowed the real me to assert itself and keep some of its vividness, but then later, this adaptation, turned habitual, proved to be self-defeating. Let me illustrate: Rather than conflict with strong authority people I sensed in my life, I'd often quietly do things that made sense in terms of the real-from-birth me and at the same time do those things in ways that took me out of the orbit of the ever-present authority figures. My being in that one-room school out there in the hills was an example of that. In so many cases I arranged it so that "they" (in the great world of the mighty school districts) just wouldn't take me very seriously except for the particularly perceptive, like Paul Hanna. (And often, initially, I didn't take myself seriously.) But then I'd find myself irritated, later, when people, in so many ways, would appear to me to smile condescendingly and tolerate "Bob's doing his own thing", or toss it all off with "Well, those ideas about teaching children are all right if that gifted young man is doing them himself but they'll never work in our school. He's such a unique person." And I often still find myself doing that - helping others to toss off my work lightly as my way of not threatening authority figures. But, I'm at the place now where I'm tired of setting myself up so that my work is not taken seriously - tired of subtly defeating myself when I want what I have learned and invented (as is illustrated by the way we study children at our SIEE School) to affect the lives of large numbers of children. That is one reason my writing this book is so satisfying (but full of uneasiness) for me right now. "Hey world: Look at what I've done! This makes sense! Don't pass it by!...shudder...shudder...(as the unconsciously-held fear feelings come up from the still-alive old drives to please-the-authority-figures).

So, where are we as I'm leading up to examples of my key unfolding and bringing together experiences? What I'm saying here is that a lot of unfolding was going on - unfolding which followed direction from the real me - from the beginning of my life. I'm also saying that I became increasingly respectful of heeding the playful spontaneous thought, the quirky idea, that so often emerged from the wellsprings of my real-from-birth self. In addition, I'm saying that this was despite the approval-seeking behavior I found myself engaged in all the time. I find myself writing about this with some detail because this is one of the best ways I can think of to illustrate what I mean by "old recordings" and resulting self-defeating patterns and what I mean by the "real-from birth self" which grows tenaciously from the beautiful, zestful, inventive, enjoyable, warm person that is born into this world - the real self which also often can utilize inventively the collection of skills and the unique-ness that emerge from living out the directions set by those old recordings.

So now, I want to talk about three key sets of experiences that were such important real self, unfolding and bringing-together times for me. The first of these was when my two children came into my life.

Wow. When I stood out in the hospital hallway looking at my baby daughter Dusty through the newborn nursery window... When I was there I didn't merely experience the euphoria that fathers often report. It was something of another dimension - the old recordings just stopped for those minutes I stood there! The warm, zestful just-fine real me was flooding up. Somehow I didn't find myself feeling the "I'm not good enough" feelings; none of the "I have to please the authority figures at all costs." That all seemed distant trivia. I couldn't seem to have enough time there at that window. Then after Robin, my second daughter, was born I continued to feel, even more strongly, this delicious feeling. Almost always when I was close to Dusty and Robin the warmth and beauty and capableness that was the real-from-birth me was uppermost; the person I was pleasing was ME, not the latest set of authority figures. As the girls (and I) grew up I found our life together utterly full of "I'm completely adequate" delight to me. Take the Saturday mornings when we roamed about the city: these were times when the light, funloving, enjoying-so-much-what-was-around, me emerged. We visited the library and one special junk shop each week before we would go to a favorite restaurant for our weekly celebration of our-selves. I found myself laughing so easily, clowning, being a strong boundary-setter when I needed to be - but usually able to let the girls know why this boundary-setting was something that I needed to do to go on with our living and loving. That period was when I found myself, one day (was it when I was sitting by myself in my car waiting for a red light to change?...I can't remember) having a fantasy that was an expression of this key experience, in the re-emergence of direction from the real me in my life. The fantasy was that one night (around 8:00) some soldiers came breaking into our house to carry off five-year old Dusty and three-year old Robin. (They looked to me like a combination of Russian and Nazi storm troopers.) I found myself, in this fantasy, fighting them off with a strong, clear feeling of the absolutely just-fine person that I was. I felt sureness, power, and at the same time, the reality of this fearful scene as I grabbed a soldier's blunt nosed machine gun and pulled the trigger. No, somehow in that fantasy, defending the girls, I was ready to die as the completely adequate person I came into the world being; as the loving, lovable, capable person I was. Somehow this fantasy (which probably flashed through my head in a few seconds) could not have happened to me before Robin and Dusty. I realized right after that fantasy experience that I had never felt that way about anybody (including myself) before. Dusty and Robin didn't have to prove anything to me, didn't have to give me approval; I didn't have to "deliver" to them to get their approval - it was just us guys, the real Dusty, the real Robin, and the real, Bob - Daddy. Just as we were! Of course we were worth dying for, if it came to that. Yes, I felt that somehow I could never have had that kind of fantasy before Dusty and Robin came into my life. Never before had I experienced the pure distilled real me as I did in all the times that the girls and I were together.

Then the next key experience that I want to tell you about: I was given a grant to set up an elementary teacher education program for mid-career women* (The Enabling Teacher Education Program). These were people whose children were of school age and had at least half-time free to learn to teach and then to be hired on a paid, shared-time, partnership teaching basis.

Because it was a half-time program it had to be almost twice the usual length full-time Master's program. So I came up with a two-and-one-half-year teacher training program where the teachers and I spent most of our time in the schools (as opposed to college coursework) and which was characterized by a strong one-to-one relationship between each of the thirty-three persons and me. For example, I exchanged weekly, then bi-weekly journals and conferences with each person. In an inner-city school, eighteen of us were hired in place of one third grade teacher, by that school's courageous principal, Jack Murray. Jack was willing to try the unusual for his kids, and had faith in what we were and wanted to do - despite flak from his bureaucratic boss. I was the head teacher for the first months while the teachers-in-training worked with small groups of our inner-city third graders on a scheduled basis. I shared myself and my experience with the participants in settings that were as real as the love and warmth that welled up for each child, the anger and guilt that came up at times as we were working with some children, the tears that came from some of us at the lunch break (when we were without the children) in our inner-city classroom. I found that almost always the real-from-birth me came across in my one-to-one conferences with the people and our journals. Characteristically, at the beginning of the mid-career program I experienced fearful feelings coming up about how people were going to "find out." ..."find out" about all that stuff that seemed to be in my bones that the old recordings were reminding me about - how inadequate, unlovable and incapable I was. But you know, they never did! And they never did because they never experienced it. We exchanged ourselves - including what we saw as our professional problems. And what came across

---

*With the help and support of Richard Pearson

45

from them to me was the reflection of the real-from-birth me in myself; the strong but listening-to-the-other-guy person; the enjoying-the-nifty-little-things-in-everybody person; the person who looked at the real self in each student and not the textbook or the policy manual for direction; the person who had invented a reading program that made sense for each of our individual children; the person who took the risk of doing something on a lark that so often resulted in an important change in a student's development; the person who ran a teacher education program where there weren't any administrators and committees of non-involved people to act on half-digested over-simplified summary data but where there were those of us in the thick of the educational action who participated in the decision-making; the person who took the final responsibilities and occasionally had to make the final decisions alone; but the person who knew so well the needs and feelings of each of us, that those final decisions somehow almost always would fit everyone.

These students found me listening to each of them, and during these three years I had located a person to listen to me. I interviewed the head of the psychiatry department of the local medical college and with the names he gave me, finally found the psychiatrist I wanted - a man who was a skilled listener. He was a person who listened with what I experienced as respect for me and enjoyment of so much that was the real-from-birth me. I had put my experience to work. I knew that somehow I needed someone to listen to me so I would experience the feelings from my real-from-birth self without the fear and aloneness that otherwise would be shutting me down too often. The conviction was settling in that good listening to the other guy was most important for teaching that way with children. And that good listening meant, for me anyway, someone to listen to me so that direction from the real me was not only emerging at unguarded times but - direction from the real me sometimes crowded out the "I'm not quite all right" anxiety - upstaged it. More and more I found myself feeling that I was "worth it." I was worth the honest appreciation I felt more and more. All those people in our mid-career program couldn't be THAT wrong. Robin and Dusty believed in me so clearly. I wasn't kidding them. I couldn't.

Then a third key unfolding-of-my-real-self experience happened during my five-month sabbatical, visiting British elementary schools in 1971. The mid-career project had closed in 1970. (The teacher shortage of the '60's had turned into a teacher surplus market so that the experimental teacher training program's State funding was cut off.) The program had been an intense thing for me. I felt a vague, undefined feeling of needing to delay getting back into the routine teaching of courses at the University. And I felt that my wife would give me approval if I provided a trip to England for the family. In this case I was getting the green light from both sides - from the real me and from the self-defeating patterned me, reacting to the anxious "I'm not measuring up" recordings by seeking to please a person whom I sensed at times to be in the authority role in my life (whether or not that was her intention).

For my time in England, I purposely didn't set an itinerary or pre-structure myself in other ways. I let it be a time of spontaneity and discovery. (I found myself just not getting around to writing in advance of my trip, for permissions to visit this or that school for instance.) So when I got to England I did a lot of drifting from school to school once we got established in an apartment and found a school for the children near London. I quickly found that I wasn't all that impressed with the much-touted British primary schooling. American education literature at the time described British schools to be full of inquiring and eager students whom I didn't find, as I observed in many schools and worked in one school for a couple of months. I felt, for example, that the ways children were being taught to read tended to be insensitive to individual differences compared with the individualized ways I had worked out.

But one thing soon began to move me deeply. That was the beauty from children's art and craft expression that I felt all through so many of the schools I visited. I remember the first time I was aware of the words to express it. I was eating a hamburger by myself at a Wimpy stand in London - at a little chip of a table next to the window. My thought was how I was looking down at my camera and touching it fondly. It was through my camera that I was seeing and celebrating so much of the children's warm, vivid, beautiful real-from-birth self direction that they were expressing in their art work and through crafts. ...And in full-of-rules England? Maybe, I felt, BECAUSE of all the bureaucratic rules and restrictions one felt growing up in England, this expression of following one's real self was encouraged for children as a kind of an escape hatch? Anyway, I found myself bringing home, to our apartment, materials for the girls and me to express our real selves - to make beautiful paper mache masks, for example. We took to the enjoyment of it right off. I took colored slide pictures of our masks. I treasured these and my colored slides of schools full of children's expression - art work which was beautifully exhibited and respected by teachers. I found myself wanting to spend days and days in schools which to me came across as big art studios and craft workshops for children in which academic work was going on, too.

Yes, I remember how it was sinking into me that through these non-verbal ways so much motivation from the real-from-birth selves inside these children was being expressed and celebrated.

One time I admired a gorgeous, vivid, Bengal tiger embroidered on a foot square piece of burlap containing about ten different colors. The tiger's steady, strong, clear eyes made contact with me in such a warm and lovely way. It was exhibited in a just-right nook in the central corridor and art museum, of the school. I finally found the tiger's creator - a thin little girl of nine wearing a slip of a dress that was as drab as the English weather outside; a little girl who seldom raised her eyes from the floor when we talked. But as I talked with her and wrote to her I became convinced that somewhere inside her there was a real-me tiger's warmth and power...a celebration of her real self that had been there at birth.

I left England with something of my infancy rekindled in me. Something that had to do with letting the real me express itself in tune with the vividness, fun, quirky, warm, fascinating loveliness of the world around me. I could do this. (I came home and began a course in ceramics, and taught teachers how all of us could express the beauty we felt regardless of whether we saw ourselves as artists or not.)

I was drawing from such a sweet kind of confidence that was building, in England, during those beautiful times I immersed myself in children's artwork. As I look back on that scene, my own experience was beginning to tell me that direction from my real self was really the stronger compared with my often self-defeating approval-seeking behavior reacting to direction from anxious "I'm not all right" recordings. It was a special kind of strength - like the strength in a tender blade of grass. There it is, I felt, that blade of grass, coming up through a tiny crack in the concrete pavement. Pretty soon more grass will come through and the pavement itself will begin to crumble. Sure, they can fill the crack, "kill" that blade there but next Spring or even later that summer new blades will come through in new cracks. As I write about this now I realize why "God Bless the Grass," sung by Pete Seeger, meant so much to me when I first heard it some time ago.*

The "real me" grass was pushing through the pavement of old self-defeating patterned behavior, all over the place, when I got back from England. Our school

---

*For the lyrics, see Introduction.

was just beginning its second year. I found myself in a complex of new unfolding and bringing-together experiences, mostly involved with the school. When I would be at the school during those second and third years I would often sit at the art tables, in the middle of the large YWCA basement we rented, and paint, draw, sculpt - I who had been so afraid to do any artwork as a boy (except the sailboat that my uncle John taught me to sketch which I did over and over again - about two or three thousand times). So often the image that would come out of me would be a sunburst. Dusty and Robin were in the school. Susan, Leah, and an increasing group of people who wanted to let direction from their real-from-birth selves prevail, I sensed, came to work with us on a part-time basis.

And those years were tough, in some ways, too. During this time my wife and I separated. The spectre of not living with Dusty and Robin every day, being away from the little ways that we brushed against each other around the house seemed almost overpowering at times just before the separation. But, as I look back on those rough months the girls and I just hung in. I had fears of losing the easy genuineness of our relationship...Robin (seven-years old)and Dusty (ten-years old) ...but the bond between the real selves in each of us was something that prevailed even though I was living a twenty-minute walk away from them. It was like the blades of grass, again. Our relationship, grounded in direction from our real selves found the cracks and kept right on growing.

We used the telephone so much. Robin would call, I would answer as John Fong, proprietor of this magnificient little hand laundry where all sorts of neat people came and went. I'd find myself smiling as we both enjoyed the warmth and lightness of "those guys at the hand laundry," - a place where people could be together and work hard (working in a hand-laundry is hard work) while they felt the safeness, warmth, fun, and action of people's just "being." Oh yes, we'd laugh a lot about the distressful ways that some of those neat guys would get themselves into jams over and over again (as they lived out some of their self-defeating patterned behavior) but it was all right not to be perfect, in the hand laundry.

As I write this I'm smiling, now... the hand laundry...yes, the hand laundry was so much like our school. And as I think about it now, I guess I was John Fong at the school.

Me? John Fong? ...alias Bob Newman, Director of the SIEE School? Yes, I guess it does fit. In my playful fantasy over the phone with Robin I'd be John Fong, feeling a responsibility for the hand laundry; feeling a need for us to get each order out on time and well done, but feeling that I didn't have to be perfect; enjoying how others enjoyed my warmth, my capability (I really knew the business); but more than anything else, how people there seemed to enjoy me for just being me. I felt accepted and enjoyed in an easy way in the hand laundry and found myself being important in the lives of all the others there - helping them to enjoy being themselves and feeling good about how everyone just seemed to know that they were OK. ...and helping them to get the orders out on time and well done.

In reality, the school was developing along the hand-laundry model rather than industrial-military model on which regular schools were based. I mean we were a community of hard workers where each person was doing a particular job (collars or wet wash or...) and where no one worried all that much about who was boss over whom - except that all realized that John Fong was the person in the laundry who took the final responsibility and had to make the final decisions at times. He accepted this. They accepted him. He accepted them.

But what helped me, alias John Fong, to move out this way with my real self in the school? As I look back over those first few years I see several things. First is Susan Manes, co-founder with me of our school. Somehow Susan saw the real-from-birth me - even more clearly than most of the people seemed to, when she was a student in our mid-career program. Susan reflected this just-fine real-from-birth me back to me so naturally in the easy ways that she found to let me know how much she appreciated the real me. And Susan set this self-appreciative tone in our school as she taught the children too. I saw her do this with child after child. She taught me so much about taking the risks of expressing honest appreciation and being interpersonally aware, in a heightened sense, so that one easily found those special qualities to enjoy and appreciate in the other person.

In another way, Susan helped me let direction from the real me dominate, in the school and in other parts of my life. She persuaded me to begin co-counselling training. In co-counselling, the assumption is that we all need a warm appreciative listener to help us listen to ourselves. And, furthermore, this isn't something that only an esoterically trained professional counsellor or psychiatrist can learn to do. Almost anyone who isn't under an undue amount of distress can learn to help another listen to her- or himself. The co-counselling training is built around the practice of people sharing two hours of listening, each week. Now, on Sunday morning my co-counsellor and I usually meet in a quiet office space downtown from 8:00 to 10:00. He is my counsellor for an hour and then we reverse.*

I found, that during these years, and now, I was listening to myself - in tune with the direction from the real-from-birth-me - in another way, too. I found that it felt good to get up early just as the sun was coming up, sit in a comfortable chair drinking a large cup of coffee and eat an English muffin spread with honey and butter. I found myself nursing that large mug of coffee for about a half-hour or three-quarters of an hour most mornings. This would be a time, as I looked out the window toward the horizon across the valley, ...this would be a time when I would find myself relaxing all over but feeling sharp and alert. I'd find so many little things that happened yesterday coming up again in an easy comfortable way. So often, what seemed to be perplexing situations yesterday dropped into place and I found myself with right-fit decisions about what to do today. Little things often asserted themselves - such as how I needed to get an estimate for repainting the rusty spots on my car. Somehow, my world... Well, how will I express it? Somehow... Yes, I have it: So much of the time during this quiet time I felt tuned to the just-fine real-from-birth me. This summer, as I write this chapter I find that my best writing is just after this time of quiet - time that feels so good, time when I seem to be able to listen to, to express and enjoy me.

At the same time that I was enjoying the real me I found myself enjoying sharing my real self with children and helping them to enjoy the ways that their own real-from-birth selves were coming out in their lives. During the first years of our school this moved from my casual one-to-one relationship with children to my becoming the child-study leader in our school. I worked out a child-study program aimed at helping me become tuned to the just-fine, real-from-birth self in each child; helping the children enjoy their own real-self direction; helping teachers sense this lovely essence of distinct individuality in the children with whom they worked; and often helping teachers sense how a child's habitual protective behavior patterns were blocking direction from his or her realness.

---

*Co-counselling training is taught as part of "re-evaluation counselling" training. For more information about who to contact for training information, write for a list of area reference people in the U.S. and overseas:

Re-Evaluation Counselling
719 2nd Avenue North
Seattle, Washington 98109

CHAPTER 5

ROB

How our child-study program brought us in tune with the real
Rob - helping Rob to help himself.

Rob came to our school when he was eleven and entering the sixth grade.
I had lunch with him about a week ago. He now is fifteen going-on-sixteen, and
a sophomore in high school. I guess one reason I find myself wanting to tell
you his story is that Rob was and is a boy who did, at age twelve and thirteen,
what I might have done too if I had the kind of school, home support and self-
awareness that Rob had.
    Another reason I'm telling you this story is that it is a good example of
how our child-study program helps teachers to work with heightened awareness -
special sensitivity to how the real-from-birth self is showing through in each
child; expanded awareness to how children might be behaving in habitual real-
self defeating ways that at one time probably helped them adapt to powerfully-
felt pressures from the adult world (remember Sean adopting the "I don't need
loving" stance to accomodate his mother's needs to be psychologically distant
from him?); and finally (and most important) how teachers and children can enjoy, with heightened awareness, their real-from-birth selves while enjoying
that fascination in the other person.
    I hope that as you read through this true story you will take special note
of my role as the child-study leader. I lead our monthly all-day child-study
meetings when we study about four or five of our children; I gather much of the
background material through observations and intervues with children; teachers
and I spend a great deal of our weekly or bi-weekly conferences talking about
the children so that our perceptions of each child are tempered and adjusted.
    I begin the story of Rob with the lunch that Rob and I just had. This was
the first time that I had talked in a sustained way with Rob for the last two
years. I had had short conversations with him and had talked with his mother
so I was not out of touch but I wanted to have another time to sort out my perceptions; I wanted, also, to check them with Rob. What came across to me was
a person who was clearly in touch with himself as he moved through his life
scene. For example, when Rob told of his continued enjoyment of playing games
with his friends he told of often not coming out the winner. As I listened I
got a good feeling for his enjoying what he was doing, being with his friends.
I explored this with Rob "What comes across to me, Rob, is that you don't need
to win to enjoy yourself. If this is true, how do you account for it?"
    Rob easily and lightly came back with "Yeah, that's right - I just feel
like a winner." I added, "...all the time?" He nodded. We both knew, I felt,
that we were talking about being in touch with his "I'm just fine" feelings and
how there were many times that the cares of the day would stir up old fears and
make it hard to be fully aware of this confident steadiness from deep inside.
During our lunch I was reminded of the way that Rob allowed much of his authentic inventive intelligence to work freely in his life. I knew that he under-
stood what I was trying to say, because he often provided an analogy - often
humorous - as feedback. At one point in our conversation I was explaining how
when I was growing up and well into my thirties, I was like two different people
at the same time, one who was striving hard for the approval of the authority
people in my life, willing to be led and manipulated by them to avoid their
withholding approval; at the same time, at a deeper level usually, I was

responding to the "I'm just fine" inventive keenly enjoying real-from-birth me
that was alive and well and growing through the cracks in my approval-seeking
behavior patterns. I paused. Rob smiled and came out with "Yeah - like you
were Dr. Newman by day and SuperNewman by night?"

I didn't have to ask Rob for this feedback, he seemed to sense that I needed
him to keep responding to let me know how well he was understanding what I was
trying to explain and how it wasn't too "heavy." I remember the feeling I had
when I sat down to lunch with Rob; that what I was going to try to explain was
going to be difficult for me to do. I needed lots of feedback. Rob picked this
up easily, without my having to tell him.

I found Rob able to accept honest affirmation from me without being too
bothered with uneasiness, without having to resort to mild self-putdowns or
other ways that I find most people tend to fend off honest appreciation from
others when it comes in straightout ways. Oh yes, there was an occasional humorous little self-negation in response to some specific appreciation but it came
across to me as if he were doing this just because that's what one has to do in
most circles. It didn't seem to come from down deep inside.

When he first came to the school about four and a half years ago, this
wasn't the way that Rob came across to most people at our school. I had known
his mother as she was working as a secretary in an office with people I knew.
She described Rob as being able to read almost any book in the library, to understand complex logic, as having fascinating hobby interests. She also told about
how he seemed to be going through withdrawing kinds of behavior at the suburban
middle school he was attending. She worried about his feeling sleepy much of
the time; his seemingly dutiful but bored attention to his homework and everything else involved with trying to fit in at school.

What Rob had to do to get approval, to fit in, was at odds with what seemed
to make sense to himself deep down inside. He began to be more and more critical
of himself - taking it out on himself because of his unhappiness with the school
scene. This struck me because I've found this kind of strategy to be universal
with sensitive-to-the nuances schoolchildren who haven't blocked their real-
person adaptive intelligence. Some become cynical about school and soon learn
to settle into "playing the game." Others slog on but feel something's wrong
with them because they still believe what the school people say - that what
doesn't seem to make sense to them is "good for you." The rub often comes when
a child gets older - at about Rob's age then - and he becomes more and more
sure that a great deal of the school-related academic and social tasks seem
trivial and not related to the values that he accepts, perhaps from his parents.
Yet he still doesn't want to be open with his teachers about how he feels this
dissonance. He's learned the school code all too well: don't question the
school's assumptions. Then, often, as a consequence, I see withdrawal disapproving-
of-himself behavior because somehow he doesn't feel he "fits."

From almost the first day at our school, Rob's apparent dissatisfaction
with some of himself was picked up by several of the children in his group who
also had come to our school with a lot of uneasiness around feelings of "Am I
all right?" Rob wasn't a cool cat. His manner was open and trusting, basically.
That made him a sitting duck for others who had anger-laden needs to see themselves as more adequate. And there were several children in Rob's group whom
I saw as bringing plenty of angry, fearful, self-doubting bewilderment to school
that year.

In looking back on that group now, four years later, David (Rob's teacher)
and I realize that we've learned a lot. We've learned more about the maximum
number of children, with these scars of being hurt in previous schooling experiences, that one group can accommodate - especially when led with the expectations
that David held. David expected each child to exercise self control and empathy

toward others. At least three of the children in that group of eleven seemed to have strong needs to react against the feelings of powerlessness and inadequacy that they had felt all their lives by striving to exercise power and control over the others in the group. The most dominant two of these were new to the group that year. David's previous year's group (the first group he had taught by himself) was dominated by children who had come up through our school and seemed to have had their needs for attention and respect reasonably well satisfied when they entered his group. But those children had left our school for junior high. So this year - Rob's first year - David found himself feeling off-balance the first few weeks. His previous year's way of keeping a low profile wasn't working as it had. As I saw it, however, the children definitely felt that David was in charge. Not one of the children seemed to feel that he or she could push David very far. As he had done the previous year, David intentionally kept his presence somewhat removed from the interpersonal dynamics in the group. I suspect now that if he had those first few weeks to do over again, David would do some things differently. For example, he probably would be quicker to express his feelings when he sensed one child putting another down hurtfully. But there is a limit to what one teacher can do in muting the expression of the hurt that several of these children had felt in previous situations. We go through this kind of thing every year at our school; we have to ride it out when children begin to react to the respect for themselves they sense at our school. Often the hurtful powerless-feeling anger that some children suppressed in the previous school situation comes welling to the surface. Our job is to allow them to express this, but not to hurt others or themselves, in doing it.

Rob, apparently was expressing some of the hurt and anger that he had suppressed in his previous schooling situations, but toward himself - in self put-downs. For example, Rob would make jokes at his own expense. He let people know that he wanted them to like him but that, in some areas of his life, he didn't like himself very much. At the same time the children must have sensed that Rob had a lot going for him - a lot of his real-from-birth self was at work for him in his life. They must have sensed that he could absorb a three hundred page history book in an afternoon and a morning. Also, it was obvious that Rob could be one of the funniest people around. Several children soon found out he had many of the adult mysteries figured out - such as the actuarial logic of the insurance business. They found out that he knew more about the various rock groups than did many disc jockeys. This all added up to both a threat and a vulnerability - a threat to some of the children's shaky feelings of adequacy and an invitation to them to put Rob down. Rob spelled out for the other children his doubts about himself - those areas where if someone needled him, he could feel a great deal of pain. He wasn't "covering himself" as the others had learned to do - as so many children learn to do so early in their lives. One of the things that drew me to Rob was his lack of coverup behavior. He showed clearly his warmth and lovableness. As a little boy I had taken the route that Rob had apparently taken. I had withdrawn a lot from situations and other children and had suffered the hurt. But like Rob, I apparently didn't shut down my trusting warm feelings in the process as much as I would have done if I had "played it cool."

The other children must have sensed Rob's frustration and anger at the conflict in this part of his life - how he knew that he was adequate, lovable, trusting, inventive, and able to enjoy the world in quirky fun ways, yet at the same time was getting messages that he was not quite right; not fitting in as easily as he felt he should be doing.

David suggested that he be in the first group of children that we studied that year. In October in Rob's first year at our school, Rob and I want to a

room in the back of the YWCA, where we had our school then, for our first intervue. It took about a half hour or forty minutes. It was warm in that room I
remember, and the light was bad. But it was away from people - a chance for us
to share our real selves. Here is my writeup of the intervue.

REN:* Where were you born and when, Rob?

Rob: In Syracuse at Upstate Hospital, on May 13, 1962 - Mother's Day.

REN: What's one thing you like about yourself, Rob?

Rob: I laugh with young people...and old people...and my mother.

REN: And one of your favorite foods?

Rob: My favorite food is macaroni and cheese. I cook for myself when my mother
      goes to her University classes (that's on Monday, Wednesday and Thursday).
      I like to cook up chicken and I make rice cup-o-soup. When I go camping
      I sometimes cook hamburgers - but I get a little help. Joyce told me I
      could cook the hamburgers when we go out to her farm next week. I like to
      make chicken covered with pineapple sauce. You take the can of pineapple
      and probably wrap the slices in tin foil and then take the juice and soak
      the hamburgers in the juice before you cook them.

REN: Have a question for me, Rob?

Rob: Yeah. What about where you were born and all those things you just asked
      me?

REN: I was born in Los Angeles, California, September 27, 1927. The best thing
      that happened to me that I can remember was when my daughter Dusty was born
      and about two years after, Val, my other daughter, was born. (When Robin
      was born I really was afraid. I wasn't at all sure that I wanted another
      child. I remember I was looking for a new job right then and kind of unsure
      about the future, and some other things.) My favorite food is, well, one
      of them is homemade soup. I make it myself. One of my hobbies is to fix
      up things that have integrity in them but people have let them run down -
      like strong pieces of oak furniture.

      You ever been afraid, Rob?

Rob: I am afraid of the dark sometimes. When I go to bed at night my mother
      fixed up a night light in my room. It's like a desk light with a floures-
      cent bulb.

REN: Any dreams you can remember?

Rob: Can't think of any.

REN: Here's a question that I invented a little while ago. I call it the
      Giant Memory Machine Question. Imagine that there was this machine over
      there on the wall of this room that would be slowly taking away all of
      your memories - memories of things you enjoyed - except for those memories

---

*Robert E. Newman

that you told it about. What's one of your memories that you wouldn't want the machine to take away, even for a little bit of time?

Rob: I wouldn't want to lose the memory of the day I went to Roseland Park. I went with friends who live near me. I liked that day because I went on the rides.

REN: You mentioned that you earn some of your money. How do you do that?

Rob: How do I earn money? Well, I have one paper route that is coming in a week. I got the route (selling GRIT, a weekly paper) by clipping a coupon in a comic and sending it in. I get 7 cents out of every 20 cents. If I sell 50 papers I get $3.50 per week. The first time I sent this in I didn't get an answer. The next time I wrote I got an answer. I'm going to sell it by ringing doorbells around where I live.

Then there is the LIVERPOOL SALINA REVIEW. I called and they didn't have anything open. They said that in a week there might be an opening. I just called and asked the person who answered the phone, "Hello, I'm interested in a paper route."

REN: Rob, what's one way you feel the school might be improved?

Rob: How might the school be improved? Well, I put up an idea box about changing the school. After two weeks, all I found in it was rubber bands. Nobody gives a shit about the School because if they did they would put ideas in the box. I gave David a suggestion: We should be grounded four days instead of two weeks. Just about our whole group is grounded because of noise in our office area and because people have left without permission. Jeff and Doug and (can't remember others) are the only ones who haven't been grounded.

REN: What about the good things about the school?

Rob: The good things about the school? Well, you can learn old stuff (that you have to learn so much of in school) and relax. In my other school I got tired going from room to room and almost fell asleep I got so tired. Here you have time to rest.

NOTE: (REN) There was a kind of pitter-pat noise in the ceiling above Rob and me. (We were in the Y's staff room at the back of the building) I said that it sounded like chipmunks up there. Rob said, "If it is Chipmunks they gained a lot of weight." (Later we went upstairs and found a nursery school up there.)

Rob: I know that I have a good sense of humor but most people don't laugh at what I say. When I tell jokes people don't laugh. Like when my mother says, "Funny he doesn't look Jewish" people laugh. When I say it they don't.

Oh, I just had an idea for the idea box. I'm Jewish. Jewish people should get Jewish holidays. (REN: I explained to Rob that our school's policy is that anyone can stay home any time he/she want to if that's OK with parents. He said that he and his mother didn't know about that.)

REN: Let's see - my last question. Well here's one: What's one thing you really care about?

Rob: What do I really care about? Well, when I see a dead dog I walk over and pet it and walk away. I don't feel too good, because dogs are nice. I have a cat who acts like a dog.

REN: Think of anything else the teachers should know at our child-study meeting?

Rob: I can't think of anything you should tell the teachers at this staff meeting that is coming up.

Oh, I sometimes make jokes (that people don't laugh at) by putting my head down and faking snoring when people talk too much...

In my intervue with Rob I found myself sensing that I could get right to questions that dealt with his and my real-from-birth selves. I didn't have to touch on those areas delicately as I have to do with children who might be made uneasy by my questioning flat-out, "What's one thing you like about yourself." To some extent this was because I had had several occasions, before our inter-vue to get to know Rob. I often found myself telling him what was "up" with me right then as we met in the hall and talked for a few minutes. When it came time for our intervue I found myself enjoying Rob easily and liked his easy trust of me. We liked each other - it was obvious to me. At the same time I found it easy to identify with Rob's hurting as he was so open (and appeared to me to be so vulnerable). I sensed how close to the surface his real self was - how somehow, despite all the flak, he was living close to his real-from-self birth self even though in parts of his life he seemed to feel so disappointed with himself.

About two weeks after our intervue we on the staff met for our regular monthly child-study day and shared our perceptions of Rob's actions and relation-ships (along with studying three other children). Staff people were drawn to Rob's honesty about his feelings but they felt his hurting, his frustration and anger, and as usual in this kind of situation, they had various feelings them-selves around "not knowing what to do."

Some of the written comments the teachers brought to be read at the begin-ning of this child-study discussion follow. These show the teachers' concern for what they saw. I asked teachers to try to tell what they saw as opposed to trying to interpret it, although we all knew we had to be human and try not to be coldly clinical. "Being human" meant, to me, reporting their interpretations as their feelings as opposed to judgmental facts that they would pass on to the other staff people. Their feelings were facts if they were clearly seen by the reader as just that - feelings the teacher was reporting. Or, in the case of Joyce's writeup (below) the feelings and reactions toward Rob that she reported as coming from "the children" were what she got as the central tendency of the thinking of the group - not at all necessarily what was "true." Joyce was our art teacher. Here's what she wrote for staff people to read at the beginning of our child-study meeting:

No matter what medium is introduced in art period, even toothpick and plexiglass sculpture, Rob makes his name out of it and some-times his mother's. In private conversations with him he seems so adult-like. I find myself caught up and interested as he so often becomes animated when talking about his stamp collection, for in-stance. Whenever I see Rob he is isolated (isolating himself

usually) from the rest of the group. He likes to read out on
the steps by the boys' and girls' rooms. At the farm last
week he was always by himself, spent a lot of time playing
"farm golf" which he invented. (You hit a rock around with a
stick.) There was a lot of trouble on the **overnight** at the
farm concerning where he would sleep so he wouldn't be picked
on; so that we could avoid his accusations of people stealing
his things, throwing things at him and all that. The other kids
typically say that he starts a lot of it, "is asking for it"
always thinks he's being misused when he really is not being
bothered, etc. But I've noticed that they pick on him sometimes.
He "acts like such a big deal," so they say.

As I read Joyce's writeup and the reports of the other staff members, I
brought my interpretations to them in my mind and feelings. I could because
there were descriptions of behavior, incidents, examples and the like. There
were plenty of interpretations of the facts there also. These were usually
less useful to me. As I read the writeups I'd find myself separating the interpretations from the reports. That was reasonably easy to do because when the
teacher didn't clearly label an interpretation as that, it was clear in the context of almost all the writeups. Also I knew these teachers and had worked with
them. This was more data for me to use in understanding what they had written.
I knew how much to rely on the judgment of Joyce, for example, in interpreting
interpersonal scenes where self-esteem was clearly at issue. I knew how children who were hurting, particularly in their self-esteem would gravitate toward
Joyce - how she had such fine intuitive sense of what was going on with the
children who came to her.
I wasn't limited of course to using the observations that the teachers
made. I had made my own observations and shared with Rob in our intervue. I
wasn't therefore, confined just to the teachers' writeups.
I had focused much of my data gathering around what it was like to be close
to Rob's magnificant real-from-birth self. I found that as usual, teachers'
reports seemed to focus on the corners of this young person's behavior where
they sensed the hurting was, as opposed to enjoying his all-right-real-from-
birth self. His hurting and their hurting - as the teachers found themselves
a part of his scene - was apparent to me as I read the things that each teacher
chose to write about; how each teacher chose to express it. These written comments from the teachers didn't describe <u>the person</u>, Rob. They tended to deal
with those parts of his life, his relationships with the children in a particular group where each teacher sensed that his hurting seemed to show through.
For this reason I have always found myself reluctant to share this kind
of child-study writeup with parents who almost always seem to be asking, "Is
my child all right?" Now that federal law* makes it mandatory that parents
know about and be permitted to read all material that is written at school about
a child, the staff people and I have decided not to write this kind of teacher
report for our records. We now meet at child study meetings with teachers
reporting from their notes, with much of it oral. I feel that this is the best
we can do under the circumstances. I just can't see adding to a child's distress by giving parents writeups from teachers which don't address themselves
to the question that I must assume the parents are really asking: "To what extent is my child all right?" The parents are going to draw answers to their
question from what they read. If they were to read these writeups they would
come up with the wrong answers to their question.

---

*The Buckley Amendment In The Freedom of Information Act - or as it is some-
times called "The Sunshine Law".

I see it as a key responsibility of mine to help parents (as well as staff people and me too) be in touch with the alive-and-well manifestations of a child's real-from-birth self - those delights and warm fascinating aspects of the child which have grown from birth and are there for the seeing if we can be helped to sense them clearly. In Rob's case I felt these magnificences as clearly as I felt his hurting in the areas on which we found ourselves focusing. Part of my job, as I saw it, then, was to help staff people not to lose sight of Rob's real-from-birth self - his keen enjoyment, for example, of so many of the fascinations in the world. This losing-sight of aspects of the child's real-person happens, I've found out, when caring teachers feel themselves hurting in response to their involvement with the hurting of a child. They are not thinking as clearly as they might, had they not been so distressed.

So when you read this kind of writeup, keep in mind that the staff people, who are writing, are sharing Rob's hurting, which is a beautiful thing as you contemplate their caring and nurturing empathy. Keep in mind, as you read, that these teachers were writing about one part of Rob's life, at only one time in his development. Keep in mind, also, how important it was for me to help all of us remember that what we were doing had great potential for helping Rob to deal with the hurting that we all sensed in him. It was essential for us all to see that not only were we doing this to help him remove particular roadblocks to his moving out from his real-self center; we were also doing this so that he could learn a process and an optimism. He could learn what I have learned from my personal experience: I can come to take charge of my own life in ways that allow me not to let self-defeating behavior patterns stand in the way of my being and enjoying the real-from-birth me.

Here are the writeups of two more of the teachers. First, Anna, the creative dramatics teacher:

In group activity in drama, Rob does not really want to participate, as I see it. He walks away or somehow separates himself from the total group or from a partner. Rob is seldom chosen by other students but I've concluded they do not feel negative about working with him. When Rob is firmly and strongly urged to participate by me, he is excellent in both planning and playing of a dramatic situation. He has shown good concentration, characterization, clarity, precision, and humor in his work. He has responded enthusiastically to any kind of solo performance. Rob seems to want to be firmly directed into participation by me. Children don't really urge him to join in activity (basketball in the gym, for instance) and I feel Rob feels unwanted by the group. Rob's around a lot in the Y halls and lobby. He is not creating a problem but I feel using it to separate himself physically and mentally from the group he feels does not really want him. He seems often to want to isolate himself both physically and mentally from the group. Rob also takes the "clown" role on some occasions which does bring him some approval.

David (his group's teacher):
On the first couple of days of school Rob and some of the other kids started off antagonizing each other. I wasn't able to pinpoint any particular reason or incidents which started it. But it quickly developed into what we later started calling "circle games," i.e., Rob does something to somebody's office (because they had done something to his) and then they do something back to him, who then, in turn, does something back to them etc. etc. ad infinitum.

I noticed such things going on between Rob and Pete, Rob and
Cynthia, Rob and Bill S., and briefly with a couple of others
(Bill M?).

During a meeting we had, Rob announced that something had been
stolen (my word) from his desk. Bill M. told him that it might
be because someone didn't like him. What struck me about the exchange was that everyone (including Rob) seemed to accept without
question that there were people who didn't like Rob. This was only
after a couple of days of school.

Rob is always having things taken from him (presumably stolen) but
he (in almost all cases) finds the missing item which was, he
reports, returned secretly or moved to another spot in his desk
(hidden from him). I keep getting the impression that he misplaces
things and then blames it on those who are out to get him. (And
they seem to be.) Some of the missing objects were a part of the
"circle games" being played earlier, but that was only during an
overlap period between those games and the missing items stage.
Rob doesn't view himself very positively (to put it mildly) and
constantly interprets others' actions as designs against him. He
objects most strongly to certain actions of others which he himself duplicates.

I remember the dialogue at our child-study meeting when we took up Rob
after going over my intervue write-up and the teachers' writeups. So much of
it had to do with how Rob seemed to be getting in his own way in securing for
himself what he seemed to want and have every right to expect - the warmth and
enjoyment of the other children and the respectful appreciation of himself. I
remember our talking about how we just couldn't expect Rob to untangle this
self-defeating circle without our stepping in and somehow helping him see the
magnificence of his real self - and giving himself credit for so many neat
things about himself; those neat things that were so plain for us to see even
though we, too, were caught up in distress and anger when we saw some of the
children and Rob himself putting him down.
I remember how so much of this discussion brought up strong emotion in me.
As I sat there listening to staff people tell stories about what Rob and these
children were into I found myself feeling anger, tears, trembling - all those
feelings that easily slipped into my consciousness as my feeling Rob's dilemma
stirred up old fears and frustrations from my own life. But I found that I
didn't shut down. I didn't have to withdraw by doing something I've seen so
many psychologists and teachers do when they talk about the hurting of a child
- withdraw by using clinical language, (eg: "In this case, we find a child
who is seeking to maintain his negative self-image while at the same time he
comprehends the congruence between those same actions and universally held aspects of self-esteem.") (Yuk.) I didn't withdraw this way or in some other way
to insulate myself from hurting as I identified with Rob's hurting. One very
important reason that I didn't have to do this or protect myself from the
hurting in some other way, was that the other people in our meeting supported
me by allowing me to discharge my feelings. I found myself with the courage to
take a few moments to let go with some angry invective, release a few tears, to
tell them how feelings of being scared were coming up in me. I remember how I
felt both able to keep my awareness high and at the same time feel the loving
support of the other staff people. I remember too, how others in our staff
group took this time, themselves, to experience Rob's hurting and some of their

own restimulated old hurting while at the same time being aware of how it all seemed to fit together.

When we left the child study day we didn't have a recipe or recipes for what each of us was going to do to help and support Rob. We left with heightened awareness of this magnificent kid - this young person who was intuitively brave enough to be his honest self even though it showed the world that he wasn't satisfied with himself - made him vulnerable to others who needed to raise their self esteem at his expense; this child who showed that he wasn't afraid to be afraid; who, for instance, fought back at fearful feelings of inadequacy even though he did it, perhaps, by projecting his self criticism on others and then getting angry at them for holding those feelings.

We felt his courage, too, in making himself available for help. Our staff people were much more ready to help now. They had an awareness of Rob's scene so that whenever the right time presented itself they found themselves responding in ways that showed their sensitivity to Rob's behavior - both his actions that showed his real-from-birth self and his actions that showed real-self defeating behavior. Joyce responded in her ways, David in his, and so on.

One day about two weeks after our child study meeting Rob and some of the children in his group were having a particularly acrimonious kind of argument over something that Rob accused two of them of doing to him. The same old story; only this time things were different. The staff people now shared a common understanding as well as a heightened sensitivity to what was going on. This was potent preparation that made it much easier for staff people to move decisively while supporting each other. Both David and Susan Manes happened to be on the scene when this fight was taking place. Susan found herself taking Rob aside. David listened to the complaints of the others. Susan helped Rob to appreciate his angry feelings as perfectly all right. "It's just fine that you feel angry, Rob. It's obvious that this brings up a lot of hurting. Let me hear it again." At the same time she didn't affirm the kind of never-ending circular argumentation that had been just going on between Rob and the other children. Rob must have felt Susan's appreciation of his courage to take a stand against being put down (even though at least some of it might have been caused by his self put-down messages to the other children). Somewhere in their discussion Rob and Susan began to talk about Rob's coming to work in her group (which met in a church about a block from the "Y" where David's group met). They talked about his taking a vacation from this scene which seemed to both Rob and Susan to be loaded against him by this time. Rob was interested and doubtful at the same time. He knew the children in Susan's group, as Susan worked only half time and her group merged with David's group most afternoons, but they were younger than he was (from seven- to nine-years old). He felt that he was supposed to be with his age group, the older children. With Susan's support they decided to try this for a week if it was agreeable with his mother. (Even though Susan had not worked with Rob before this at all, her involvement with Rob through our child-study program helped her to pick right up at this moment and do things like discuss it all with Rob's mother).

At the end of the week Susan and Rob decided that they would continue with his staying in Susan's group. Again Rob was drawing from his courage to do that which was outside the norm. But in this case he had Susan's strength and sensitively aware insight to support him in seeing his action as an affirmation of his real-from-birth self rather than a disappointment to himself because somehow, again, he turned out to be "different."

Susan had come away from the child study meeting thinking of how Rob was asking for teachers to help him both be himself (different from the norm in some important-to-him ways) and yet feel the pride and warmth toward himself which would draw others to him and which would help him to reach out to them from his comfortable self-realization.

What did Susan do in helping Rob help himself? During this morning classroom time, Susan constantly interrupted Rob's actions when he put himself down
in his apparently unthinking habitual and often humorous way. She constantly
gave him incontrovertable proof of his value. For example, in the daily ten-
minute "power writing" that Rob would do (daily timed writing practice beginning with a sentence stem or title supplied by Susan, such as "There was a cow
walking down Main Street...") Rob would sometimes dash off something that was
not near his ability and if anything, showed some degree of contempt for his
ability. Susan just wouldn't accept this. "Rob, take whatever time you need
and go into the next room and do this again." At these times he seemed, to
Susan, to be asking her to help him do what they both knew that he could do and
wanted to do well. Or sometimes Rob would mildly put himself down when he did
something well and, again, Susan just wouldn't have it. He might say, "Sure
I know that I got 100% on that math page. It just was such an easy page." Susan
would listen to this but seemingly effortlessly reply, "Well, Rob, it was easy
for you but that's a reason for you to be joyful about what you can do. For a
lot of people that page would be hard."

And when Susan invited Rob to be part of her group she not only sensed
clearly what he needed, she felt she knew that her way of teaching would fit
his needs. She knew that she was constantly asking children to look at the fine
ways that they were doing things and the ways that she was proud of herself too.
Her doing this humorously helped her to be so radical as to encourage them all
to appreciate themselves honestly. For example she showed them how a part of
her appreciating herself was her enjoying the embarassment of her mistakes - her
courage to laugh at the fear of making mistakes. When she misspelled a word and
one of the children caught her mistake she'd turn to them with a serious look
and a twinkle in her eye, saying "Teachers never make mistakes." It was fun
for all of them to be able to laugh at those little ways that she didn't measure
up.

Susan knew, too, that it would help Rob right then to experience how she
was "up" most of the time in their classroom. It seemed too easy for Rob to
let his heavy feelings about not being at the norm get him down. Susan felt
sure that her "up" light way would be a good role model for him right then.
(One reason Susan was able to be this way honestly was that she was co-counselling
with another trained co-counsellor once each week. They helped each other get
off a lot of heaviness in their own lives. During a co-counselling session
Susan sometimes would, for example, beat on a pile of pillows and she might rage
at something that happened earlier that day in her classroom - something that
had stirred up feelings of anger. Often this would be followed by tears, trembling, yawning, and then laughing.)

Susan found herself insisting on Rob's moving out so that he would bring
out more of his uniqueness. She insisted on his reading THE HOBBIT rather than
a book on weather predicting, despite Rob's insistence that "Oh I don't like
that kind of book." She, felt as Anna Stave implied in her child study report,
that Rob seemed to be asking teachers to help him take the first steps in involvement with sensitive expression.

She sensed that Rob was asking, by his actions, for a teacher to take over
for him, temporarily, where his own controls were either lacking or directing
him away from accepting guidance from his real-from-birth center. She saw
clearly that she had to change the controls on Rob's automatic pilot, to use an
analogy from flying an airplane, until Rob could get used to the new route and
manage the controls on the automatic pilot himself. She had to do this while
Rob was gradually finding that it felt safe and comfortable to fly this new
route for himself. Who knows what needs Rob apparently satisified, as a young

child by beginning his humorous self-deprecatory verbal behavior? It apparently either began or certainly was conditioned by his needs not to threaten other children at school - to survive with the "I'm not all right" anxious messages that he must have been getting, deep down, as he saw himself acting and feeling differently from the norm at school.

It's hard to think of his being helped at his former schools by most school people who constantly found themselves reinforcing the code: uniformity, concern for achievement test "results" from the group and striving to minimize the differences and exceptions so that children could be handled smoothly in group lots. For example, how often were Rob's teachers praised for the variety and different directions apparent in their classrooms as opposed to praise (when they got it at all) for smoothly choreographed groups of children all seemingly responding to the same music, or at best three different melodies all blended together (as with three reading groups)? When a child lagged behind the group, he or she was sent to the reading teacher or other specialist to be returned, hopefully, to the norms.

But whatever were the causes, it was obvious to us that in the beginning Rob needed our help in resetting the controls on his automatic pilot. Susan did a beautiful job in helping Rob help himself this way. There was just too much fear, down there in the unconscious reaches, for us to expect this twelve-year old to change the controls himself - it apparently just felt too scary to him to let his agemates feel his magnificiences without blunting them with self-diminishing humor. This outside assistance was needed in just one corner of Rob's life, however, not in all of it. In most of Rob's life it was apparent to us that he was drawing from his real-from-birth self. For example, teachers noted that when he dealt with adults and not children he quickly moved out of the suspicious, funny-at-his-own expense role. His easy self respect showed through very clearly. (Remember Joyce's child-study report?) Then, his humor was a delight.

Rob's humor showed his delicate understanding of human nuances. He showed this in his dramatics characterizations. It was also obvious in his ability to sort out meaning and logic in supposedly complicated and esoteric fields such as weather predicting. During the next year at our school children began to see all this clearly in Rob and at the same time find themselves drawn into the fascination of his inquiries. His humor often helped other children to see the light side of the heavy business of growing up. People, both children and teachers, were finding that Rob was a person who would listen; was a person who could identify with others' conflicts and concerns.

During Rob's second year, David made his room into the science workshop. David and Rob (who then was back in David's group) shared their attraction to the order, wonder, and beauty in the natural and physical world. David's easy non-judgmental acceptance of people was right for Rob, too. When they would argue, neither would find that the other kept a grudge, I noticed that Rob showed a non-judgmental way of relating to others. Rob apparently was quick to practice this behavior by watching and living with David. (Once before, with Susan as his model, Rob had learned how satisfying it could be to take the risks of being "up" and self-appreciative.) Along with finding David as a model for self-respecting non-judgment independence, Rob appeared to benefit from David's leaving so many things up to the children to decide for themselves. David was there supporting the children by his example, setting the tone for accepting oneself and helping children hassle things out in meetings when living together became difficult. (Almost all children found David to be a trusted friend as well as a respected teacher.) When David's way of teaching was functioning well, as it was in Rob's second year, children seemed to make longlasting strides in setting their own automatic pilot controls - developing strong and sensitive-to-others controls from within themselves.

Why wasn't it this way when Rob entered, a year before? For one thing, as I discussed earlier, several of the eleven children in David's group during Rob's first year had entered that year or the year before with only partly healed emotional scars from feeling oppressed in regular school settings. There was a considerable amount of latent and expressed anger from those children in that group. This tapped the pockets of anger in many of the other children. When Rob entered David's group the balance was way off - towards children's needs for self-indulgence at others' expense, towards a population of children dominated by those who were hurting a great deal from former situations which left them with fear and bewilderment. Some of these children left at the end of the year - much the better for their experience in our school. And, too, many of the children in David's group at year's end seemed to be responding easily much of the time, to the warmth and "I'm just fine" feelings emanating from their real-self centers. It was a group dominated by these children that Rob entered to begin his second year.

Things at home were also supportive for Rob. At Susan's suggestion, Rob's mother Sara began two nights out each week to be trained in co-counselling. This allowed Sara to understand and come to share Susan's frame-of-reference. Sara did this in addition to keeping up with assignments in her two University courses, her demanding job, a nagging physical ailment at the time, doing the School's business work (to pay for part of Rob's tuition), typing dissertations, and learning to say "no" to many other things so that she could have the satisfaction of special times with Rob. The close relationship between Rob and his mother appeared always to be supportive to Rob, but during this crucial time his mother was able to think particularly clearly, because of her listening to herself, her getting off frustration and tension in co-counselling sessions.

Rob's behavior this second year in David's group seemed hard to believe when we remembered those first few weeks the year before. It wasn't hard to believe when we stopped and remembered our child-study of a year ago when we sensed Rob's centered-down courage but apparently self-defeating behavior pockets. When Rob came to our school, he was not denying his real-from-birth self. In fact he seemed to be taking much direction from the warm, just fine, inventive center in his life. The rub came as he saw himself separating from the norm of behavior of others his age. That was where he needed our help - so he could help himself. Oh, I realize that there were undoubtedly other strong forces contributing to this conflict in his life but at least his self-doubting because of his "difference" seemed to be a significant part of the explanation.

Here's David's writeup for our second child-study session on Rob, fourteen months after the previous year's child-study session, suggesting the degree that Rob was now in charge of his own life in the areas where, before, he seemed to be caught up in self defeating behavior:

> I think back to last year's child study meeting on Rob, and it's almost as if it were a different child we were talking about. I can remember having so much anxiety over Rob and his outlook of himself and his relationships with his classmates. But I don't feel that state of panic now as I think of Rob in relation to these things. His classmates like and respect him; and I get the feeling that he realizes this. Even if he's bickering with someone, it's simply a matter of ROB COHEN, classmate and friend, involved in an argument; not the Rob Cohen, whom nobody likes anyway, struggling through another threat to his survival with another member of The Enemy (i.e. almost everybody). People go to him for help: Bill for math, Jeremy for the metric system, David for

spelling. At class meetings he gives his opinions, and they are listened to and reacted to on their own merit, not with personalities getting involved to gum up the works.

Rob the weatherman, Rob the math student, Rob the metrician, Rob the stock market whiz, Rob the research historian. (Glenn, an active member of the Syracuse Peace Council, came to school to give a talk on the JFK assassination. We had an hour and a half session and then he and Rob went off for an interview. Glenn tells me that Rob has apparently read almost an equal amount on the subject as Glenn himself has. Rob turned Glenn on to a couple of sources which Glenn has been having trouble locating, and Glenn gave Rob a great deal of printed matter and loaned him a couple of books. Phone numbers were exchanged and they'll be keeping in touch to enhance each other's information sources.) Rob the second best basketball player in the school (Bill's got the height over him), Rob the feeling human being...I was talking to Sara over the phone the other day. She told me about the woman who lives near them in the apartment building they live in. She apparently has a great number of "emotional problems" which often create tension between her and her neighbors. Rob is a friend of hers and often goes to watch TV or play cards with her in the evening. She became involved in a particularly bad scene with the neighbors a while ago in which she behaved extremely irrationally. The result: everyone in the place was terribly angry toward her and tried to get her to move out. She was upset and Rob went to spend the evening with her because she needed a friend (his words). Sara says that he said he didn't agree with her or her actions, but she needed someone at that time. He was her friend, so he went to stay with her.

Sara says that she wants someone to pay attention to Rob because he is so competent that everyone (Sara included) always just assumes that Rob will be all right and can take care of himself - and he always does. Sara also expressed her concern over the fact that she has had a particularly heavy schedule this year and has had very little time for Rob. To my knowledge, Rob doesn't have any friends at home. His social life seems to center around school, during school hours.

I prepared a writeup, for that second child study, of my second intervue, with Rob. I got it to the teachers a few days before our child-study day, as was our routine. Here is my writeup:

Intervue And Thots With Rob Cohen. 1-9-76 REN

Rob and I went into the Church's narthex for our intervue. As we passed through the sanctuary he said that this was the first time that he had been in the sanctuary. My thought here is wondering how many other things are right around the corner for Rob and he's missing them. Sara and I talked the other day and I again was reminded how easy it was for Rob to give adults (and others too) the message that he really doesn't care if they give him their special attention - while at the same time he so basks when honest respectful attention comes his way from an adult who enjoys him.

I'm writing this up in my office as the sunshine is coming through the window.

Wow. There's a lot out there and Rob is so well equipped to take so much of it in. I just thought of what David said the other night - how Rob had just read the Warren Commission report all through, in his research on the assassination of President Kennedy.

Then I think of the "inside-out" kind of direction. I think of Rob at a recent family co-counselling training workshop. I think of the stand-up-straight, genuine, hugable neat person - Rob - there.

Now To The Intervue:

Rob: Yes, the other night I tried to photograph a commercial on TV but I didn't get my camera set up in time. I sort of dreamed, then, that I called New York (to the TV station) to see when that commercial would run again. I did wait for a while with my camera ready to see if the commercial would come on again. The commercial was about a Dick Clark album. I wanted to get a shot because it's my favorite rock group. He put this album together - 25 years of songs. It had one picture of the rock group - BTO. No, the real name doesn't matter, it's a real long name - people just call it BTO.

REN:* I've got to sort of get focused in on where we are here so I can kind of switch gears. There was so much that just happened this morning - so many people, so many feelings. It's...It's like I sort of have to finish the feelings in so many of the cases that I just...That is, I just spent a moment with a person and a lot of feelings came up then I was off and did the same thing with another person without letting things sort of sift down. I talked to Mio, Mary, Dottie, Cal, Susan and in each case there was something that was.....and Susie. Like Mary; I need to close each one of these "touches" with a sort of imaginary bookmark - to kind of put things gently where they belong and then I can come back to them later. For example, I need time to finish my reaction to Mary's few words about our lunch today. Just the look on her face and a few words was all that she gave to me: "Yes, (lunch is fine) if that's OK...? (We set up this luncheon thing a few days ago.) What went through my head was, were, thoughts like to what extent does Mary see me as...Well, how does Mary see me? Where in her whole range of past associations do I fit? Or, to what extent is the way she sees me really a present-time thing - Bob Newman - person. So much of the time, I find myself seeing people in terms of old material - my father, mother, teachers, yes. Mary and I are going to lunch to talk about Mary's taking some college work. A lot of old material full of a lot of old stuff there, probably, for Mary?
REN
NOTE: I then explained how I had learned in my co-counselling training to do an "Identification check" before we begin working together in pairs, as counsellor and client - so that old associations and all can be worked through and out - so that present-time reality will be who that person really is and not this reality mixed with other past realities and past recordings that are so easy to come up.

Do you have anything "up," Rob?

---

*Robert E. Newman

Rob: Yes, my classroom project is about weather. I got the weather station outfit for Christmas. Now, I want to expand. Want to buy a little weather forcasting device. It has a 38 page booklet with a sliderule computer and charts and instruments. One problem, though: David thinks it's a waste of money because it does cost a lot - $8.25. It's in a brand new Edmond Scientific catalog. My mother knows I like catalogs so she got that from a friend. I'm asking David if he can use the school's money to buy it. So David thinks it's a waste of money. I think that if it'll help me I think it's worth the price. Because David wants me to do the project... My predictions have been a little off the past few days and I can do better with these tools. Now, I look at my instruction booklet and dials and then sometimes I guess. 70% of the time I'm right. The weatherman gets 60-70% accuracy so I'm doing all right. Like today the weatherman predicted "80% chance of snow" and look at the sun out there. I predicted 2 inches of snow during a 2-3 day period and about 2 inches came. I do it by watching the instruments not the newspaper or TV. That's cheating. Anyway, TV doesn't help. Most of the time they are wrong when it really comes down to it. The $8.00 kit has a booklet supplied by the national weather service. It has tables for predicting weather if the barometeric pressure is such and such. David asked me to bring the catalog in. One thing that was eating him was that I saw the same thing in another catalog (with a minimum order of $25) and it was much cheaper. The other catalog is a giant catalog that David has - from a few years ago. It has over a thousand pages and is full of science stuff. I'm saying this because you asked me what was on top, in my mind.

REN: You know, Rob I'm really feeling 100% <u>here</u> now. That's neat.

I really want to hear you talk about where you are at as a person. That's hard to sort of get into - to lead a person into, anyway - hard to explain. Let me think of a question. How about "What's a new and good?" You don't want to do that? Well, OK, then let's just chat.

Rob: Don't really have anything to say.

REN: Well, do you want to try the new and good, then? OK I'll start. I just looked up and saw the sun coming in through the stained glass in the sanctuary. Sunshine. Yes. Ever since my recent co-counselling training at the Kirkridge workshop (I was there for five days) I've been smiling and thinking that "Bob Newman is Good! People aren't going to 'find out' like I so often sort of felt all my life until not so long ago - find out I was "bad."

You're yawning, huh?

Yes, Rob I've always seemed to feel, way down inside, that I kind of had to be especially good - kind of to make up for something I'd done wrong - like, for example, I HAD to do well at school because I owed it to my mother or something like that... Huh, you're yawning again. I'm putting down your yawns in my notes because I'm...

Rob: I'm yawning because I'm tired. I woke up in the middle of the night last night. My mother had to come in and stand me up. She had to shake me.

REN: That could be. But I notice that you only yawn - that deep kind of wide-open-mouth yawn - when I talk about this kind of feeling lousy about myself; then you start to yawn - right on cue!! Yes. Maybe the two of us have something in common. Even though I'm 48 and you're 13.

Rob: Yes, I'm 13 and I'm just getting into it.

REN: No, you're getting out of it - you're getting out a lot of heavy old material. And I don't need to apologize for being pretty sure that I am right. That's part of my old material - to sort of ask for permission to be strong and assertive - in expressing sensitive aware kinds of things.

So, anyway, back to my new and good. My new and good is that I'm going against my old behavior pattern. I'm doing a lot of fun things like going around mumbling to myself "I'm a bad guy - Terrible Robert the maniac." Then I start to laugh - that deep kind of laughing and then celebrate it and laugh again. I can laugh because it's ridiculous. In present-time I'm a super person.

Rob: I'm covering my mouth or I'll yawn and you'll write it down. (He's smiling and I get a warm neat feeling. We both laugh.)

Well, anyway, my new and good is that we've almost decided on a new car for ourselves - a yellow Hornet sedan. My mother and I have a little thing to work out yet. She wants an AM radio and I want an AM-FM stereo. I think we'll have an AM only.

Why is that a new and good? Well it's nice to get out of the back of our present car where my legs get crushed. I ride back there when we have a passenger. There just isn't any legroom. People's feet just get stuck. (Smiling) Notice, I haven't yawned in two pages of your notes?

REN: THE MAGIC SHOES QUESTION: (I pointed to my shoes there on the rug and said) If those shoes were magic and you could put them on what would you tell them?

Rob: My answer is going to sound really weird. I'd like to extend them to size 19. I always wanted to hold a record. A guy in the army has size 18.

Then, too, I'd like to kick field goals - like what you'd call getting a lot of foot in it. That's the way you get your kicks. (Rob smiled here, a bit embarrassed as I didn't respond quickly to his play on words. I felt a bit of his old self-putdown humor here.)

REN: Why do you want to hold a record?

Rob: When I went to camp, at Jamesville, I was unofficially the world's record holder for getting the most 10-leaf clovers in anyone's life. I guess I want to hold a record because I'll be known publically as the world record holder.

REN: Yes, but like if you have size 19 shoes, won't people also laugh at you?

Rob: Yes, but just as long as I'd be recognized - that's the point.

REN: But, how could you be recognized for <u>what you've really got going for you</u>

Rob: Don't know... You mean for 10-leaf clovers or something like that?

REN: Something that you could be recognized for right now - something that people would approve of and celebrate WITH RESPECT rather than something that made you out a kind of freak.

Rob: Don't know.

REN: I mean the headlines would read something like "Weather predictor at 13 beats the multimillion dollar weather bureaucracy" or "13-year-old stock market whiz never fails".

Rob: How about "13-year-old in County league hits record field goal in big game."

REN: But my headlines were real possibilities, yours was fiction??

Rob: Your first headline is true because the weather bureau is so bad. A kid in Arizona used a penny and flipped it and was right 90% of the time. He predicted a big storm for the plains states and the weather bureau didn't.

I can't believe that you've written 10 pages about me (I was on the beginning of the tenth page of notes as Rob talked.)

REN: Any questions for me, Rob?

Rob: No, I don't have any questions for you, Mr. Newman. I just feel like the interviewee.

REN: I keep wanting to get back to what we can do here at school in the next 5 months so that you might be "recognized" for some of what you can do.

Rob: I talked to my mother about scheduling a meeting with the University College* president. I was the youngest person ever to go to UC and they advertise "A College for the People." That ought to be something that I could be recognized for.

REN: I know Marty Fass who is the public relations director for UC. Right now is their registration season so he'd like to get an article out and prove the "A College for the People" thing...I bet.

Rob: This spring I'll be beginning my third year at UC.

REN: I'll call my friend Marty Fass. But let's think this through. I want to get to something that you do or will do about the UC thing that people will read about and be full or respect for you - not just that you are different.

Rob: How about how I spend an average evening at a class - how I prepare; or the two classes I have taken - a chess course last year and a metrics course finished last month?

---

*University College, Syracuse University's community adult education college.

REN: Let me tell you my thoughts about this business of getting you in the headlines. I have to sort them out for myself; I just know that it feels right when I think about it - when I think about getting you in the headlines in ways that brings respect from the reader. Yes. I see it as kind or a next step... A kind of next step to break through the "force field" that's getting in your way, that says "Oh, those things like my ability to predict weather, stocks etc. are just ordinary...I'm just ordinary..."

That's a lousy force field, Rob.

Rob: Yeah it is. (He had a serious look in his eyes as he said that.)
REN
NOTE: Then Rob and I talked about breaking self-defeating patterns; so that the "person inside - that person, who kept on telling us that we weren't worth much" - so that person inside just can't deny it. And for me, I told him, it's important to do it some of the time in a way that makes me laugh or have fun; like that time I found myself going around downtown doing my shopping shouting out to everybody "I want to introduce Bob Newman - world's champion bad guy!" - except I was doing it inside as a phantasy as I was walking along looking at people's faces. Then I'd start to laugh at the kind of ridiculous caricature - so 100% in the wrong direction!

(Then Rob ended our intervue with the last word:)

Rob: Could I just put one more thing on your note sheet: "I haven't yawned in the last 8 pages!"
REN
NOTE: We then went upstairs and called Marty Fass at University College. Rob talked with Marty about his attendance at UC, stocks, weather, etc. I understand at this point that in addition to the newspaper article, Rob is to go on TV, on the Mike Price "Open Line" show, and is going to get involved with the weather bureau people but the last this is vague - see David.

NOTE #2: After I talked with Sara before Christmas I jotted down these notes:
Rob's Problem:
1. "You have my permission to ignore me."
2. "I'm really not interested in what I'm doing."
3. "Oh I don't know what I might do, like going to the bike shop to work or going to the Mall."
4. "Don't appreciate me openly. I can't deal with that."

BUT HOW THAT'S CHANGING: Now when I affirm him he lets it sink in; no wise cracks or other forms for handling the awkwardness he feels; I think he really enjoys it even though it obviously feels a little awkward. Now he's speaking up for what he's interested in. Still, much of this has to come from me (using myself as the example of the supportive person here) but the point is how easy it is to get him going. So, the point is that it's up to us, staff people, to ignore this self-defeating pattern of Rob's (#1, 2, 3, 4) and get through and take over for Rob from time to time. Don't set him up so that he will feel he might fail

but, speaking for myself, I'll make some initial decisions for
him - like the thing about recognition and his self-defeating
patterns.

That's another thing. I find that I can talk directly with Rob
about his self-defeating patterns - but maybe one of the reasons
is that I'm living this all in my own life. Anyway it's a neat
feeling as I write this - about Rob Cohen...

I remember that after my phone call to University College's public relations man, Marty Fass, Rob and I stood in the hall, talking. I told him, again,
how I saw what we were doing. It was important for me not to have this thing
backfire. I didn't want Rob to see the publicity as "bragging" - nor did I
want others to see it that way. I wanted to be sure that Rob knew clearly
what we were doing. We were taking an important next step. This was one more
exercise in turning around his previously self-defeating habit of helping himself and others not to take himself seriously. (Shades of Bobby Newman!) This
was going to be hard for him - to accept a celebration of himself as being true
and lovely while at the same time feeling the uneasiness that probably would
come up in different ways. It was important to see if he could handle this
uneasiness and not negate the appreciation by humorous self-depreciation, quickly
changing the subject, some sort of heavy self-analysis or similar ways to dodge
the full appreciative impact on himself of the the real-from-birth Rob.
     As it turned out, the newspaper reporter invited Rob and his mother to
come to the newspaper office where they had a relaxed interview. The article
came out in the City News section of the Syracuse Sunday newspaper. I felt
good about what the reporter said even if the headline writer came up with something a bit close to what I was afraid of - making Rob out to be some sort of
a way-out person. What was in the article was true and not exaggerated. Rob
was different from most kids and in exceptionally fine ways.
     I took a risk by suggesting this newspaper article. It could have turned
out so that Rob would have been seen as some sort of strange kid, but it didn't
work out that way. I expected that Marty Fass would handle it sensitively.
He did. I sensed, also that if we goofed Rob and I would be in this together.
I could help him learn from it all. And I wanted Rob to experience my following
quirky ideas from my inventive real-from-birth self even if they appeared to be
a bit risky at times. Like Susan and David, I too found this an opportunity to
help Rob learn from what I do well.
     I hope that it is clear how all of this illustrates how each of us - Susan,
David, myself and all the other staff people who had participated in our child
study of Rob - was thinking for herself or himself; not following some recipe
from an authority. Because we were thinking for ourselves out of heightened
awareness and understanding, we found all sorts of times and places to make
decisions on the spot that made sense in supporting Rob and in bringing to bear
our strengths to help him help himself.
     So much irritation comes up in me when I think of how teachers and others
in "helping professions" are intimidated not to think for themselves - are
brought in to sit at the feet of high priests with labels such as psychologist,
psychiatrist, reading specialist, principal, and guidance director. So often
this is the occasion for the teacher to receive the order (no matter how benighly
given) to carry out. And in the area of one's self esteem - the concern of
almost all serious helping of children - the carrying-out just can't be done
by command or recipe. It has to be done intuitively. It has to be done easily
and naturally and at the moment that it will have the right effect.
     Sure, in our child-study program I have a lot of well learned skill, in-

Rob Cohen, 13

A math genius?

By MARIE FLETCHER

To one who considers it an accomplishment of some merit if the checkbook balance jives with the bank statement each month, Rob Cohen is a marvel.

At 13, Rob has turned a hypothetical $10,000 into $22,000 in the stock market, devised a mathematical formula which gives him an 84 percent accuracy in sports' score predictions, and become a student at University College of Syracuse University.

Recently, Rob completed a metrics measure course at U.C. Fellow classmates included several engineering majors who were participating in the course for degree credit. (Rob is not eligible for college credit due to an age requirement at U.C.)

How did the others react to so young a student as Rob in their midst?

"At first they couldn't believe it," Rob says, "but after awhile they treated me like the rest."

Before enrolling in the metrics class, Rob had completed a U.C. mini-course in chess strategies.

This semester Rob will be sitting in on a computer programming course at Syracuse University, (computers being his latest interest.)

Rob's mother, Sara, asserts that a great deal of study goes into each new mathematics project her son undertakes.

For example, she notes, when he decided to invest in the stock market, Rob spoke with people who owned stocks, studied theory of market transactions, read news accounts and ultimately kept a detailed daily record of the market and his transactions.

Probably most noteworthy about Rob's stock market accomplishment, is that he made his hypothetical money during a three-month period when the market was in decline, his mother explains.

Rob enjoys this type of "learning by doing," he says. And in keeping with this, he has begun to explore electronics by putting together his own radio.

At the Syracuse Institution for Enabling Education, where Rob is a student, he has become an amateur meteorologist for fellow students. His weather predictions have been accurate 90 percent of the time, he notes.

Photography, (Rob takes and develops his own pictures), stamp collecting and the drums, are also among this talented teen's extracurricular interests.

It would seem that Rob believes the old saw "All work and no play makes Jack a dull boy," for he's also a member of his school's basketball team and bowls.

When making predictions about his own future, Rob feels he will use his mathematical prowess as an accountant.

valuable experience both professionally and from trying out in my own life what I'm doing with children and staff people. But it's infantilizing to other staff people for me to be seen as the high priest-type authority. My goal, as the child study leader, is to help each staff person (and myself) move out from our child study of a particular child and think for ourselves.

I see this being done in several ways simultaneously. First, of course, there is the actual study of the child, like Rob's study, to give each staff person data; the sharing and the trustful support each person receives is so important in letting out our own feelings so that our own fearful and often anger-laden restimulations won't act as colored glasses in distorting our seeing what's really going on in parts of the life of a child. (Remember my initial perceptions of Sean?) This study-time is also a time for us to pause and come close to the child's beautiful real-from-birth self and the unique ways that he or she is expressing it in her or his life. This, in effect, defines our direction and suggests both how we might bring more of this magnificance to bear and how we might help the child remove roadblocks to taking direction from his or her real-from-birth-self - help the child see and feel this centered-down direction as it shows itself in his or her behavior.

Another way that I find I can help staff people (and myself) think for ourselves with the heightened awareness from our child study, is through our one-to-one conferences. As I've said before, in this book, at least half of the bi-weekly (or so) talks I have with each of the staff people revolve around this child or that one. I find that my conferences with staff people seem, almost always for me, to be times when the just-fine, easy to laugh, easy to cry, real me is right there. I find that it's important for the two of us to get away from concerns at the school for these meetings. (The Treadway restaurant across the street fills this bill admirably for me.) I find it easy to blend the ways that I'm growing to take guidance from my real-self center and my work in helping children to do this; easy in this scene over the lunch or breakfast table where I can give undivided attention to the staff person who is with me and he or she can give this so important gift of appreciation to me. As I experience it, staff people too feel this relaxed, almost heady, sensitive appreciation of themselves and of the children we're working with.

Grounding our study of children in sensitive appreciation of the child's real self is a key thing. For one thing we couldn't do it any other way. We don't invite parents to send children to our school to be labelled as children with personality disorders. We invite parents to send their children to our school so that we can help them, (the parent, the children, and ourselves) to come close to the child's lovely real-person center; the real self that was there when the child was conceived and born and is still at least poking through the cracks in the concrete of behavior the child took on to survive in a world fraught with distressful adult needs.

Parents won't stand for schools' probing around children's behavior to label this deficiency or that deficiency. Parents know that that just isn't the whole picture of their children. We at our school have to, and want to, and are able to work within the total balanced picture of each of our children.

This allows us to share our hunches with parents. But this sharing, too, is something that I find has to be done with sensitivity. Let's take some time here to explore some of the difficulties of sharing our tentative conclusions about each child with parents. This is difficult both for parents and for teachers. Much of the problem has to do with parents' and teachers' fears, as I see it - parents' fears of not doing an adequate child-rearing job and teachers' fears of "practicing psychology without a license."

Let's begin by reminding ourselves that our first conclusions, as to how a particular child might be blocking out some direction from his/her real self, are really not "conclusions" at all but are at the level of partly non-verbal awarenesses. Oh, yes, there usually are strong hunches that come up; I almost always come away from a child-study with some strong hunches that I can put in words. But these are invitations for us all to follow tentatively - to check the validity of these hunches by acting on them, each in our own way, while watching closely the subtle results; modifying and changing our emerging conclusions, as we increase our sureness. Of course after we've done this process with child after child, it's easier to make stronger hunches in the first place; but it's also easier to jump to the wrong conclusion too early in living with a child. In Rob's case we hit it, so-to-speak, right from the beginning. Rob made it relatively easy for us as he was so up-front with his behavior. What was inside was so visible on the outside. So much of his distressful behavior (such as his apparently projecting some negative self-images on others and then getting angry at them for holding them) seemed so transparent.

Because our "knowledge" is tentative - particularly at first - I find myself reluctant to share too much, too soon, with parents. But we can and do let parents know the process that we are using and specific awarenesses of their child's neat real-person-centered behavior. Often in the early stages of getting to know a child, we can talk with parents about this corner or that corner of the child's life where there seems to be some conflict. They can help us with their perceptions. But all of that's often not easy because, again, I find so often that parents are seemingly always waiting for a judgment: Is my child OK? (Am I OK?) They don't want to leave things tentative. There's just too much at stake. There often seems to be defensiveness there, right below the surface. I know that in my own case, when we were doing a child-study on my daughter Robin, I felt as tense as a violin string. The feeling was kind of like, "Well, if you find something wrong with her I'll just have to accept it - I can't argue with you. You'll just feel that I'm defensive. You'll just feel that you can be more objective. You'll just..." Yes, that's the feeling; I sense that many times there is a deepset kind of angry powerless predisposition on the part of many parents when they are involved in discussions of what they are quick to see as "deficiencies" about their children.

Can you blame these parents for looking at our child study process as a quest for deficiencies? They are a product of their own schooling which year-in and year-out conditioned them to expect teachers to tell them about their deficiencies, not about how the teachers enjoyed the neat expressions from their real-from-birth selves. School was a place where you learned if you were measuring up - and hopefully what was wrong with you if you weren't. If you didn't hear from the teacher you could assume that everything was all right. The schools to which almost all of these parents went were places where these parents (then children) were manipulated by keeping their fears of being close to their "I'm not all right" feelings, high. So how can we expect more than fear-laden re-run behavior from most loving parents at this time when they sense the questions to be right at the heart of the "Am I all right" scene?

There are also parents who find themselves taking this discussion of their child as the time to put down their child - unloading some of the hurting that has come from living with their child. Most of all, I dislike finding myself in this kind of corner with parents. Oh how I wish that some parents could feel it was OK to find a counsellor whom they could trust so that they could get off so much of this frustration in living with their children - so much restimulated fear and anger from when they were children.

I just don't have the time to involve most parents every step of the way, in the ins-and-outs of our working with their children. I'll never have time remaining to concentrate on working with their children. The day only has twenty-four hours and some of those I need just for myself.

A great deal of my expanded awareness is at the tentatively held nonverbal level; but parents want to know "Just what do you mean?" Should I call parents each time I modify my hunch? I modify my hunches all the time - that's part of my method. Parents' love and concern for their children would mean meeting after meeting if I tried to involve parents every step of the way. Total parental involvement would mean premature verbalization on my part and pushing teachers, who are less experienced in our process, toward uneasy feelings of "Do I really know what I'm doing...?" If I suggested that they meet with parents early in the sequence of a particular child-study.

Teachers are easily pushed toward fearful feelings of inadequacy because so many seem to accept the taboo that "only High-Priest Authorities should be involved with studying the sacrosanct psychological questions" - the follow-the-leader thinking that utilizes the medical specialization analogy to rationalize not allowing teachers to study children "psychologically." (If you're having trouble with your feet you should be referred to the podiatrist.)

But if we accept the responsibility to teach a child, we are working with that child's feelings of self-esteem and fearful uneasiness. If we choose to ignore this fact for whatever reason, we just lessen our teaching potential. In practical terms we limit our effectiveness to helping those children who can learn "the material" without much help from a teacher at all and we have to live with our consciences as we sense that our teaching is bringing up all sorts of self-esteem issues in each of the children.

However, because the self-esteem issues are so basic, as we teach we have to protect children from being labelled as "psychological problems" by some teachers who seemingly see their job as cataloging particular children's deficiencies. Teachers and other professionals who are traditionally psychologically trained people often follow the medical analogy, always seeking "what's wrong" as opposed to coming up with an awareness in the light of expanded sensitivity to the ways a child takes direction from his or her just-fine-from-birth real self. Children have enough "I'm not measuring up" fear in their lives already from being continually managed by the giving and withholding of approval as they are growing up at school; they don't need more of the fearful "this is what's wrong with Mary" message from school people.

I have talked with many teachers caught up in the fears basic to all this. These are sensitive-to-the-hurting-in-children people. They feel that they can't refer a child whom we might call "Ginny" to the psychologist (if they ever could get Ginny on this harried person's list) because that would be saying that Ginny probably will be labelled with some psychological deficiency. No, they can't do that because they know that even though Ginny is dealing with something in a corner of her life with which she needs help, she certainly shouldn't be labelled as a child with a "psychological problem" (which freely translated means a child on the way to becoming a loser - a "weak person," "disturbed" having a "personality disorder" or whatever). These teachers have trouble talking with Ginny's parents because of the reasons I've just touched on in the paragraphs above. Then, too, these teachers haven't had the training that the teachers in our school are getting as they participate in our child study program. How can they be articulate and reasonably confident when talking to parents? They feel their aloneness. They don't have the support of someone like a child-study leader. Not only don't the teachers have this kind of support; usually it's the reverse. Usually they find themselves in the "You're guilty until you prove yourself innocent" corner. If they don't handle "it" in just the right way, the principal or other authroity will accuse them of "practicing without a license" or some other "how dare you try to act like a high-priest" admonition. So what do so many of these perceptive and caring teachers do? They retreat. They don't seek help in studying Ginny's habitual self-defeating behavior apparent in parts of her life, as contrasted with their heightened awareness of Ginny's real-from-birth self. They never become skillful in doing this (and there's plenty of skill involved) because they never are supported as they might be; as they might be in learning along with a child-study leader - working together studying the Ginnys in the teachers' classes.

Thus teachers withdraw from this area of concern which, in school people, is so permeated with anxiousness about dealing with the "I'm not measuring up" fears in children - even though the school and the family are the places where so much of this uneasiness is generated and played out in children's lives.

The essential question, in my mind, isn't <u>should</u> a teacher, in the schools, do what I'm trying to explain in this book. The real question is <u>how</u> should we, in the schools, go about it so that a teacher can be supported in helping Ginny to bring back to her life the beauty and power which was there in such abundance when Ginny was born and still clearly is there in much of her behavior even though she finds herself habitually moving away from some of its direction in her pockets of self-defeating behavior. We should save the good psychiatrist or psychologist for helping children whose functioning is severly impaired and who are so far from their real-from-birth selves that, effectively speaking, they are out of touch with that lovely and strong center in their lives.

So how should we support teachers in helping children to take direction from their real-from-birth selves? My proposal is to help teachers study children as you have been reading in this story of Rob, starting with heightened awareness of each child's beautiful real-from-birth self. This is what we do at our school and call our child-study program. Let's take this opportunity to consider further what it's like to do this child-study well in a school setting - how the priorities, organization and training of the staff people can make it work well. Let's consider, how these factors helped in our study of Rob.

First, my role - that of the person on the staff who effectively acts as the child-study leader. When I say "effectively" I am referring to several conditions. I am referring to how I take the leadership in our child-study program and <u>at the same time</u> take a leadership role in the school. I see those two roles as important to be combined. Because I took the key role in studying Rob's enjoyable real-from-birth self, his conflict, his classroom relationships I found myself right at the heart of our school culture as well as having a sensitive awareness of Rob. When I do this over and over again I soon come to know our whole school from deep inside out. I live, in our school, in the world of what is going on with children where it matters most, as I see it; where children are both taking direction and keeping themselves from being in touch with their centers of humanness - their real selves. Because I sense myself near the centers of the children, each teacher and I have a partnership right where it counts.

Then, too, I am the only person in the school who knows almost all of the children this way. I am in a perfect position to work with staff people in building and in changing our overall organization to support what we want to do with children and to help each staff person take the next steps in growing as a professional.

I'm not saying, by the way, that the director or principal is the only one who could be the child study leader. I am saying, though, that the person or persons who take this role need to be, also, people who are in leadership roles in the school setting. In a large elementary school, for example, I'm making the case for a child-study leader to be the team leader for teachers of a grade or a sub-group of fifty to seventy-five children.

As both the child study leader and the school's director I find that I am in the best position I have ever seen for helping staff people grow as professionals. Consider my relationship with David during Rob's first year at our school. David and I both faced the struggle of helping to heal the hurts of three or four children in his group while at the same time not allowing their fearful, angry, bewildered expression of so much previously-suppressed distress to hurt other children. I found that I didn't have to know all the specifics of David's routines - so many of the literally thousands of details that a good teacher keeps at his fingertips. But at the same time I found myself close to what really concerned both David and me. This was a far cry from the typical supervisor-teacher relationship. Usually, the supervisor is seen as one person for the teacher to please. Often the supervisor can't help the teacher very much, because so many of the teacher's problems are grounded in children's fear and struggle to see themselves as just-fine, warm, lovable and capable individuals; problems that come in a large part from the messages given to children at school that continually pull them in and out of the fearful area of seeing themselves only in terms of what the school and parents are telling them are their deficiencies. The supervisor doesn't know each child's real-from-birth self.

But as the child study leader, I do. I make it my business to come close to the real-from-birth self in each child. With this sensitive awareness I can be the advocate for each child. I can act to protect him or her from well-meaning teachers, parents, other professionals who seem to spend almost all the time and awareness they have for each child ferreting out his or her deficiencies. These professionals do this to such an extent that they lose touch with a sensitive feel for each child's unique expressions of his or her real-from-birth self (if the professionals were ever close to it in the first place).

And as the child-study leader I can protect the children, also, from the unthinking and conditioned ways that some teachers find themselves managing children - with fear around not measuring up. I can, as I've been trying to explain, focus teachers' sensitive attention to the unique manifestations of the real-from-birth self that we find in each child - that permit us to bask in the human magnificence that was born into each child. Then, too, I can help teachers and help myself look at children in terms of what it might be that each person seems to need. The essential teacher-child relationship, then, can be characterized by this sort of message: "Let me help you, Sean, tell me what you need. Even if you can't understand completely, Sean, here's what I need..."

As I look back at the time Rob came into David's group, David needed help in getting in touch with what Rob needed and in clarifying his (David's) questions as he found himself in the ebb and flow of the fearful anger that he felt passing between the children in his group those first few weeks. So David asked for this help and got it. He put Rob "up" for child-study at our first session, in October. By doing this he was also putting himself (David) "up" in the sense that he was asking me and the other staff people to help him in coming close to Rob's real humanness, in coming up with some clear hunches about what seemed to be Rob's needs; and in the process to help him (David) to be much clearer about what his needs were as the leader of this group - the person who also had to think about helping the other children come close to their real-from-birth selves for guidance. So David set in motion a process that helped Rob pull himself up by his own bootstraps.

I hope that you sense my point here. I hope that you see how I feel that it's almost impossible, in most instances, for the usual school supervisor, principal, lead teacher or whomever to help a teacher get in touch with the self-esteem needs of children. It's almost impossible because understanding these needs is a matter of heightened awareness; it is a matter of human sensitivity that allows the helping person to be seen and experienced (by the person being helped) as "safe;" it involves the helping persons coming close to the child; coming close to the teacher and allowing the teacher to get close to the real-from-birth person in him or her (the helping person).

Rob's study is a good one to illustrate how the child-study program and its leader can help the teacher who is at the first stages of becoming an experienced teacher, too. David had come to our school two years before with no training or experience in school teaching. He first had worked along with staff people as an assistant for a six month training period. Then the year before Rob entered, David began with his first group which was, as I have said, dominated by children who had been well served by the school - children who could be relied on to exercise empathy and sensitive-to-the-other-person controls in interpersonal relationships. Then David faced this tough next-step new situation which both drew from his real person strength as well as his unsureness. David's firm real-person feelings of being "just fine" showed through clearly. Remember how he was able to think of Rob's needs first and his concerns for having to succeed with Rob in _his_ group, second - as he supported Susan in taking Rob into her group? Another way David clearly showed his strong "I'm adequate" feelings was how he openly allowed all of the staff people to feel the bewilderment he felt during his second year as a regular teacher - bewilderment with some of what was going on in that group of children. I remember so clearly how he stopped us all, at the child-study meeting, asking me to explain again my hunch about Rob's being caught up in a habitual self-defeating pattern of negating himself while at the same time Rob seemed to feel his just-fine real self. David insisted that we not move on until this changed in his mind from an apparent contradiction to something that came across to him as logical. He sensed that I saw this as perfectly logical, but at that moment it just didn't make sense to him.

One of the hardest things I find about helping beginning teachers is to do it in such a way that they find themselves, like David, pulling themselves up by their own bootstraps. So often the first response of the beginning teacher is one variation on the theme of "tell me what I'm doing wrong." This comes right out of the childhood years that these people spent in schools expecting their teachers to define their deficiencies. But defining the problem is often at least half of its solution. The beginning teacher can't abdicate this task and needs to learn to think independently about teaching. I find that I have to insist awkwardly sometimes, that they stop, begin again with their feelings about a particular problem they sense they are having, get in touch with their needs and what part we both feel I can play in helping them meet their needs.

I don't know how I can expect teachers to lead children by being in touch with the needs of each child as well as their own unless I model this kind of nurturing relationship between the two of us.

CHAPTER 6

HOW CHILDREN MOVE AWAY FROM THEIR REAL-FROM-BIRTH SELVES

How this happens particularly at the elementary school.

As we begin this chapter I want to say two things: First, I hope that you have come to sense what I mean by the natural, warm, inventive, fascinated-with-life essence born into your children, my children, into each of us. When we were born we had no doubts about our perfectly good and capable selves. And in the process of participating with me in enjoying the beauty of Carrie, Pedro and the rest, I hope that you have come to feel how easy it is for children to be nudged away from following the direction of that natural beginning in their lives.

Second, I hope you have sensed that I feel there are lots of people who want their children to lead lives in tune with their natural verve and loveliness. There are lots of us like Pina, like the parents of Rob, Marian, Jim, Dusty, and Robin.

Unfortunately, it is my observation that those parents are swimming upstream against the current of our culture's dominant child-rearing tone; swimming upstream particularly against the cultural squeeze that takes place for children in our elementary schools, in spite of the many teachers and other professionals who try to work with children's authentic selves.

Let me elaborate. As children grow up in the United States today the prevailing childrearing culture, particularly that of the elementary schools subconsciously nurtures "I'm not measuring up" deep-down fearful feelings which are directly opposed to the natural predisposition that is born normally into each child.

When the human baby comes into this world he or she is for all practical purposes, perfect. When you were born you could easily tune in on a sunbean that danced along your crib - yours was the gift of expanded sensitivity to nuances and subtleties; you were born with a yen to be in cooperative relationships - warm trusting relationships with others. (Even as in adult, with all of the compromising of your birth heritage that you have found yourself making, in fear and from oppression... ...even with all of this accommodation you can see the essentially cooperative nature of human beings reflected in, for example, the daily newspaper and the nightly TV news. "News" is when you're <u>not</u> cooperative, not easily working to fit in with the needs of those around you.) You were born with a fascination and wonder in living - for enjoying and savoring the little things, the commonplace, like the stickiness of your babyfood, the lovely warmth of your mother's milk, or the fascination of the cracks in the sidewalk. You were born with the inventiveness and creativity that can easily be seen in children's art work. You were born easily expressing your sensual and loving feelings to others - naturally hugging and being hugged, comfortably and needfully touching with others whom you could easily love and from whom you could easily feel love. You were born feeling completely adequate and good - not doubting this an iota as you felt the pre-natal comfort of the world of constant perfect nourishment in your amniotic security.

Then you were born and began to experience discomfort and began to find that your needs weren't taken care of completely. You began to sense that you were physically powerless in a world of relatively powerful giants called adults (and smaller giants called children).

You were also born with ways to protect yourself to heal the hurts and fears that you felt from your powerless state. You could cry and somehow felt better afterwards. You could shake and tremble when you felt fear. This would help you not to panic, to be able to sense what security you had in spite of how you hurt. At first, adults would support you when you cried and when you shook. This helped a lot. But soon you felt that adults didn't want you to use your crying and shaking to heal and alleviate your hurting. In fact, you felt fear when you cried and trembled as you sensed the displeasure from adults, especially if you were a boy.

It soon became completely clear that the bargain in most families was for the baby to please the adult and then the adult would increase the comfort of the baby. It might have taken about three years for this essential bargain to have come up to the level of consciousness, but finally the child took to the adult-pleasing role rather than suffer a constant fear and hurting from being outside the law that mandated that children strive to please big people. (Adults often call our last ditch efforts not to accept this as "the terrible twos stage.")

Almost all of us as children, found ourselves trying to please adults, looking for signs of what the adults wanted us to do and doing that, at least for the moment, to gain the approval we needed.

Because we as children were looking for what the adults wanted, we found it out easily and usually did that. So it was the exceptions, the times when we didn't do what the adults wanted, that got the responses from the adults. "No" was the common adult response to the young child. There were few verbal or nonverbal "yesses" because they weren't necessary.

The "no" came through directly or subtly (slightly raised eyebrows or just a "no" which came across below the level of consciousness.) Often the "no" was emphasized, because a simple "no" wasn't emphatic enough to result in instant control. The emphasis was almost always experienced by the child as a variant of "you're bad." Of course, all of this just seemed natural to the adult who had been brought up this way herself or himself.

Families varied, of course, in the degrees and kinds of control the adults in them exerted through the granting and withholding of approval. There were some family settings where children weren't manipulated very often by the giving and withholding of loving support. In those relationships people dealt with each others' needs. The usually unspoken "no" message might have gone like this: "Hey Marie, I just love you loads but you've got to stop banging those pots and pans out there while I'm trying to entertain daddy's friends for lunch. I just can't deal with your needs right now." In a setting like this, two year-old Marie found no-strings attached love coming to her from her parenting adults - usually in floods. She found the big people around her sensitively appreciating her real-from-birth self; felt continually how much joy and lovliness she was bringing to the lives of the big people simply by her presence. Marie's trusting, full of wonderment, warm, able to "get it out" self was a gift of the highest order, as Pina expressed in my intervue with her:

> ...Times goes so fast. If you're not close with your children in
> the early years... ...very difficult to be close later. ... It's
> just such a beautiful miracle to watch unfold. I didn't want to
> put our children in a day care center for others to watch... ...and
> not me.*

Marie was continually being reminded that the big people around her were in contact with her feelings of being just-fine - those feelings that were just part of being alive - like the air she was breathing - when she was born.

---

*For the full quote see Chapter I.

Relationships didn't revolve around people managing each other by arousing fear of being "bad" in the other.

But nevertheless, children like Marie felt their smallness and vulnerability in the broader cultural press - a world that often seemed to assume them to be inadequate until they "matured" into adults. Perhaps this came through to Marie from a drugstore clerk's condescending pat on the head accompanied by his pained tight-sounding "that's a good girl, put that toy down." Perhaps it came through to her from a sibling who resented his new rival. Perhaps it came through to Marie at those insecure moments of parental distress when the usual unconditional love of her mother or father suddenly seemed, to Marie, to vanish amid angry hurtful threats aimed at her.

With a rich abundance of freely given unconditional love fortunate children like Marie could absorb what came across from some adults as reflections of the child's "badness." For these children the "I'm not OK" fear was dormant in their lives.

In most children's cases, however, the love from parenting adults often was conditional on the child meeting the big person's needs. These adults had been raised that way themselves; receiving love had almost always been conditional on their pleasing adults. Those adults, as children, had done what adults wanted them to do when manipulated this way. Now they, in turn, as parents easily sensed the child's need for big people's approval and used this need in controlling their children. In this way the beginning of a life-long game of giving and withholding approval set in for most children. For the fortunate few, like Marie, this game was held at bay until the press of culture set in with full force at the elementary school.

At the elementary school the life-long game of giving and withholding approval became institutionalized in the struggle of adults to manage groups of children packed into small spaces called classrooms. When the child didn't do what the teacher wanted, the youngster not only felt the feeling of being "bad" but the full weight of the institution would come on that child if necessary, to insure compliance with the approval-seeking rules of the life-game. (This again, as opposed to managing children by the adults asserting their needs and at the same time trying to sense the needs of the child. With this kind of assertive interaction the result wouldn't have been a sense of "they think I'm bad when I feel a need to do something differently." The feeling would have been "they don't like what I'm doing because this makes them hurt.")

In addition, in the elementary school it was not proper for teachers and others to express unconditionally to children the ways that they liked them except when the children did what the teachers' wanted them to do - when children measured up. Think back on your own elementary schooling. How many times did you feel the words or actions of teachers giving you the message that they liked something about you - just unconditional appreciation and loving coming to you? It didn't come physically. (Hugging and touching was taboo except for older female kindergarten "grandmother" teachers.) It didn't come from just-for-you attention. (How many times can you remember your teacher just listening and enjoying you without an instructional reason?) It didn't come through words. (Those words came so seldom that they were experienced as awkward by both teachers and children alike. "I like the ways that your eyes sparkle in the sun this morning, Harry," was left unsaid by the teacher.)

While children in most homes and elementary schools were looking to adults to give them signs of approval and disapproval they were, at the same time, growing less dependent on checking with adults. They found that they knew what to do and what not to do. They were internalizing the messages from adults and setting up their own authority substations inside themselves. Not all was this simple. The messages that children got from adults were often conflicting. "Be honest" was the dictum that adults would mouth but in their actions they would sometimes find themselves lying and cheating, often with elaborate rationalizations. So the rules got salted away, at the substation inside each child, in a kind of unclear jell, but the process got salted away with sharp clarity; "Find out what they want and fit in with that."

Then the shock of puberty reminded the children that they soon would become the adults who would be expected to take over from their elders in the approval-disapproval dispensing life-game. Boys began to feel with clear jolting reality that the women who would be attracted to them would expect them to strive to become approval-givers and withholders over increasingly large number of adults. For the boys (and now increasingly for girls), "getting ahead" meant, to a large extent, striving to compete with others for the power roles as approval-givers and withholders. In this setup, money had, among other things, become a symbol of the power to manage the lives of others through regulating the approval flow. If you earned a lot of money you were given credit for having this power.

While boys were being forced into the fearful position of having to "make it" competitively against men for this power, girls were being forced to accept what many saw as the unfair portion of the power-pie- power to give and withhold approval only over children, except for the same kind of power covertly exercised over their husbands and male lovers.

An interesting byproduct of this division of power developed, to the disadvantage of men. Boys found themselves learning to be closed, not to show their real-self feelings of warmth, their natural-from-birth bent toward cooperative trusting. (How could you elbow someone else out potentially, or defend yourself against someone who was being forced to do that to you, if he knew your secrets? Be cool. Learn to defend yourself and keep your posture of alertness always covered by "kidding with the boys" or swapping predictions about the outcome of next Saturday's game, or...) Women, on the other hand, were allowed to show and develop their natural lovableness out in the open. It didn't seem to matter all that much if women cried and were "soft" and trusting - those beautiful expressions of their real selves from birth. So the necessary (and logical within the assumptions of this life-game) rationalization became the final subtle hammer blow to many little boys who exhibited this "weak feminine" bent. Feeling themselves "weak and feminine" was just too much of a fearful threat to stir up their anxious "I'm not measuring up" feelings deep inside - just too much to take. They came around; they conformed even though they lived the rest of their lives with a nagging conflict between their real selves and their society sanctioned selves. This conflict was often apparent under their adolescent moody fears and resultant depression and banding together with other boys for support.

During this adolescent period children found themselves doubting, deep inside, that they could ever cope with the awesome task of winning in the life-game of approval-seeking and giving. Adolescent children tended to withdraw from adults and adopt other adolescent fear-reducing lifestyles. Even the child who didn't feel a need to move away from adults or follow other adolescent patterns did it - to fit in. This was a time when the real-from-birth self seemed to make a rear-guard stand in many subtle ways. This was a time when the real self seemed to retreat as a possible director of behavior. This was a time when many children withdrew fearfully into following the Elvis Presleys and other theatrical heroes who promised them feelings of power and surcease of the gnawing fear of "Will I make it successfully in the life-game of competing for power, of approval-giving and withholding?"

Most young people came out of this period with what the anthropologists call "enculturation." That is, they found that their substation inside had become well able to generate the guiding rules and boundaries followed by their parents and which they had felt from their early upbringing. These included the subtle ways of rationalization of differences between what were laid in as dictums (e.g. "conserve and save") and what they saw as the behavior they felt the adults were showing (e.g. Consume!, but don't consume grossly or too conspicuously. Do it discreetly and with finesse - not a Cadillac convertible but a Mercedes town sedan) so that you and others will feel that you are a powerful (and not-to-be-tampered-with) giver and withholder of approval. By this time the substation inside was unequivically generating the formula for winning, "Find out what they want and fit in."

I see this clearly in what adults seem to want from elementary school. One thing that is clear to me is that they want their children to learn to "fit in." I see this clearly in other ways too - in the simple things such as how it is that I don't feel that I look good any more in a narrow tie, why is it that those who pride themselves on resisting the dictates of the fashion gurus have, for themselves so often, such a narrowly proscribed range of choices of what feels "right" to wear - within the guidelines of what other "noncomformists" are wearing.

This desire to fit in is very plain to me in the rebellious movements of our times and in the history of such movements since World War I in the United States. Many "dissidents" of the sixties, for example, didn't move to build alternatives and change the institutions or the "system" they opposed, but opted instead for brandishing the symbols of revolt - the shouting, yelling, milling "take-overs" of college administration buildings, the hair styles, the "Black Power" bumper stickers, and on and on. To me this was an invitation to the "authorities" to clamp down and force these people to fit in. It was as if the people were pointing out the areas in society which were too permissive, had too few strong boundaries to force them to fit in. Take for example the weak college campus police forces of the early sixties that since then have grown 500% in number and in written rules, regulations, and riot-quelling strategies. It's as if the "rebels" were asking the authorities to keep them in line. A relatively miniscule amount of this rebel energy was turned to building alternatives that collectively might result in a better "system" - ways out of the "mess." I see the symbols of "I'm not going to fit in" as being, paradoxically, the best allies "they" have of keeping the rebels (who really feel such a pressure to fit in) in line. It's as if these symbols were sedative pills available for angry young people to take. The pills were available for people who didn't like the system that they were growing into but who were fearful or lacking in something to try out instead. "Just take the pill - just join in the sumbol-waving, then 'they' will squash you, then you can feel that you tried but couldn't fight it and then settle back to try to fit in, enjoying the comfort of pious self-pity."

I see this in education, too - with people of all ages. The teacher, rare principal, even rarer superintendent who waves the flag of "open education" or (in the thirties) "progressive education," invites the "system" defensively to squash them. These symbols are too threatening to people's ingrained need to "fit in" that people learned as their mother and fathers did before them.

The educator who works to make an approach to education work that values each child's unique manifestations of warmth, and adequacy-at-birth, and THEN invites "them" to evaluate it... ...those educators can make changes. Those are the educators who really are the risktakers because not only are they not fitting in, they are putting their own ideas to test, as opposed to the much safer route of just criticizing the other guys' ideas. It's even safer, in a sense, blatantly to criticize the "system's" ideas (by waving symbols of revolt) because then, for sure, you'll never have a decent chance to try out yours.

These are enough examples of the degree to which we are immeshed in the life-game of "find out what they want and fit in" learned particularly in the elementary school, from those who had the power of giving and withholding approval - parents, teachers, principals. Let's go back to our over-simplified but true-to-experience story of how it is played in the evolving sequence of years in the typical life.

After adolescence, the young people in their twenties are faced with showing signs to themselves and others how they are winning at the life-game - how they are succeeding in fitting in. As a final training, pacesetters in this game have gone through college where the dominant theme for academic success is "Find out what the professor wants and give it to him." By this time society symbolically has expressed its view that enculturation has taken place by first granting the young person a license to drive a car (around sixteen years of age) and three years later a license to raise a family.

As people advance through their twenties into their thirties and forties an interesting thing seems to happen to many people whose real-from-birth selves haven't been pushed too far down into their subconscious - "never to rise again," as the folk song goes. The real self begins to make itself felt again. Often this takes the form of restlessness in one's job or in one's marriage, dissatisfaction with striving to win at fitting in the game of approval-wielding power. More and more people begin to ask themselves what meaning their lives have for them. Translated, I see this as asking to what extent are my actions in line with the real-self, the spontaneously warm and open just-fine person who was in tune with the wonderment of living, at birth. Just getting and appearing happily married, raising a family, making money, having a stable of the standard possessions to show myself and you that I have power over others in the game of approval-giving and withholding... ...all that isn't enough. As many people in the United States move through their thirties into the forties they begin to feel the restlessness of having lived a life with at least a conflicting roadmap.

One teacher expressed it to me this way:

I found that there were two sets of blueprints in me, each having varying degrees of strength from time to time. The two blueprints were constantly struggling for dominance. The anxious "I'm not adequate..." being rewarded by my peers and authority figures, and the "real me" being rewarded only by my own enjoyment and constant renewal. The struggle between the two often caused anxiety within me that I didn't understand, and still does from time to time.

Gail Sheehy's book Passages has become an overnight bestseller in the United States as many adults "find themselves" in its dozens of illustrations of the struggle to fit in turning at least a bit sour, especially between the ages of thirty-five and forty-five. These are the words of a 43-year-old man who is seen as a successful designer:

What I've discovered over the last year is how much of what is inadmissible to myself I have suppressed. Feelings that I've always refused to admit are surfacing in a way I am no longer willing to prevent. I'm willing to accept the responsibility for what I really feel. I don't have to pretend those feelings don't exist in order to accommodate a model of what I should be.*

*Sheedy, Gail. Passages (N.Y.: E.P. Dutton, 1976), p. 360. (By permission.)

You might ask, aren't there some people who grow up "in good shape," being able to keep in tune with their real selves that were beautiful and capable from birth? Yes, of course - think of Jim, in chapter one, for example. However, it takes sensitive vigilance, subtle support and some firm boundary setting to help a child make it with growing "OKness" through a cultural mold - the elementary school - that is built on managing people through threatening to make them feel bad. It takes just as much help (more?) for that child who's finding basic guidance from the "I'm just-fine" real self as opposed to the child who you see clearly losing in the conflict of struggling to assert that self, or the child who seems to have been forced away from orienting life around his or her birthright. There is the little six-year-old, for example, whom you feel is so comfortable and "secure"... Those children are particularly in need of having us pay attention to whether they are "coming from" their real selves or not. I think of a parent who recently told me how she was "secure" at school; at the top of the honor roll, was liked by the popular children at school, was accepted into the best clubs, was seen as creative and clever... ...and then, she said, "BOOM." It hit her after she had three children and found her relationship with her husband as enhancing to him but she felt exploited. She found herself stopping in her late twenties and asking herself, where's ME? Who am I? How am I fulfilling the real me potential for a satisfying life? What first started as boredom and irritation with her marriage soon turned to deep questions as to what she had done with her life. She, like our designer friend above, began to acknowledge her real me feelings and began to follow their guidance in her life, but with a great deal of confusion and anger. Hadn't she played the game by the rules? Hadn't she won? Well, then, how come it didn't feel that way?

I hope it's clear that I'm not writing all of this because I want to help children to be blindly conforming participants in the managing-by-fear, striving game that I've just described. Like the parent I just discussed, I've found that it's not worth it. I'm doing all of this because I want to help parents and teachers, particularly elementary school teachers, help children move out and live in line with the peculiar set of attributes that they were born with as human beings.

I've expressed this definition of humanness so many times up to this point I hesitate to do it again, but the emphasis is needed; so here it is again: We were born as warm, loving people, fascinated and responsive to the natural details of loveliness in each other, in nature. Each of us was born with a power for creative adaptation - inventiveness or problem-solving intelligence - that is uniquely human. We were born to need and want to live with each other cooperatively in groups, reaching out and responding to each other in warmth and trust, wanting others to consider our needs as we consider theirs. We were born without any qualms about ourselves basically. We felt morally good, we chuckled easily, we felt free to let out our feelings of hurting, we felt adequate, we felt our power, we felt lovable, we felt loving.

Fortunately for all of us, those attributes add up to a life direction that is satisfying and rewarding for the individual and essential for an open society. Our society is woefully short of capable people who allow themselves to enjoy the loveliness in others and themselves and at the same time have learned how to be assertive in expressing their needs and helping others to do the same. Yes, they will fit in. They will fit in if they learn, at school, to extend their capableness by skillful use of such tools as reading, writing using a library with ease, and basic concepts from the sciences. I'm emphasizing, here, how important it is that children not only learn to draw upon the humanness with which they were born, exercising it in the school community, but also learn how to extend their capableness so that they will be sought after in the job market and can easily find a comfortable niche for themselves.

Now let's pause here to consider what we've discussed and what more needs to be said. We've been discussing how society subtly molds children to be adults who learn to manage each other through fear - fear of feeling the "I'm not measuring up" anxiety laid into each of us when we were little, particularly at the elementary school. This is most commonly done by persons in power positions acting to extend and withdraw approval to get others to do as the power wielders wish. One of the striking features of all of this is how intricately it is all done, how subtle are the rules of this game that children learn so well as they sensitively absorb what the big people "want" from what the big people do in their lives; how little of the teaching is done verbally and above the levels of consciousness; how much is done unconsciously as neither the ones in power positions nor the learning-to-be-power-wielders sense a choice or an alternate route for them to use in orienting their lives. My emphasis in this chapter has been on how this is played out through the child's elementary school years and what logically as well as psychologically follows from that, in the lives of people. I haven't tried, however, to deal with <u>all</u> that there is acting on us strongly as we grow up and live out our lives. I haven't even touched on the role sexual relationships play in all this, for example. I haven't discussed how much self-satisfaction some people find in learning and exercising their job skills, their child nurturing skills, their hobbies, regardless of whether they get approval and get ahead, regardless of whether they fit in.

There are many loopholes in the rules of this game. Children adapt to the game of pleasing the big people in their lives but find ways to allow their real selves to be assertive (as I did, for example*) - to allow one's real self to continue to grow, usually covertly or in relatively permissive areas like recreation. What we become conditioned to is not all bad. Many of the rules make a great deal of sense in light of the humanness with which we were born. The problem is that the process of managing people by giving and withholding approval, which is locked-in in the elementary school, is so deeply imbedded in our culture. It is so deeply imbedded that often we don't even realize how we are threatening to immerse the other person in his or her anxious "I'm not measuring up" feelings as we manipulate them and are manipulated by them.

I hope that in reading the case studies of children in this book you see three things at work to change this way of living together, particularly during the elementary school years. First, I hope you felt, in our child study program, how we work to become aware, sensitively, of the attributes of humanness in each of us and nurture them. Second, I hope you are sensing how we help children, teachers, and parents learn to deal with the habitual ways that we subvert ourselves - how, for example, Carrie, (Chapter II) and her parents settled into accepting her protective withdrawal from feeling deficient as a loser academically. They found themselves moving to accept it all as being part of her nature. "She's just kind of lazy, not an egghead." (At first this lessened her subtle anxiety. Later in her life it would close all sorts of options for her.) And finally, I hope that in these case studies you see a positive alternative to managing children by playing on their deeply held fears of not measuring up. For example, I see our school as being a place where adults assert their needs to children, ("It really bugs me to hear you swear so openly, Pricilla. We're leasing our space from a church - and the lease comes up for renewal next month... ") and I see our school being a place where children assert their needs to teachers ("It just feels good to swear some of the time the way my Daddy and Mommie do.") I see our school as a place where children and adults listen to each other and exercise the beautiful-from-birth yearning

---

*See Chapter IV.

to live in a mutually supportive way with each other - where people "hear" each
other's real selves.

I hope that in this book you can see how children in elementary schools
can be led sensitively and sometimes firmly in ways that help them to move more
and more in line with their real selves and become less overpowered by the need
to fit into the adult world by learning to please adults at the expense of their
real selves - by accepting a deep down image of themselves as somehow deficient
especially when they tend to follow their natural-from-birth real self
inclinations.

One of the best ways I know of to do this is to understand well the nature
of those "I'm not measuring up" generating substations laid down in each of us,
perhaps even from the first shock of being born. So let's get on with this
discussion of how, as children, the uneasy music from deep inside always seemed
to be playing with the theme of "I'm not all right" apprehensiveness particularly if we didn't feel the approval of adults. (The messages come to us whether
we saw ourselves as conformers or as some of the few children who felt the lone-
liness of outside-the-law persons.) As we first discussed in the study of Carrie,
I like to call that constant fearful conditioning - first from without and then
as the substation grew, from within - the recordings of "I'm not measuring up"
anxiety that were set in motion for the child's lifetime.

Along with this acceptance of the deep down "I'm not measuring up" anxious
self image came the growth of behavior patterns adopted by the child to neutralize these fearful self-diminishing feelings - to secure the message from adults
that "I'm measuring up." Children like Carrie, adopted the "I'm just not an
egg-head - I'm just lazy, really, when it comes to schoolwork" self image to
protect her from the hurting "I'm not measuring up" feelings from her daily
immersion in the first grade low reading group. I, Bobby Newman, adopted the
behavior pattern of always trying to please the handiest authority person rather
than grounding my actions in what made the most sense in terms of my "I'm OK
from birth" gyroscope softly purring as it spun within those oh-so-dimly-felt-
self images of the loving, trusting, capable, lovable and inventive person that
was me, Bobby Newman, when I came into the world.

So, I'm saying, in all of us are those deep-down recordings somewhat dor-
mantly playing the fearful theme of "I'm not measuring up" over and over. Then
as we find ourselves in situations of distress we feel the uneasiness of the
anxiety around experiencing the self-diminishing feelings of those old recordings.
The fearful apprehension of bringing up these feelings seems to be more pro-
nounced when we find ourselves in situations with feelings somewhat similar to
the feelings we had as the self-diminishing anxiety laden, feelings were laid
in. For example, for me fearfulness often impairs my clear thinking when I
feel a distressful present-time situation involving feelings of my suddenly
being all alone confronting someone (especially a woman) I sense to be a particularly powerful authority figure in my life. This is a similar feeling to
the feeling I must have had as a child as I found myself responding to my
mother's warm loving enticing while at the same time feeling alone, small,
fearful and "bad" as I felt competitive toward my father for whom I felt affection and who loved me too - an intensification of the standard Oedipal conflict
in young children. It was more intense in my case because my mother didn't
like my father and seemed to want to have a close relationship with me instead
of him.

Another way of saying this is that we are each more "vulnerable" in some
ways and areas than in others - depending on the specific nature of the original
scenes where the hurting and resultant fearful recordings were laid in.

Thus each of us has a generalized kind of "I'm not measuring up" recording
theme that is playing deep down there from childhood. In each of us, moreover,

we have particular feeling areas where these sometimes dormant anxieties are more volatile, more ready to flood us with fear - the anxious feelings of child-hood scene - when excited by feelings in day-to-day situations that resemble our feelings when anxieties, or recordings, were laid in.

Each of us developed, unconsciously, and from forgotten occasions, what I'm calling self-defeating behavior patterns. We have adopted them, particularly, in those areas where we are most vulnerable to feeling the self-diminishing anxiety. Originally, these now self-defeating behavior patterns seemed useful. They actually were very useful. They made it possible for us to move away from the fearful "I'm not measuring up" apprehensiveness that was so strongly pro-voked in certain life situations. An example is how Sean (Chapter III) probably learned to orient much of his behavior so that he was continually getting "I'm all right" messages from his mother. As Sean got older he found his originally protective pattern of "I don't need anyone; I'm strong and powerful" just get-ting in his way more and more. His playmates submitted to his leadership but didn't want him for a close trusting friend. If it hadn't been for our child-study program I probably could not have reached Sean. More and more his ori-ginal "protection" turned out to be a facade which alienated others from whom he wanted warmth. In effect it intensified his fear around feelings of not measuring up. Thus what originally probably allowed Sean to survive in a dis-tressful tight situation later became habitual and more and more self-defeating for him.

Often, too, these later self-defeating behavior patterns contain the dis-tressful perception of the world that the child felt was there when he or she first began to use this behavior pattern to quiet down anxious "I'm not measuring up" feelings. This perception contains the feeling of threat that the child first felt - perhaps as an infant.

I think of a child who came to our school at four. Let's call him Rockky. The teacher would tell Rockky to come to the group, Rockky would walk the the other way. Rockky seemed to have to defy the strong figures in his life even though it put him constantly in the fearful outside-the-law state, down inside, as he pugnaciously took on those adults and bigger children who were more power-ful than he was. As I studied his behavior, his perception of the world became apparent to me. He saw his world as a fearful place, peopled with powerful people who were out to hurt him. This must have been his perception of the world at some earlier time in his young life, and he tenaciously maintained this perception. His anger and defensiveness were, to him, perfectly logical and moral in light of his distressful perception of his world. It went some-thing like this: "They are out to get me; they think I'm not OK; they're not going to push me around; I'm worth more than that; I have to stick up for myself in this alone spot I'm in. I feel strong at those moments when I defy them. I feel worth something, then, too."

As he grew older, and as we worked with him, all this seemed to become clearer and clearer in his behavior. Each year our child-study program focus on him became clearer. I grew so much to enjoy his indomitable courage to be adequate, lovable and capable in his own eyes, given his perception of what he was up against. The threat that he felt was probably real at one point in his young life, when these defensive behavior patterns and his view of his world set in. He had just refused to be conquered; but, as a matter of fact his per-ception was dead wrong when it came to the safety that he might feel in our school, with our teachers.

As he grew older, and as we worked with him all this seemed to become clearer and clearer to us. At seven-years-old he could describe in words his perception of the world - that it was full of people who were no damn good, people who would get you if you didn't get them first. (I thought of my father's almost identical language as he "explained" the world to me as a child.) Rockky's parents put him in another school when he was nine - even though, as I saw it, he was coming along so well in accepting his perception of the world as not squaring with his real world all that well. For example, his obvious affection for some of our teachers, for the basic warmth and love that they had for him, how they enjoyed so many things about him... ...this didn't square with the protective perception he had adopted as a child: "People are no damn good."

When his parents took him out of the school we were beginning to move in on his scripts and perception of the world with the warmth of our love for him and the strength of our subtle assurance to him that we wouldn't let him hurt us and that we would keep him from hurting others. We were strong and loving. When he would start his tough-guy scripted routines, we just wouldn't have it. Sometimes this was just by a teacher pausing, looking at him, and smiling - and often he'd smile and "forget it." Often it would be by asserting our needs - "Hey Rockky, cut out the 'awful awful' stuff, I just don't like to see you that way." Or sometimes it would be that we'd just take over, be more powerful than he was (while he knew at the same time that we felt loving toward him) and prevent him from doing some kinds of behavior. For instance, we sent him home one day when he continued to try to keep the level of uneasiness in the group high. (He'd sometimes try to hatch plots with some children against others, whisper obscenities into the ear of one little girl who found this hurtful, and so on.) "No, Rockky, no more of that sort of stuff in this school. That's that." All of this was being done within a context of helping Rockky feel, in many ways, the things that we and other children genuinely enjoyed about him, the ways that he made us feel good.

As I said, his parents decided to move him out of our school before I felt we were in any degree "finished." I hope that he got the right teachers - people who would appreciate his courage not to buckle under, his straightforward honesty, and people who would not accept his threatened view of his world when it obviously didn't fit. Then his budding "Hey, they're not all out to get me" new perception of the world could be strengthened.

This makes a sobering point. That is, changing deeply-seated behavior that at one time successfully protected a child against threat often means changing a child's ingrained perception of his or her world. And that's tough, when this perception of the world grew from some acutely hurtful life-scenes.

This makes another point clear, I hope. That is, when helping children to change self-defeating behavior and perceptions of the world, often it becomes necessary for the teacher to step in and act on what the teacher sees as the real-from-birth person and/or the real world for that person... ...step in and lead the child step-by-fearful step into the new behavior even though the self-preservation instincts of the child will be fighting it. Those instincts are drawing strength and guidance from the anxiety-laden "I'm not all right" old recordings holding that old scene as present-time reality. With some children some of the time, and with some children all of the time (it seems!) that in-stinct will resist tooth and nail the teacher's attempts to convince the child that life now, with that teacher and these children just isn't all that filled with fearful self-diminishing threats. Therefore, often it becomes necessary and the most caring thing to do, to interrupt this instinctive survival behavior caused by the threat of resurgence of the old anxiety-laden feelings. Inter-ruption so often means making the child behave in ways consistent with a per-ception of the world that he or she doesn't feel. This will feel both sweet and sour to the child if she or he feels both the loving and the strong inter-vention from the teacher. This is not easy to do. The dynamics are as delicate and sensitive as they are full of potentially fearful confrontations. The teacher just has to be in touch with the child's enjoyableness - has to feel

loving feelings toward the child, has to be able to feel that "I like Rockky's..."
This sensitive awareness of the special things that the teacher can touch in
Rockky doesn't at all mean that the teacher has to like Rockky's behavior, of
course. How can the teacher? What I'm trying to say here is that the teacher
has to feel (and hopefully, express in words) warmly, the things that she or
he does like about Rockky. The teacher needs to feel that, given Rockky's
conditioning - how he was hurt and how he found ways to defend himself against
this hurting - given all this, Rockky is doing the best he can. With this kind
of sensitively aware understanding and feeling, the teacher will be able to
deal with Rockky's resistance better. The resistance can be seen as logical.
Rockky just won't see the teacher's intervention as a loving act. He'll probably be angry and confronting to the teacher as he's prevented from acting on
his scripted angry feelings toward others. ...what a definition this is for
really caring for a child.

Therefore, the frame-of-reference that I am building for you has little
place for the Rousseauian beliefs that if you will just leave children alone -
not interfere with their behavior - they will somehow find the right path to
living out a life in concert with the real person who was born into them. I
am saying that the crux of the matter is for the teacher to enjoy sensitively,
the child's manifestation of his or her real self and by contrast, it will become apparent to the teacher how the child is moving in seriously self-defeating
ways. Then, it may become necessary for the teacher to lead the child in concert with the child's real self until the child has the "feel of it" - until
the new behavior direction becomes habitual enough and until it proves not to
be hurtful in the present-time real world of being with a teacher and in a
school where people obviously enjoy the child's real self orientation, with
heightened awareness.

"...with heightened awareness..." We need to discuss this here. It is
the goal of much that I do in our child study program at our school. It is my
aim that we study children with heightened awareness and that we come out of
the study with an even more sensitive feeling for the child. I don't, as a
child-study leader at our school try to teach people the frame-of-reference
I'm discussing in this chapter, in the abstract - even though it is most valuable to me in understanding, enjoying, and being sensitive to a child I'm
studying. I use this frame-of-reference well. As I use it I find myself sharing
it more and more with our staff people. In that way I am offering my frame-of-
reference to each staff person to use for himself or herself in sorting out his
or her sensitivity and enjoyment of a child we're studying. I'm doing the same
things in this book. I didn't at first, present to you this frame-of-reference.
I wanted you to get involved in the results of my using this thinking and understanding, before we discussed the processes and understandings involved. In
our school, then, I offer my frame-of-reference to staff people to use all or
in part but my immediate goal is to share my increased awareness and sensitivity
about each child in ways that help each staff member to see and feel the child
with increasingly heightened awareness. Each staff member is thus invited to
come to his or her sensitive understanding and enjoyment of a child in ways
that he or she finds most useful.

Our child study work illustrates how helpful it can be to a staff if one
child-study leader uses this frame-of-reference and shares his or her appreciative insight with the other staff people. The other staff people can then
add to their resources and the perceptions of other teachers who work with the
children, what the child study leader has learned from intensive training and
experience.

Several days before our monthly child-study meeting, I pass on to each
staff person a typed copy of my dialogues with each child, my thoughts as I

reflect on the dialogue, my feelings as I talk with the child's parents and teachers who work with the child, my perceptions as I look back at the last time we "did a child-study" on that child. If my frame-of-reference has value, I feel people will come to use all or parts of it as it fits in with their ways of heightening their sensitivity about the child's real self, about the ways that the child is getting in his or her own way, not following the clearness of the real self that began as her or him from birth. My goal is to help each teacher increase his or her awareness of the subtle, illusive beautiful real self in the people we focus on (both parents and children). In so doing I know that the other side of the coin will come into view - the self-defeating behavior patterns and views of the world arising from the child's survival instincts.

In me, the sensitivity with which I can tune into the real self beauty and distressful conflict in a person is growing as I use this frame-of-reference in studying children; and as I use it in my own life in helping me to bring my own behavior in concert with my real self. It's difficult, really impossible, for me to assess my growth in sensitivity without a benchmark - a point of perspective from which to view the present. For me, the only time that I find myself noticing how I've grown in my sensitivity to the essential humanness and its conflict in a person is when I look back and compare where I am now with where I was at a previous time. Here's an example: About five years ago I saw a couple of W.C. Fields one-reelers. I laughed so hard then at his amazingly clear and light ways of blithely ignoring and pointing up the absurdity in many of our ideas of appropriateness, authority and sex roles. Last night I again saw scenes from favorite W.C. Fields movies. I still enjoyed his theme, enjoyed the way he artfully used the caricature form, but was jarred by his deliberate insensitivity even though this was all part of the expression that he was weaving so well. I found myself wincing as Fields, the dentist, casually ground out all of a person's teeth instead of the cavity he was supposed to fill. I squirmed as the patient dutifully spat out the crumbled and broken bits of his teeth.

The essential point here is that my awareness has heightened as I have sought and found the beautiful bits of humanness to enjoy in myself, in child after child, their parents and the special relationships in my life. This, I see, as my "learning" as I follow with raised consciousness, the directions from my own real self. The frame-of-reference I've sketched in this chapter has hastened my learning by helping me to understand and talk about what I'm doing.

Another way of looking at this is to hold in mind a baby in her or his crib, fascinated and in tune with a sunbeam dancing on the wall. I was born with that sensitivity, that awareness. Each person reading this book was, too. As we help our real selves and the real selves of others, to unfold we get nearer, again, to our beautiful human consciousness... ...that sensitive awareness that is our heritage by birth. We can use this skillfully and articulately with children and in our own lives.

References For Further Reading

(These books were useful to me as I learned from my experience with children.)

Harris, Thomas A., I'm OK, You're OK, (New York, Harper and Row, 1967).

Hayakawa, S. I. et al, Language in Thought and Action, 4th Ed., (New York: Harcourt Brace World, 1978).

Jackins, Harvey, The Human Side of Human Beings, (Seattle, Washington, Rational Island Publishers, 1965).

Jackins, Harvey, <u>The Upward Trend</u>, (Seattle, Washington, Rational Island Publishers, 1977).

James, Muriel and Jongewand, Dorothy, <u>Born to Win: Transactional Analysis with Gestalt Experiments</u>, (Reading, Mass., Addison Wesley, 1971).

LeBoyer, Frederick, <u>Birth without Violence</u>, (New York, Alfred A. Knopf, 1976).

Maslow, Abraham H., <u>Motivation and Personality</u>, (New York: Harper and Row, 1954).

Maslow, Abraham H., "Some Basic Propositions, of a Growth and Self-Actualization Psychology," in <u>Perceiving, Behaving, Becoming</u>, 1962 Yearbook of Association for Supervision and Curriculum Development, NEA, (1201 Sixteenth Street, NW, Washington, D.C. 1962) pp. 34-49.

Rogers, Carl, <u>Client Centered Therapy</u>, (Boston: Houghton Mifflin, 1951).

Sheehy, Gail, <u>Passages</u>, (New York, Bantam Books 1976).

Steiner, Claude M., <u>Scripts People Live</u>, (New York, Bantam Books, 1974).

CHAPTER 7

THE ONLY THING CHILDREN HAVE TO FEAR IS FEAR ITSELF -
NAMELESS, UNREASONING, UNJUSTIFIED FEAR*

How elementary school teachers can help children take guidance
from their inborn selves rather than follow behavior patterns
originally learned to protect against fear.

Let's start by appreciating elementary school teachers who suddenly see
themselves unwittingly using children's fears of not measuring up to manage
those children in their classrooms and at school. That's a real jolt to many
teachers who care a lot about the children they have been teaching. That's a
tough spot to be in. That's an uneasy place for me, too, as I try to reach
teachers who at this point often seem to feel a lot of fear of arousing their
own "I'm not measuring up" anxious recordings. Some tend to react in what comes
across to me as thinly veiled angry ways. What I sense inside some of these
people is first a defensive, "Hey, quit telling me that I'm hurting children;"
then this tends to melt into a kind of outrage at seeing themselves caught up
in a life game from which they want to protect their children.

So many of these teachers, so much of the time, find out suddenly that
they are caught up in the fearfulness of what we are talking about. This both
helps them to realize how true it all is and at the same time makes them feel
that the path ahead isn't all that simple and light. As I sense the reactions
of many teachers, they find themselves in a conflict. On the one hand they
want to change the institutionalized management of children at their elementary
schools - change the patterns and tone so that children won't be pulled away
from taking direction from their real-from-birth selves by teachers' intensi-
fying and playing on children's deep "I'm not measuring up" apprehension. On
the other hand these same teachers find themselves conditioned to "find out
what the principal wants and give it to him." Many seem to feel a sense of
powerlessness from what I interpret as their own deep uneasiness when it comes
to the risk of bringing up their own "I'm not measuring up" predispositions.
Why shouldn't they feel this way? Most elementary teachers were star products
of elementary schools. It's the rare teacher who as an elementary schooler did
not feel a compelling need to please her or his teachers. Not pleasing teachers
was unthinkable - just too fearful to contemplate.

Then, too, I know the discouraging welter of authority roadblocks that
many teachers sense when they think of making even some minor unorthodox changes.
They feel that they are seen as petty functionaries in bureaucracies called
school districts. The teachers who want to change their own impact on the lives
of children also have to deal with their caring concern that they don't "experiment with children." If they follow along with existing practices and children
are hurt - well it's just not so scary because they receive some support from
the approval they feel from doing what the authority figures tell them to do.
But if they move out deliberately in a way that leaves the established authority-
sanctioned path, they are sitting ducks for strong uneasy feelings of inadequacy.
Both their concern for each child and their old childhood fears of "crossing"

---

*From Franklin Delano Roosevelt, who in his first inaugural, March 4, 1933,
said: "...the only thing we have to fear is fear itself - nameless, unreasoning,
unjustified terror which paralyzes needed efforts to convert retreat into advance."
This is attributed to Henry James Thoreau, who wrote in his Journal, of September
7, 1861, "Nothing is so much to be feared as fear."

the authority figures will fan the heat from the anxious "I'm not measuring up" message coming from their own elementary school-made recordings.

So where does that leave us? It leaves us with a healthy respect for those teachers who are going against these fear feelings. I say "feelings" because in each teacher, as in myself, those _feelings_ are real but they might or might not reflect accurately the real obstacles to a real-self oriented learning situation for children.

So let's start right where we are - by discussing the importance of the knowledge that anxious, distressful, "I'm not measuring up" fear feelings are almost always a flashback to old childhood or infancy feeling states rather than being feelings which are warranted by present-time dangers and threats of danger. This includes the knowledge that our defensive irritations and frustrations are often protective shields used in our attempts to keep from re-experiencing all that deep down anxiety and fear.

That's why, for example, it often is so difficult to resolve a fight between children - especially older children or adults. The real issue almost always is not known consciously by either of the combatants or by the well-meaning teacher or mediator. The real issue, often, is that each person is desperately wanting to protect her or himself from anxious "I'm not all right" hurtful feelings while the surface issue is perhaps expressed rightfully by Ben who says "The front seat in the bus is MINE this afternoon, Carl; you _promised_ this morning, when I let you have it!" The real deep-down issue inside Ben, however, probably is the fearful old feeling state of "I am _too_ all right," along with self-protective anger feelings that were present when these feelings were laid down years ago. And, too, it probably is Ben's fear of letting all those anxious feelings up that is causing him to stamp his feet and have such a tantrum.

The truth in what I'm saying has been brought home to me time and time again when working with children in situations such as I just described. Often I've found that, when in the process of mediation I can genuinely express appreciation to Carl and Ben - a way that I find each of them eminently adequate, lovable, and capable, and they find themselves feeling this, then seemingly all of a sudden all that there's left is the mop-up task of face-saving.

I remember the fight between Glen and Rolf with Harold playing a key role on the sideline, some time ago. (These boys were nine and ten-year-olds.) It was intensified by Harold's needs to exaggerate the awfulness of the injustice involved and made more complex by Rolf's being sent home, thus involving the parents. Leah called me the morning following the fight and its escalation among the boys. She decided that we just couldn't let this slip by and try to "forget it." She wanted this to be a learning experience for the boys. The apparent triggering issue was that Rolf allegedly laughed when another child fell from a tree causing Glen to get mad at Rolf for this immorality. One thing led to another between Glen and Rolf, egged on by Harold, until Leah found herself standing between two boys about to come to blows. That was when she sent Rolf home in what she later described with a smile as a "survival act on my part."

I remember my talk with Leah on the phone early the next morning when she called to discuss what we could do about all this so the next time this sort of thing happened the people involved would be more able to deal with it, drawing from the loving, cooperative parts of themselves. We decided that I would come down to the school and the boys and I would have a meeting. Rolf and Glen would be there along with four other children (each boy was to choose two). The others would be people each "principal" felt would make him feel safe - someone who he felt liked him. Leah couldn't be there as this was her morning off and she was committed elsewhere. Well, when I got to the school for our meeting I found that our intention that this would be a reflective discussion and a chance for the boys and me to try to move the scene out of the hurtful "I am too, all right" angry defensive track was misperceived by the boys. I found that the boys had perceived our request as a trial to see who was most not "OK." Each boy had chosen two schoolmates who he felt would stick up for him in the questioning that he assumed I was going to do - people who would defend him. Glen chose Harold and Matt. As it turned out, Matt was also chosen by Rolf, along with Jerry. We all went up to a quiet room on the fourth floor of the YWCA, where we had our school then. The sun was coming through the windows. We sat in a circle on the floor.

It took me quite some explaining to get most of them to "hear" how this wasn't going to be a trial to fix the blame on this person or that. I finally got across to all of the people, except Harold perhaps, that we were going to speculate on the ins and outs of a question that Leah and I wondered about. The question was, "to what extent does Rolf get in his own way at times and sort of push other people around in a (perhaps) unnecessary kind of insensitivity." (I had talked with Rolf before about the possibility of his getting in his own way, and he had allowed that there was some truth in it but, at that time, I had wondered to what extent he really felt it. You should keep in mind too, that Rolf and I had had an intervue earlier that year and that in other ways I felt that Rolf had learned to trust me.)

I told the boys that before we would begin trying to talk about that question I wanted everyone to say one thing he liked about Glen and one thing he liked about Rolf. I began first. I told them how I liked Glen's subtle awareness in being easily able to pick out enjoyable things about so many people. When I had intervued with Glan he had told me one specific and right-on-the-button enjoyable thing about each teacher in the school. I told the group that one thing I liked about Rolf was that he had that rather rare ability to accept criticism when he felt his critic wasn't trying to hurt him. I illustrated this by an example between Rolf and myself. Then I called on Matt who told how he liked Rolf's honesty even when it was hard to be honest. I asked Matt for an example, "...like the time?" He gave one. Then he told how he liked how Glen would speak up in their class meetings and wasn't afraid to say how he really felt. I called on Jerry next, who expressed something he liked about Rolf but just turned his eyes to the floor when I asked him to tell us something he liked about Glen. I asked Jerry if this was because, deep down inside, he felt that Rolf might still feel that he (Jerry) was here to stick up for him (Rolf). He said, "yes." So we moved on. Then I asked Harold to say something he liked about either Glen or Rolf. There was silence. Harold's look came across to me as somewhat defiant but uneasy. I knew that Harold seemed to have an investment in keeping this incident a "big deal" so I just waited. Silence. So I found myself telling Harold matter-of-factly, that I wanted him to go downstairs to his classroom because this just wasn't for him. He quickly got up with what came through to me as "Go ahead with your goody goody kid stuff; I'm leaving;" (You can't fire me, I quit).

We all knew Harold well and just accepted this as we went on. I sensed, too, that the children were confident that I would make this all turn out all right. If I felt that it was all right to deal with Harold's expression of his own anxiousness about relationships (as I saw it) that way, my feeling was that the others would go along with it. We finished going around the circle with almost everyone easily able to express appreciation for both Rolf and Glen - including at the end, Glen's telling an incident when he liked what Rolf did and Rolf finding himself rather comfortable telling one time when he felt good about something Glen did.

After that we were able to talk about the question that Leah and I posed. By this time I sensed that the real deep-down issue involved had been dealt with.

The feelings of fear that each boy felt - fear of bringing up their "I'm not measuring up" feelings of self doubt were laid to rest. Harold's influence in trying to involve the other boys in his fearful perception of what went on tended to fade away in the light of our dwelling on the "OKness" of Glen and Rolf - in the satisfaction each of us felt in drawing from our real-self, warm appreciative natures. And Harold's stirring up each child's fear of being in a situation where others were ready to attack one's fragile feelings of being adequate, lovable, and capable, was quieted by my assurance, between the lines of our meeting, that this was a school where people like Leah and me just wouldn't let this psychologically "unsafe" atmosphere prevail. This was despite the fact that Harold and some others, at times, seemed to find it hard to feel safe at our school, or anyplace else.

So, as I said, we finished the meeting by each person reflecting on the question of whether Rolf might be getting in his own way from time to time. This caused a flare-up one time when Matt said that he felt that Rolf cheated in a math game. Rolf denied this flatly, but in the context of the "I'm all right" feelings that we had established, this flare-up quickly died down and did not dominate the scene.

At the end of the meeting it seemed to me that none of the children who were there felt preoccupied about which boy was the bad guy. Perhaps Rolf learned a bit more about the degree to which it seemed to Leah and to me that he got in his own way by his awkward attempts at being a "tough guy." After the meeting, during the next day, I talked with Rolf, who in his characteristic honesty said "That was a really great meeting." Glen convinced me that he felt good about what happened upstairs too. It seemed to me that we had addressed the real issues which were first, a concern with being "all right" and, second, the issue of whether Rolf was trying to feel powerful at times by acting out the cool-cat Hollywood image of a tough guy that comes through all the time over TV and through the behavior of some kids on the streets.

I hope that this tended to reassure the children in that group that our school was a place that was safe for them. I say "safe" in the sense that this was a place where we staff people would protect each child in two essential ways. First, we would protect the children who felt less physically strong from those they perceived as being stronger. Second, and this is most important, I feel, we would protect the fragile and growing "I'm adequate..." real self inside each child when he or she was at our school. We would protect it in the sense that we would guarantee to each child that he or she would come each day to a school where he or she could learn to act out of feelings of being essentially adequate, lovable, and capable - without all the game playing that might protect oneself from the fear of restimulating the self-diminishing "I'm not measuring up" feelings.

I need to explain this a little further. I don't mean that at our school we were guaranteeing to the children that there wouldn't be threats to their feelings of being "all right." I'm speaking here of guaranteeing that there wouldn't be an UNDUE amount of this threat. We were guaranteeing that we would see to it that the appreciation and comfort level at the school would be high enough so that one could act on the feelings one had of warmth toward others, toward cooperative and creative participation in the life of the school; so that one could expect others to enjoy one's real self aspects and that one would feel open enough to reveal them easily. We were also trying to help each child hear the message that "We'll help you deal with the put-downs that you will feel, fear and anger that you sometimes come to school with in the mornings, the hurtful-to-you needs of some other children, some of the time." We knew that there would be some children who in some ways were more vulnerable to anxious "I'm not adequately measuring up" fears than others. For these children (like Jim in Chapter I) our message was, "We'll do special things to help you help yourself maintain your sensitive awareness and yet deal with any threats of 'I'm not measuring up' anxiety that you might feel."

What about helping children to feel safe who seem to feel that there are massive amounts of threat to their psychic integrity all the time? I think of a girl we'll call Carol who came to our school seeing her world as threatening - filled with people who were out to get her. She was physically strong and had learned to hurt children so they would fear her. She projected the image of the tough-guy loner to the world. Her real-self warmth and loneliness-for-a-friend came through, however, to her teacher, David, in the journals she wrote - page after page of them. On those pages also came through her feelings that she just wasn't worth much at all - just not adequate in any way that counted. How might we move inch-by-inch with Carol and people like her, helping her to feel that it's possible to feel safe, to feel she's in a school where she can begin to act on her real-self feelings of warmth toward others, feelings of enjoying others' reaching out to her with openness, feelings of being an adequate person?

First, Carol needs all sorts of special support, obviously, to help her get in tune with her real self. To begin with we know Carol isn't evil. I see her as behaving in the best ways that she can, given the battering that her sense of self-adequacy apparently once took or perhaps still is getting outside of school (where we have such little control). But it won't help Carol at all if we buy her perception of the world. No, as a matter of fact, it won't help Carol even a little bit if we humor her by glossing over or in some other way accepting her perception as our perception. The way that we can help Carol's ever-so-fragile "I'm all right" feeling begin to come out of hiding, is to let her feel our enjoying of her real-self behavior and at the same time not accept the behavior arising out of her perception that the world for her is chock full of generalized fear. And above all, to help her feel safe, we need to keep her from threatening other children (as I prevented Harold from doing, for example, in our meeting with Rolf and the others). Paradoxically, she frightens herself more than others when she acts the bullying tough-guy girl, or when she intimidates others into following her in making life miserable for a particular child. When she does things like that, down deep she feels her own vulnerability to reprisal from her followers turning on her, from adults "getting" her.

Right from the start I hope it's clear that we MUST keep Carol from threatening others. That's going to be hard because we need to keep her in sight all the time, and be aware of so much of her behavior. Fortunately she's not very slick about it. One thing we can all enjoy about Carol is her openness.

Very often the Carols of this world aren't slick and sneaky. They seem to be inviting adults to prevent them from hurting others, because when they hurt others they find themselves in a vulnerable-feeling position with those they want to like them. This exposes the conflict. They have a need to react to the threats they "see" and feel from their view of the world even though that view is contrary to present-time reality at school. On the other hand the Carols so want to be accepted and liked by the others at school. They sense, despite their perception of the world, that they are safe in this classroom scene. This conflict leads to erractic behavior - with the child drawing first from her view of the world and then from her sensing the reality of the immediate safe scene; all the time she yearns to have trusted friends in this immediate classroom scene; she finds herself pulling away into the loner role as she reacts with her deep-down learned distrust of "them out there."

Again, it seems to me that often this kind of erratic behavior is very clumsy. The Carols are expressing these frustrating and angry conflicting feelings openly - pleading, by their actions, for the teacher to keep the angry reacting-against-the-perceived-threatening-world feelings from becoming hurtful actions toward others in the school - the children from whom the Carols of the world desperately crave acceptance. We also see another paradox: a child who seems to go out of her or his way to "bug" teachers openly is often really asking for the love, close supervision, and teacher-maintained boundaries that her or his defiant "I don't give a darn" facade belies.

Carol, at our school, can see in the commonplace trustful behavior of others how somehow her perception of the world just doesn't fit, at least at the school - despite her viewing the school scene as it were through dark glasses that color relationships as massively threatful. Massive threat was real in her life once and maybe still is in the outside world for her but it's not that way at school. All of us on the staff just won't let it be that way. If we can't make our school a potentially safe place for each child we should just close up and find work elsewhere.

This feeling, on the staff's part, was expressed strongly just this spring. We found ourselves at the end of a long hard winter and a sudden burst of fighting (three incidents) between four or five of the oldest boys brought the whole question to us with sudden immediacy. Leah, again, seemed to speak from our deepest convictions. It began at a staff meeting with Leah expressing that she just couldn't live with this. Other business at the meeting seemed to pale into the background. Next followed a special parents' meeting to which we invited, especially, all of the parents of children who were showing this kind of tension from time to time. That was a difficult meeting for me to lead. What we were talking about seemed to bring up a lot of fear as parents and staff people (including me) began to get in touch with old unsafe feelings they had had when they were little; as people began to talk about their own conflicts and frustrations.

The meeting began with talk about murder, hitting, and violence on TV. Then it got more personal. "I tell my son always to hit someone back when they hit him. 'Stick up for yourself', I say, 'don't be a patsy'." Then other people talked about how they spanked their own children and some of their conflicting feelings about this. Always the general tone seemed to be that hitting another person was moral if the other person was in the wrong. In my mind I knew that in every fight I could remember at our school each combatant saw the other person as in the wrong. After the meeting, in another room, one of the teachers just cried and cried, supported by Susan and myself. A tremendous number of this teacher's deep down fearful old feelings were coming up. We deeply admired his courage and his ability to cry to discharge the old distress that was coming up. I think we helped him to appreciate himself. All of our support and his crying helped him, too, to be clear the next day as he worked all of these conflicting feelings through with his class.

During the next week we did succeed in relaxing the scene in the school among most of the older children. One of the things we did was to have a meeting with the older children where several of us on the staff found ourselves telling the children how scared it made us feel as we watched tension mount and when this led to open angry fighting - as we relived distress from our own childhoods. Some of us spontaneously told stories of how it was for us when we were little and had to deal with feelings of being unsafe. David, whom many of the children saw as both gentle and strong, told how it was for him "on the bottom of the pile" almost always as a child. Then, too, we drew clear boundaries for children. If you were involved in angry physical fighting you'd go home. That was that - unless those involved could figure out another way to put a stop to it. After this was tested - after we sent some children home - children and staff people began to talk in a businesslike way about other ways we could deal with the immediate problems and the fear there was in this for all of us.

Because we had involved the parents, often a telephone call to a parent would provide us with the support we needed at home. As you might imagine, all of this had to be handled with great sensitivity. In some of the cases the parents and teachers seemed to have more problems dealing with their conflicting feelings than did the children.

One of the disturbing themes, for me, in all of this down-to-earth staff-parent-children dialogue about safeness at school, was how many people seemed to feel that the world, for them, was an unsafe place - this dialogue seemed to tap, in so many of us the fears of getting close to those old deep down anxieties laid down in us as children. This wasn't voiced openly but, to me, was an unspoken assumption with many of the parents at that meeting about stopping fighting at the school, for instance. These parents, too, were trying to make it through that tough winter. We were at a night meeting when people were tired. This added to our vulnerability to those threatening fears that each had had laid into him or her as a child when many of the big people in our lives had manipulated our deep-down anxious fears around not being adequate, loveable or capable, in order to manage us. Perhaps the next morning, or in the first beautiful sunshiny spring day in a few weeks we would find it easier not to have that old fear stirred up.

That deep-down anxious fear is there, easily brought to the surface in many of us, in me; easily passed on to children whom we've trained to fit in with our view of things. It's important to me that in elementary school we see this fear as it is - old fear we sought anxiously to protect ourselves from in our childhoods. It is not present-time reality, not the nature of our world now even though it seems, sometimes, that way.

My perception of generalized person-to-person threat in the United States today is contrary to that deep-down fear that sometimes floods up and colors my reality. I say that despite the parade of interpersonal distress that nightly appears on the TV news. I see people's relationships in the United States as having unsafe pockets in them - areas in which we have to learn to protect ourselves - but in general I see the safe scene in our school as being "how it is out there." I certainly don't feel safe on most of the streets of New York City at night, but I certainly DO feel safe on most of the streets in the United States, most of the time - almost all of the time. I certainly am wary of the full page ad asking me to smoke some brand of cigarette with the subtle promise that I will be admired by people like the woman in the ad. Yet I certainly am not disbelieving of what most store clerks tell me about what they have to sell. I believe the TV news staffs when they select the distressful material they show because it is "news" it's not at all the usual, the commonplace.

Carol's perception is not accurate according to the facts as I see them. My leadership at our school is implicitly based on the assumption that the "world out there" is full of people who are trying to live comfortably with each other, trying to conduct their affairs with face-to-face trusting relationships. This is the natural born-in character of relationship for human beings.

And this isn't at all just idle cocktail party disputation. This assumption is the key to the notion that what we are teaching our children is REAL. What most elementary schools are implicitly passing off as "the real world" is a watered-down version of what Carol sees. These schools are preparing children for living in Carol's perceived world.

I feel that we're dealing with a bedrock issue here. What I am talking about is my assumption of reality that assumes a basically non-threatening world of people with cooperative intent. It is at the other extreme from much of the subtle message taught by the life of many elementary schools. The message is taught by the real and symbolic threat to each child of not measuring up - the basic motivational lever. This threat, to restimulate the anxious "I'm not adequate" fear in each of us is woven subtly and intricately into the way of life of the schools. It is just part of the air we breathed at the schools so many of us attended as children. It's the fearful substance in the ways that schools have institutionalized the power to withhold and give approval, as the way to control children. Granted, some school people soften the harshness, use parent teacher conferences rather than report cards, for example, but in almost all cases the hard core message is still there. Well intentioned teachers and school people just don't know a practical alternative that will support what they have accepted as necessary methods, teachers' role, and school organization.

In this book I hope that you will find in my examples and discussion an alternative to controlling children's behavior by threatening to restimulate their anxious "I'm not adequate..." feelings.

Let's get right into the core of the question whether we need to base so much of our need to control children at school on manipulating their "I'm adequately measuring-up?" anxiety. Parents have sanctioned schools' playing on children's fears because that's the way it's done in nine out of ten families almost continuously. Teaching is hard enough, one might say, with so many children in small rooms and with the pressures that teachers feel to get each child "up to the next level." It can feel overpowering to try to change what seems to be the way parents are conditioned, the way the administration is conditioned, the way the children are conditioned, the way... I realize how discouraging it often is and how full of feelings of self-diminution for teachers as they feel what appears to be the dead weight of the school bureaucracy demanding that each child make it to the next level successfully and expecting that they, the teachers, will use all the fearful institutional props (grades, fear of repeating a grade level, threat of being sent to the principal, being kept after school, lecturing, and other threats) which can stir up "I'm not all right" anxiety in each child.

Last night I had a dream that I took a sabbatical and was working in an urban school district - teaching second grade, I think. I remember the scene was just before Thanksgiving vacation. I was writing a report to the principal of some of my perceptions of each child, on a giant long sheet of 2 ½ foot wide butcher paper coming off a big roll there at the end of a table. I remember that I felt uneasy but that I did it anyway, in big bold felt-tip pen writing. I remember, too, that I felt even more uneasy as I found myself saying things that I enjoyed about each child - things that I felt would just not be taken seriously by this principal for whom I felt a kind of mixture of feelings. I felt feelings of having to please him, felt that I could see miles ahead and he was only looking at the next few inches in the lives of these children, felt that we were both trapped in the bureaucracy... Well, anyway, I finished this giant missive, folded it and went to the teacher's lounge. There I began talking with an attractive but tired-looking woman teacher in her forties. She had her report to the principal on the table next to where we were drinking coffee. It was on a form in triplicate, which had each child's name listed in the left column and next to that was the child's reading test score from the last grade. Then in the next column she had pencilled in the reading test scores from the standardized tests that she had administered just that week. There was about a three inch by 3/8 inch line for "comments" to the right of each child's name. No comments were written in. I noticed the form and felt anxious "I'm not all right" feelings. I hadn't even thought to give all my children the uniform pencil and paper reading achievement tests this close to the beginning of the time I had first met them! I hadn't seen this form at all, yet it must have been in that pile of things that I get in my mail box daily. I wasn't fitting in. What else hadn't I done? (More apprehensive, alone, feelings.) Much of the dream seemed to be saying - "just fit in Bob. It's too scary not to. ...too much alone, anxious stirring up of the fear around the 'I'm not measuring up' stuff... But the even stronger anxious undertone was one of "I just can't do that... Just can't give those tests right now. Just can't..." I find I can't use the institutionally sanctioned and supported manipulation of "I'm not measuring up" fear in children to get them to do what I want them to do.

But as a teacher of a group of children crowded in one room I have to be able to manage the leadership of that class; I have to see to it that each child moves ahead in reading and what the administrators and parents see as the lesser school subjects; I have to please the parents and principal and others in the school district. I have to... Can I control my class and not manage children by threating to draw on their "I'm not measuring up" fear?

There is another way to manage groups of children that will be living at school for at least a nine-month year. Let's call that way sensitive assertiveness. This the way that I try to teach teachers to lead at our school. Let me explain. Basically the scene between teacher and children is "Here's where I'm at. Help me if you can, to make where I'm at make sense to you. Let me help you let me know where you're at." I'm speaking more of the underlying relationships between people - children and teachers - that I am trying to characterize the nature of each encounter between a teacher and a child or a group of children.

Let me give you an example that pops into my mind. A year and a half ago I felt we had to do something about the words "shit" and "fuck" that some people were from time to time writing on the walls in the church building where we were holding our school. I felt anger and frustration. I called together all of the children who met in that part of the building - the part where the four-letter words stood as silent reminders to me of the trouble the young writers' parents had with the sexual taboos and restrictions on expression of their anger, as they grew up. We met in a beautiful suite of three rooms that I wanted to secure from the church as expansion space for the school next year. (This space was not used during the week and only lightly used on Sunday mornings.) We were there just about a half hour before the buses would come and children would leave. Many people were tired; we all had had a full day behind us. First I established the rules, which I always do, for such a meeting: (1) only one person will talk at a time and I'll recognize that person and, (2) be sure you're sitting on the floor far enough from each other so you aren't touching and so you can wiggle a little if you get restless. From the beginning I found my anger coming right out in a matter-of-fact way. "Listen, I really don't want to get into how right or wrong it is for you to use those words, how or whether your parents do, or when it might be OK to use them, and all that - or for that matter the extent to which I use them. But I feel so frustrated! I want to try to get your help in supporting me in renting these rooms for David's group next year." I found myself walking up and down among the children feeling and expressing my frustration - my hurting: "Wow! How in the dickens am I going to get the church people to want to cooperate with us in giving up some of their best space if they see those words on the walls of their church!" I wanted the children to sense where I was at. Inside, for me, was full frustration, anger and some feelings of fighting a battle single-handed with my own side subverting me. I was in touch with these feelings and I wanted the children to be in touch with them too. Probably this would be enough. The writing would not go on. (It didn't go on until the next year.) If I had to use some authority and sanctions then I could and would because the need of our school, in this case, was just more important than a few children's needs to write those words on our walls. They would just have to find other ways of dealing with the conflicting messages they were getting from home; their yearning to try out "big" behavior, liberally laced with their own anger and confused sexual feelings!

A teacher reading this might say, "If my principal got together the older children in our elementary school in a scene like that the writing would just keep on - maybe more of it!" I agree, because the essential elements behind me wouldn't have been behind him or her. I want to use this example to point out the essential elements needed in a scene where children are led with sensitive assertiveness. First, using this illustration, remember that I had intervued with each child who was in that room - or almost every child. This was a time when they had come to know the real self inside of me and when I had gotten to enjoy their real-from-birth selves. This was a time when they could feel how I was trusting this fragile and beautiful part of me with them. Then, in many cases I had intervued with their parents in the same way. This was all tied together by my focusing and heightening my awareness as I typed the record of these intervues and my reflections for our staff people. Following that I had shared staff people's perceptions (their child-study write ups) of the "OKness" of each child, of how each child saw his or her world, of the self-defeating things that happened over and over in that child's life. Then, too, for many of the children in that group I had repeated this process for two or more years.

In addition, we need to add the homework that I was doing. I was learning how to get in touch with my own feelings - how to express where I'm at, even in a situation like that when I was subject to the fears and pressures of what I felt as "performing." I was growing in my own life - in separating out, for example, the confused feelings I had grown up with, about sex and touching another person, along with the near zero-level training I had had in ways to let my anger out within a loving relationship.* My "homework" was teaching me not only how to help myself but how to help others in those walled-off areas that I saw symbolized by the four-letter words on the wall.

It takes learned skill to function as a sensitively assertive leader of children. It takes skill to learn how to understand, with matter-of-fact simplicity, "Where I'm at;" it takes skill to learn how to help children feel this; it takes skill to be good at helping children to express where they are at - the part not illustrated by my example of the meeting above.

Helping children express where they are at is something that I see our teachers working at day after day. Susan Mock is one of the teachers whom I see as particularly good at this.

Susan works with five-, six-, and some seven-year-olds. Children often tell me, in their intervues, how when they are mad or crying or feeling bad, Susan can help them. I see Susan having learned just the right kind of, and time for, lap sitting; just the right kind of empathic mirroring to a child of his or her hurting; just the right way to reassure that child at that point that she or he is "OK." When children leave those moments of loving, learning-to-know-me lessons with Susan, they so often are in touch with just what's wrong - and miles away from all of the confusing anxiousness around "I'm not measuring up" feelings. Mind you, I'm not saying that these little children can always say, in words, where they are at but at least non-verbally they are in touch with their feelings of hurting under their anger and frustration.

Then, if Harriet goes back to where Sandra is (Harriet and Sandra had just had the to-do that led Harriet to Susan) Harriet can get across some way - probably with a mixture of words and actions - what she needs to lessen her hurting. Probably, of course, the whole squabble will just evaporate but it leaves Harriet with an important lesson in getting in touch with her own needs and it leaves her one step closer to being able to take direction from her

---

*See Chapter IX for more on dealing with your anger toward children.

inborn fully adequate real self.

Another example: I can't remember ever seeing Dottie, another of our teachers of five- and six-year-olds, restimulating the fear of "I'm not adequate..." anxiety in children. Often she takes the necessary role of making sure that children in this group of 27 keep within the boundaries. One boundary is that "you don't 'bug' a child when she or he is doing his or her 'quiet study time' work." But children can just see Dottie's mind work. When she has to tell a child he may not just wander around in this room today for the next forty-five minutes - he must have something to do that won't distract the others - that child knows that Dottie's head is going this way: "Almost all the children in this room are doing things that make a great deal of sense in helping them learn to read, write, handle numbers in real-life ways (games, feeling-filled writing, absorbed work in exercise books...). I'm proud of what we have going here and I can't let you mess it up even though you have your periodically recurring rather hostile itch. Now, we can negotiate what you will do; I'll try to take what time I can to get you into something that will distract you from your hurting inside, today; but I can't let you mess this scene up. And anyway, indulging you will just make you more uneasy because you'll be awaiting some sort of show-down with one of the staff people."

I remember when I began teaching sixth grade in a fairly large suburban elementary school, after two years with the children in my own one-room school. I was struck by how hard it was for me to "keep discipline" during the times when I was trying to make the standard basal reading groups function smoothly. Inside me the system I was expected to use just didn't make sense.

It seemed to me that I was embarrassing some of the "slower" children; I was boring some of the "faster" children. (Just a bit maybe, but this was enough to bring them too close to the anxious "I'm not measuring up" feelings when they found themselves not wanting to conform. I was killing what life there was in the "Dick and Jane" type reader stories by over-analysis and slow-paced oral reading. (Even a children's classic couldn't take the kind of belabored questioning that the teacher's guide suggested, and these stories weren't classics.) Then I changed the reading program to something I could justify with clear resolve. I was a member of a group of four teachers who were moving away from the mechanicalness of the basic textbook reading program to what we were calling an "individualized program." The principal supported us. I changed my reading program to emphasize self-selected reading for those who needed to build their reading fluency; those who were fluent readers concentrated on using their reading skills in library research, writing fiction, etc; for all the children I incorporated a time each week for conferencing individually about their work. Then I found that I felt all right about insisting, if necessary, on children's cooperating. I felt this way because the program made sense to me. I had organized it in the light of what I had found made sense to me about how children learn to read and write and about children's needs to feel safe if I expected them to lead out from their real-personness at school.

So where are we now in my trying to answer this question that I hear over and over from teachers:

> "All right, if we're not going to orient elementary schooling around
> power to give and withhold approval; if we're going to help each of
> us to draw from the 'I'm adequate' enjoyable, capable, real self in
> each of us... ...practically speaking, how should we do it?"

Up to this point I've begun to answer this question first, by spending quite a bit of time discussing how threatening it is for elementary school teachers to contemplate going against the current - against playing on children's deep anxieties about not being quite all right. ...how threatening this is because the teacher is a "success" product of a system that leads one to ask "find out what the principal wants and give it to him" or suffer the prospect of feeling "I'm not measuring up" uneasiness. I've dwelt on this because it's important that we know what we're up against as we contemplate taking steps to change our controlling children by threatening to restimulate the "I'm not adequate..." apprehensiveness - the same kind of fear that we, as teachers, have and the same kind of fear that is manipulated by others in the education bureaucracy to keep us in line. This is no little thing we are asking sensitive teachers to do.

We then discussed the need to make our elementary schools safe for every child - safe against the fear of feeling not-all-right apprehension. School needs to be a workshop in learning how to handle this fear. We talked about how part of the necessary safety for each child is a teacher-child relationship scene that is not based on the fear of failing and does not rely on withdrawing and extending approval as the undercurrent that keeps children in line.

I labelled this alternate kind of teacher-child relationship sensitive assertiveness. We discussed some of the key elements in bringing that about: the teacher expressing where he or she is at; securing help from children in getting this across to them; helping children to get in touch with where they are at and increasingly to be able to express that; how important it is to build a trusting relationship with each child; how children need to know and, I hope, enjoy the real person in me and know how I, too, can get in touch with conflict and fear in me because of my own anxious "I'm not all right" recordings; and how each child needs to learn to get in touch with his or her real-person feelings inside - especially in times of interpersonal stress.

Finally, in being sensitively assertive as a teacher, I stressed how important it is for me to know that what I'm doing makes sense and why. Then either through my actions or my words or both I can get across to children that I'm not insisting (if necessary) that they do such-and-such because it's just something I've been told to do or just because that's the way all the other teachers do it. I know how what we're doing fits logically with how we learn and the patterns and sequences of the subject matter - it makes clear and compelling sense to me.

Well, what's left to discuss in answering that question about how we might go about helping children to take guidance from their just-fine real selves? We need to discuss how we might help children to feel their due self-appreciation - how this might be done in sensitively aware ways. In this context, we need to discuss people's feelings of being put-down in relationships with others. Our concern, then is to help people grow in proudly drawing from their real-from-birth selves, despite the times each day when they feel, consciously or unconsciously the sting of a put-down. We need to begin by examining feelings of being put down. The teacher needs to understand as much as possible, the nature of feeling put down if he or she is to help children minimize putting each other down.

Sometimes teachers try the IALAC game to illustrate the number of times each day that we experience the fear of feeling "I'm not measuring up" apprehension in the banter and serious talk of our relationships with others. This kind of fear, triggered by someone else's action in relationships, is what I mean by feeling put-down. It can be either a conscious act on the part of the other, or an unconsciously done thing. Sometimes the person feels a conscious "I feel put down" sting and sometimes the effect is largely unconscious - with the person finding herself or himself wanting to withdraw, becoming pugnacious or using some other protective behavior without knowing why. In the IALAC game, each participant is asked to take an 8½ x 11 inch piece of blank paper and write

I.A.L.A.C. across it in big bold letters. These letters stand for "I Am Love-able And Capable." Then the directions are for all the teachers, that day, to tear a bit of the paper off each time during their interaction with others they recognize the down feeling, the feeling that they want to pull away from another, the protective anger, the out-of-patience frustration or the - sudden sensing of the fear of "I'm not adequate..." uneasiness. We are speaking of the fear of restimulation (or the outright restimulation) of anxious "I'm not quite all right" feelings in themselves. Then at the end of the day all the teachers get together and show how much of their IALAC sheets they have left. They swap stories of the incidents that caused them to tear off pieces. One interesting thing is that what tends to be a put-down for one person sometimes isn't seen as worth tearing a piece off, by another. This gives the leader a chance to make one of her or his points: It's dangerous to assume that what I see as a cutting remark, for example, might be felt as a put-down to another person. Maybe that person's dominant "I'm not all right" recordings were originally laid in with only negligable feelings of inadequacy in the area of that cutting remark - it just wasn't all that potentially restimulative. For example, it just isn't very restimulative for me to be hit by some sharp remark about my lineage or my social class background which is white, Anglo-Saxon, Protestant. The same remark of slur might really hurt a person who grew up with feelings of "I'm not adequate, loveable or capable" about being Black or Jewish.

Often in the IALAC discussions teachers talk about their feeling put down when it seems to them that there was no conscious or unconscious motivation in the person who tirggered the fear in them to do it. Advice from well-meaning people is often received with some feelings of diminished self worth because the advice is almost always given in a way that makes the advised one feel that the answer to the problem in really simple - "Why didn't I think of that?" is often the put-down feeling. Or the advised one feels that the advisor is "so much stronger than I" because this course of action would seem so easy for the advisor to do but it seems so complex to me. "Why can't I just step out and do it?"

Children often do this - put people down without malice or forethought. Think of the many times that children stare at a physical deformity in a person - a vulnerable area, often, for that person. Then some people seem to be fan-tastically unempathic - just seem to hurt others over and over again and if challenged can't seem to understand how they possibly could be doing this. I know of a clerk at a university where I once worked, to illustrate, who always seemed to bring up fear in students who had something to do with her. I'm con-vinced that this person wasn't consciously trying to feel more important or had some other deep down reason for wreaking the havoc that she did. I think it's more that this person just seemed to be particularly insensitive and unaware of the ways that she might tap the fear of not measuring up in almost all students. She could almost always be trusted to scare students, make them defensive, or give students "downers." I sometimes wonder how psychologically brutally she might have been hurt over and over again - made fearful as a child - to cause her to withdraw her natural real-person sensitivity in these relationships with students. In my mind I can see a little girl who adapted to being hurt insen-sitively over and over again, by becoming "tough" and insensitive, on the sur-face anyway, to her own feelings of hurt. She probably adapted, further, by coming to admire the "tough" image she cast. All of that most likely helped her survive then, but it is self-defeating now.

Some little boys learn, too, that this kind of "toughness" is a mark of manliness. As a man, around children at school, I make a point of letting the little boys see me react with open warmth in relationships. When Jack or Bobby runs up to give me my big hug almost every morning as I come in, I often see

Archie sort of watching out of the corner of his eye. Archie likes me and would like to hug too but is uneasy about the manliness issue in all this. Not so long ago he sort of "slipped" and gave me a big hug after I made it easy for him by asking him if he wanted a bear hug or a kangaroo hug. (I invented that on the spot: the bear hug was with his feet on the ground and the kangaroo hug was with his feet flying through the air.)

What <u>are</u> the avenues open to Archie to express warmth? Hugging isn't... Well, his heroes just never do that. Except for Dr. Newman, he almost never sees men openly expressing their warmth for each other in words, but he knows that they seem to exchange warmth, nevertheless. There <u>is</u> something that feels warm, as he learns from experiencing the relationship of the men he admires. Yes, they do, too, exchange warmth but Archie muses, it feels OK to him because it gets the other guy to know that another man likes him yet it feels "manly" too. What is this "it" that feels like an exchange of warmth but also feels manly? For example, Archie sees and hears a man he admires greet a close buddy warmly, with a smile and a "fun? put down" saying, "hey you Son of a B..., let's work on my car this afternoon?" Archie knows that the man who said that was expressing warm appreciation to his friend - and so does his friend. Then too, Archie begins to learn more about exchanging "manly" warmth from the older boys he saw the other day fooling around shooting baskets in the park. They were laughing and having such a good time making jokes at each other's expense. "Marty's so dumb he'd eat the grass instead of mowing it: (Haw Haw)" and then Archie saw Marty obviously enjoying this as he came up with, "Oh yeah, and Sam is so dumb he..."

Archie is learning one of the few (the only?) avenues men have to expressing warmth easily to each other directly - by turning the appreciation 100% around. I call that the "fun? putdown."

I suspect that children have learned to use the "fun? putdown" so much because in this way they can smuggle-in expressing warm appreciation while following adults' rules against expressing our warm love openly to another. In the rough-and-tumble of the "fun? putdowns" at school and elsewhere where young men (and older ones too) get together, I feel boys in particular, are doing the best they can to reach out with affection and still not violate the rule against open expression of warmth. If they violate that rule they will feel uneasy and so probably will the person who received the open expression of warmth - he won't know how to handle it.

I feel angry as I think about what I just wrote. I think of the contortions that little boys, in particular, have to go through to squeeze out expressions of honest appreciation to one another which come through muted, at best. When I was a kid, I needed so much clearly-felt unambiguous expression of warmth. The last thing I needed - the last thing we all needed as children - was to be cut off from the clear love of people around us. We so needed to feel straightforward honest appreciation, so needed to hear that we were "OK". And I can't think of an adult I really know now, who doesn't need this.

I think of the exercise where each adult in a support group (where people know and trust each other) turns to the next person, one-by-one, and begins "One thing I like about you, Alice, is..." Almost EVERY SINGLE TIME I've been involved in this exercise (about 150 times, I guess) I've sensed the sort of tightening up of the person about to receive the warmth as the speaker collects her or his thoughts during the pause that so often comes after "...like about you, Alice, is..." What that other person is going to say is terribly important to the person being affirmed. As I've waited there, I've experienced feelings like "you can't find anything about me you like." I've found fear coming up - rushing up - during that pause.

My point here is how important clearly-given honest appreciation IS to us.

How strong is my feeling of anger when I think that perhaps the only way a man (particularly) can express warmth to another man is by a 100% reversal - through the "fun? put-down" which often is used as a cover up for a real stinging put-down, too.

For example, I remember when I was paying my bill at a motel dining room the other day. I waited at the cash register behind a woman while her husband was putting money in his wallet after paying his bill. He saw me standing there and she didn't. I can't remember exactly what he said but it was something like, "Hey clumsy, let the man through." He smiled after he said it and I was left (and she was?) ...to sort it out. I got the feeling that his "fun? put-down" was being used as a cover-up for his blatant put-down of her. That's one of the things that bugs me so about the "fun? put-down" avenue. It can be and is so often used to express a real put-down intent but it protects the doer from retaliation - "Oh, I was only kidding. Can't you take a joke?"

Oh... I get so frustrated! It's as if there were some supermonster "up there" sitting on a branch laughing at us. "Yes," the monster goes on, "one reason men die seven years sooner than women, on the average, is that their loving feelings start withering away as soon as I shunt them into the 100% reversal "fun? put-down" way of expressing warmth, when they are little boys."

"Yes," the supermonster continues, "and I feel so proud of myself. I've done one more thing to make clear honest expression of appreciation between people an object of scarcity. Why, if people were to express easily and clearly their warm honest feelings toward each other then people would begin acting on those "I'm just fine" feelings that are down there - that were born-in each person. Then adults would have to learn new ways to manage children because they wouldn't have that ready reservior of "I'm not measuring up" fear to tap by simply withdrawing approval. And then, God forbid! later adults would have to learn to manage each other in some other way."

There's really no scheming supermonster up there. I realize that the rules against showing warm appreciation to each other weren't set up as part of a plot against humanness. The rules came about naturally and logically as a result of children learning to feel "I'm not measuring up" and learning the anxious apprehensive fear that accompanies that. This "I'm not adequate" fiction gets laid in so well that people just don't believe honest appreciation. When the straightforward expression of warmth encounters the laid-in feelings of "I'm not all right" anxiety, we reject the appreciation. We've grown accustomed (as the big band song goes) to these feelings as being part of us. Deep down, we tend to defend ourselves against anything that conflicts with them. We're so afraid of being afraid - of stirring up those anxious fearful "I'm not all right" feelings that we strongly reject attempts at clear expression of warmth.

What might we do to help children to handle this fear? As Franklin Roosevelt said, "...the only thing we have to fear is fear itself...." Well, it's not that simple but it certainly is important to help children deal with the fear that comes from stirring up those anxious recordings so deeply ensconced inside.

I make it a point to let children know from time to time that I have feelings of not being adequate or loving come up in me - lots of times. I try to get across to children, without a lot of explanation, my understanding - that these apprehensions about my self-worth were taught to me when I was little by people who were taught this way themselves; but that I was born basically adequate, lovable and capable and still am.

When I intervue a child and feel some "I'm not adequate..." anxiety I sometimes comment that I can feel this old stuff coming up and do something then and there to counteract it - such as trade "news and goods" with the child.

"News and goods" are a good way to help children build up their feelings of being safe enough to deal with the fear that is restimulated by anxious recordings of self-diminution. When I work with groups of children (adults too, often) I almost always begin the meeting with some variation of "news and goods." In its simplest form, each of us (usually started by me if the group hasn't done this before) tells something that feels good right now to him or her. For example, as I am typing this, right now, what is new and good? Let's see...? Oh, I know, it's how easily this discussion of helping children with put-down feelings is rolling out of me, and, too, it's how I knew it would if I "slept on it" after some muddiness in my thinking when I tried to write about it yesterday.

"News and goods" gives each child a few seconds of the group's undivided attention. (I encourage each child to try to see the speaker's eyes.) "News and goods" lets each child enjoy a bit of the real person in every other child. Each of us was born with the neat power to be aware vividly of the dozens of delights that are right there for us to enjoy every day. During "news and goods" time we help each other to exercise this power, strengthen it, and celebrate it.

Children also can see how our real-person awareness and enjoyment of the everyday good things can be dulled when we feel "down" - another way to say when we feel the result of deep-down fear asserting itself. Often, for example, a child can't feel good about anything when it comes to his or her turn during "news and goods." These times give us all an important mini-course in understanding a few things about how fear works - the subtle ways that fearfulness can cloud a person's perceptions of otherwise delightful little wonders of our living. This is a mini-course without any lectures or prescriptive teaching - just experiencing the text, which is each child's participation. When a child just can't get in touch with a good feeling for her or his "news and goods," he or she just takes a "pass" for today. That, in itself, is often a helpful thing - the child gets this chance to let the group know that he or she's not "up." Sometimes that's about all it takes to deal with those feelings and then, at the end of the circle when I check back with the child who passed, he or she often has a good one to share with us. Often, too, this seems to be because that child's awareness has been heightened by hearing and feeling the many other light and special feelings of "news and goods" from children in the circle.

Often I'll give an affirming "new and good" feeling that I have about a child who can't think of one to give. I might say, "One thing I like about Krista is her courage. In my intervue with her last month I remember how she had the courage to let me know just what her feelings were, about some things. She spoke right out about what she felt. That makes me think of another thing I like about her. I felt honored in the intervue because I felt that she trusted me easily - trusted me not to take her frankness the wrong way, and if I did she trusted me to do something that would allow her to straighten... Well, no, that's not it... She just trusted me, in the sense that I wouldn't hold anything against her. That made me feel good that she could see that (which is true) in me."

Often when I appreciate a child like this, at the end of the circle that child will have a "new and good" of his or her own.

Why? It's because I've succeeded in quieting down the child's fear of bringing up the "I'm not all right" recorded music enough so that the child can connect with the "I'm just fine" real self inside. In Krista's case, I helped her bring a manageable balance between her fears of restimulating her "I'm not all right" recordings and her acting on her "I'm a perfectly all right person" power.

With Krista, I was able to help her by giving her a specific incident to use as affirming evidence. Her reaction sensations might have added up to "Well, yes I guess I did make him feel good. Yes, with him, anyway, I guess I can sense the nice fairness there." If I had just said that Krista is nice, or "I like

Krista" the whole thing might have backfired. For one thing her anxious deep down "I'm not OK" strong image at the moment might easily have rejected that, as kind words by her teacher who liked her, which to an eleven-year-old might have helped a little bit but not that much. Instead, I invited her and others in that group to come to their own conclusions as I cited some of the data from which my feelings of enjoying her grew. I helped her and helped all the other children to be aware of part of Krista's real-from-birth self as I experienced it.

Another way to help children begin the day in touch with their "OKness" is newstime as we do it in our five-to-seven-year-old group. Teachers interview each child in small groups of eight or ten every morning during newstime. Usually each child brings something from home for newstime. Sometimes these are everyday things that are important to the child like an old friendly stuffed animal; sometimes something like a new toy. Almost always the thing a child brings is just the jumping off point in the teacher's interviewing of the child. The teacher then caps off the interview by writing something on a large chart paper, in front of the group, about that child - something that expresses the teacher's feeling of being in touch with that child's adequate, loveable and capable real self.

To give us an illustration of this time when each child is helped to get in touch with the beautiful, adequate, real self, I just called Susan Mock, asking if she recalled an illustration from her teaching of the five-six-and sevens. She remembers the time when Pedro brought his new, blue, downfilled, nylon vest to school for newstime. Pedro (as you remember from Chapter One) is a little five-year-old with plenty of self-respect but with some apparent uneasiness about his small size and what he seems to see as his lack of physical power. He retires, for example, from physical tussling with the other boys. In Susan Mock's words (as I remember them): "When you know a child well enough you know the significance to him of the thing that he might bring - the significance of this in his life right now. For example, Pedro brought his new downfilled vest and said something like 'This is a down vest.' I knew that Pedro is particularly interested in camping, camping equipment, and that he loves to go camping with his dad. In the course of my newstime interview with Pedro, he seemed to be able to get in touch with his feelings of love for his father and his father's love for him, just from the little things he talked about. Also, from the comments and questions from the other children I felt he saw clearly that camping was an area of knowledge that he had that was greatly respected by the kids. Then, too, I remember that one of the biggest and strongest boys in the group volunteered how when he goes camping it's sometimes scary for him in his sleeping bag at night. I could tell by the roundness of Pedro's eyes how this really was important news to him - important news about his own courage that he had taken for granted. What did I write on the chart paper to remind us of all this? Yes, I can remember. It was something like:

Pedro's Dad gave him a down vest.
They love to go camping together."

Thanks, Susan Mock. This illustration makes so clear how appreciating the real loving and capable person is something that can start off the day in a primary classroom, despite all the uneasiness that so many adults, and the children who learn from them, seem to have about openly appreciating another person.

I remember how strongly an art teacher expressed this uneasiness about openly appreciating another person one summer morning in a teacher's in-service class on "Reaching Each Child" I was teaching. "When I grew up," she said, "I

learned how phoney it was to soft- soap other people, to flatter and compliment
them so they would like you and then you could get them to do what you wanted
them to do. It's not real. And it just isn't natural. Why it just always
feels awkward to come right out and say to someone that you like something about
him. Makes him feel awkward and uneasy too. How can something that is used
so much to manipulate people, that just doesn't feel right, that's in fact unnatural, be something that we should use with children? How can you advocate
using this in this course that has so much, apparently, to do with being real?
It won't work anyway, it's too phoney."

I remember clearly my first reaction as I tried to process all that. My
first reaction to myself was that I was glad that this was the first day of our
course. How could our course of ten five-hour sessions unwind her lifetime of
defensive conditioning?: a lifetime, perhaps, beginning with the assaults on
her openness and warmth toward others, that she first expressed as an infant.
I found myself pausing as I sat at the head of that seminar table and then suddenly saying, "I feel at a loss about how to begin." I reminded the teacher
that she had plenty of time to switch to another course. But, it turned out
that this course was strongly recommended to her by her advisor, an artist col-
league of mine whom she respected. She wanted to stay.

Let me just go on with this teacher's situation for a minute before getting
back to her point about the "unnaturalness and phoneyness" of expressing warmth
openly toward another person. I want to tell you a little about how it came
out. It came out that I grew to enjoy her honesty, empathize with her, even
though I often did wish that she had transferred to another course. She seemed
to have a need to prove how "tough" she was by doing open conflict with me at
our seminar. (Carol grown up?) Yet it was apparent to me how much warmth and
human loveliness was right behind her tough-guy facade. Her yearning for people
to reach out to her with warmth came out strongly in our class discussion. The
feeling I got was of the conflict that she was carrying out in so much of her
life. ...the conflict between the tough-guy behavior pattern which probably
protected her at one point in her life and her yearning for people to reach out
to her with warmth and lovingness - to reach the beautiful warmth and lovableness that came out easily in the sculpture she did, for example. She brought
a piece to class one day; a courageous act, for her, of reaching out to us in
warmth.

It just occurred to me as I am writing this: One reason that I found myself so empathic with her was that I had done this very thing when I was in
college - balked strongly at entertaining the notion of my openly expressing
warmth with others. I remember dropping a human relations lab course because
I told the professor with some bitterness, of the "phoniness" I saw in the whole
thing. As I write this I can see now how having this person in my seminar
strongly restimulated the anxious feelings in that scene of years ago. Now I
can see why I found myself being so completely distracted by her needs. Huh...?
I'm smiling. What a good example this is, of how a present time situation can
stir up old fearful ghosts. I say "ghosts" because what was restimulated in me
might or might not have been just what was going on in that teacher's life and
it certainly isn't where I'm "at" now, thirty years later.

So it was that in my early twenties I strongly rejected what I'm advocating
here - it was just too scary for me, too much in opposition to the view of the
world I had adopted from my father, to protect me from the "I'm not all right"
anxiety I felt from the Oedipal seduction - rejection games that my mother's
unmet needs for warmth and love drove her to play with me as a warm, loving,
trusting, little person. This explains, in part, why so many "feeling people"
feel like crying when they feel, suddenly, deep love and warmth - it restimulates
so much childhood distress surrounding their receiving and giving love. It also

by the way, attests to the value of crying - how after a good cry the loving feelings remain and the old restimulated fear seems to have evaporated. I find, for example, that when I experience the beautiful warm loving from my own children I often let the tears come and when I do I find that the hold, on me, of the old "ghosts" of distress around loving and being loved seem to go where old ghosts should go - away. I have had to learn to cry despite the very clear rule against grown men crying, of course. I've invented ingenious ways - for instance I can turn my head in what appears as a "manly" pondering, reflecting pose - and cry.

What I am saying is that this subject - helping children and ourselves to express openly our feelings of warmth and enjoyment of the other person - is a subject with deep and disturbing and uneasy overtones of fear that reach back far beyond our distant memories, in most of our lives. I also am saying that the way society's rules are set up it seems as if the rule-makers set out deliberately to make it hard for us to express warmth to each other; for example, how against-the-rules it is for grown men to cry when they experience distressful fear that comes up from old hurts as they express and receive love and warmth.

This "figures," too. It's logical because, again, society's rules weren't made by rule makers supported by supermonsters "up there." They just accumulated out of the commonly felt need to insulate ourselves from the distressful "I'm not all right" anxiety that is tangled up with so much of our expressing love and receiving warmth and love, as we were ever-so-young children. (It's also tangled up with institutionalized sex roles and the needs of the early factory system for clearness about putting the profit need above the human need for sharing warmth and loving cooperation.)

We have taken another sidetrip into the some of the complexities and deep-down fears involved with openly expressing warm honest loving, and receiving this beautiful human gift from another. Now after we've done this, let's get back to the tip of the iceberg that is the only part that shows on the surface - the emotion packed question of whether we should help children (and ourselves) at school to express appreciation honestly and warmly to each other. (Then we'll go on with ways we might help ourselves to do this).

This question about the difficulties, the phoniness that people have experienced as others flattered them comes up every time I work seriously with a group of teachers - when I advocate our considering bringing more honest appreciation into the lives of the children we teach. I always have trouble with the question because it appears to me that people feel it's such a clear issue but that, as I see it, people are often dealing with much in their own lives that they aren't at all clear about - namely fear. One time, recently, a high school English teacher brought this out forcefully in a late afternoon class. This came up near the end of our day so that I had a chance to think about it during the following week. Then on the morning before our next afternoon seminar, my clear thinking seemed to bring it together for me. (Thinking about fear isn't as easy as rolling off the log for me even though I'm here writing about it here. I sometimes tell myself that I'm the perfect person to do this, though, as I've certainly "been there myself.") What settled in my thinking, that morning as I found myself turning the issues over and over, was that the very awkwardness of it all - this giving and receiving warm appreciation, this unnaturalness - was the very best argument for why we should learn how to do this in spite of the uneasiness that it brought up in us; and, with that in mind it certainly was plain that this was going to be no easy job. At the end of my quiet time that morning, when these thoughts were in my head, I sat down at the typewriter and wrote them. Then I decided to duplicate them and pass them out to the class that afternoon. Here's an excerpt from that piece:

... ...   Giving and receiving appreciation, for the most of us, is awkward.
That doesn't mean that we should, therefore, not do it. On the absolute contrary. That just supports the reasons to give it and learn how to give and
receive it with sensitive awareness. It's awkward because (1) we have picked
up the rule that one shouldn't be self-appreciative IN PUBLIC - that's "bad"
even though we know that this self-appreciation is something that is important
for our own comfort, for raising our children with the minimum of distress, for
having relationships that are mutually growing; (2) We are full of deep down
fearful feelings that tell us the ways that we aren't doing this right, aren't
as good as we should be etc. Most of the people aren't all that aware of the
presence of these feelings - hell, why should they be aware of something that
hurts that much? We just push it down and it doesn't interfere too much with
our daily routines etc. Then when we receive a bit of honest appreciation it
stirs this pot of distress. We deny the generalness of the appreciation, (e.g.
"that's not true about me ALL the time!" or we put down the person giving the
appreciation ("Hey are you kidding me?!"); or we shut down (withdraw from the
feelings of appreciation) so that the pot of distress can stay down there and
influence our moods but won't get into what happens in our minds.

Because it's awkward, to give and even more awkward to receive honest appreciation and because we need it so (in order to balance the bad put-down feelings
we take in almost every day and have inside already), expressing and receiving
warm appreciation is a big deal. Yes, it's a big deal and is something that
takes a lot of work, takes a lot of training, takes a lot of trying and analyzing what happened. (Try, for instance, what one third grade teacher did with
her class - ask the children to try telling people in their families about
things that they liked about those people, for a couple of days. Just try.
Just try and you'll probably hear children's stories about all the flak that
the people at home gave them as the youngsters tried to carry out instructions
from the teacher who was acting out of well meaning but naive understanding of
the pitfalls of expressing appreciation warmly to others and receiving it from
others.

I'm going to try to teach you a lot about intervueing with children, in this
course. Then later you will intervue with some of your children. In your intervues of children try to get close to where those children are coming from
in terms of their feelings of self-worth, how easy it is for each of them to
accept appreciation that is honestly given, how much distrust is already laid
in, already LEARNED and already getting in their ways over and over again. Begin to get a clear idea of what you might do to help Penny balance her residual
"I'm not adequate..." distress with reflections of her specialness that are her,
that are involved in her behavior and that have grown so nicely from that perfect child at birth.

Try hard - really hard - not to find yourself judging all of this after a short
little trial - "Hey, I tried that stuff and it won't work."

As I tried to express last Wednesday afternoon when I was so bushed at the end
of a long day (like so many of you) sitting there in our seminar with such strong
feelings of not knowing where to begin... Sure, what I'm talking about is different. Sure, it's not what we grew up with. Sure, it's not what happens between ourselves and those with whom we have close relationships (enough anyway).
Sure, but that's just the point. What we are talking about is not according to

the rules that have been handed down with all the distress, with all the...
Well, anyway, SURE it's awkward. AND SURE, this is something that we have to
learn.

But it's so worth it. It's so worth learning to help a child, some children,
to have mutually supporting relationships based on each person's trying to help
the other define and move with the humanness that is his/her birthright. People
don't live that way effectively when they move in and out of managing each other
by fear. They clearly can move in that direction when they support each other
to draw from each person's feelings of adequacy inside - when they can express
their clear loving warmth to each other. In a world where the weapons of mass
distruction are just a trigger-pull away from us we have no choice but to help
people strengthen their use of alternatives to balancing fear with fear. I see
the yen to cooperate as being strong and healthy, especially on the one-to-one
level, but it needs plenty of help so when people get into complex interpersonal
situations (schools, marriages, parent-child relationships, the "office culture"
etc.) ...people in those complex interpersonal situations can express warmth
without ambiguity, muddiness or too much fear, but with clear sensitive human
honesty.

The feeling that is coming into me now is "what a fortunate way to begin this
course." ...this dialogue. As I was thinking, this morning, about our session
last Wednesday afternoon I felt so good about how we were right into what was
important right from the start. ...yes... A bunch of tired teachers, students,
who somehow met on some ground that was important - touched each person's life
... That's the feeling I have when I think back on the faces at our table.

I'm smiling. I'm looking forward to this afternoon's class.

     OK, if we do want openly to express some of our enjoying-of-the-other-person,
if we do want to make it easier for the other person to reach out this way to
us - (and for us to appreciate ourselves) - what are some thoughts on how we
might proceed, with aware sensitivity? How might we proceed into this area
where we have been denied experience all through our lives (especially if we
were once little boys)? How might we proceed when we want to help our children
at school take some shaky steps into this area?
     First, it's important that we take time and train ourselves to "listen"
to children - to heighten our awareness of the self-esteem conflict being played
out in the children we teach. The next chapter deals with that question. But
let's finish this chapter with some rather everyday things that we might do,
given this expanded sensitivity toward children's self esteem feelings - everyday kinds of guidelines that we should have learned as we grew up but didn't.
Here are the guidelines that I find valuable in expressing and taking honestly-
felt warm appreciation, assuming that the appreciation is given in a context of
sensitive appropriateness:
     First, when you are expressing your honest enjoyment in another, to that
person, try to be specific and as factual as you can. "When you smile, Sarah,
it makes it easier for me to think clearly. I feel reminded of the beautiful
natural things all around me - the things that are really important. Not about
so much of the trivial stuff that I find myself worrying about during the days."
This gives Sarah specific information to consider. It invites her to be able
to check it out. "Huh... He sees THAT in my smile? Well..." I have given
Sarah a factually specific bit of information that is hard to blunt by the
usual defenses against receiving appreciation expressed by another. If I had
said, "Sarah, you have such a beautiful smile," then it would be easy to blunt.

First, if Sarah's self-image didn't include that awareness she could just not accept the comment. It wouldn't get to first base. She really wouldn't "hear" it. Second "Sarah, you have such a beautiful smile," is so general that it just doesn't give her much of a way to check it out. What is "beauty" anyway? "Beauty" is such a general and cliche-level notion that it just doesn't give her any help if she were to look in a mirror and ask herself, "Is my smile beautiful?" But, with the specific expression I gave her, she has the data to question more specifically. It leaves little doubt just how I react to her smile so often. Then Sarah can muse: "Does my smile reflect the kind of natural essence that Mr. Newman is feeling - to others? Well, maybe it does; I remember others who seem to see in me a kind of realness..." Of course all of this musing happens in split seconds and usually below the level of conscious verbalization. I'm just trying here, to put it into words so that I can make a point.

Basically, what I'm saying is, try to learn to express warmth in ways that the "I'm not all right." image (in so many disguises) can't discount. I'm saying that these images tend to be held at high levels of abstraction. That is, we tend to hold generalized ideas as opposed to specific characterizations of our not being adequate, lovable, or capable. A feeling that "People don't like me when they really get close to me" is the kind of image that might be floating around the lower levels of consciousness of a person, rather than "On that canoe trip last Saturday, John, Betty, and Carolyn didn't find anything to enjoy in me." When you express appreciation at low, specific-instance levels of abstraction, it can slip by the first line of defense against self-appreciation, which is the generalized abstract negative self-image.

Reaching for this specificity presents a problem to the person who wants to express warmth to others. It means that the person needs to get in touch with his or her own feelings - to try to be articulate and down-to-earth about what it is that is enjoyed, at that moment, in the other person. One way that I find that I can exercise this kind of specific sensitivity is by clearing out some of the fearful distress that seems to block that kind of loving sensitivity - in me - it's sometimes just too threatening to my own fear of self-esteem conflict for me to get in touch with adequacy and lovableness or capableness in others and in myself. When this kind of fearful uneasiness is high in me I find that I just don't seem to be aware of the specialness that I might enjoy in others - in myself, too.

One way I find to deal with this kind of fear in myself is to pause and to appreciate the little things I can like about myself. I found that the best way for me to learn to express this self enjoyment is with the support of others. For example one time I was with a group of about six parents and teachers where we each took a turn in expressing specifically a little something that we liked about ourselves. Then we would all help each other to let that enjoyment sink in. We used starters like these phrases to get going:

I'm proud of the time when...
I like the time I...
I'm proud of when I...
I like how I...

One way that we helped each other, in that group, was to establish the rule that we weren't going to claim that we were all OK - just that we were picking out specific times or things that we could think of to enjoy about ourselves. This is so important. Expressing appreciation, whether it be self appreciation or appreciation of another can be such a heavy thing if we make it an act of judgment of the person's worth. No, put that aside. We're not dealing with her or his basic worth, our overall enjoyment of that person, whether we would want to be close with that person. We're just picking out something that strikes us as special, something that we enjoy, something that does something for us.

"...something that does something for us." That's important, too. Often when someone is hung up and can't seem to express in words something that he or she enjoys specifically about another, he or she is really hung up because the person feels about to be a judgment-giver. That's heavy. The person then feels trapped in the corner of needing to give some final statement about another person's worth. Don't get trapped like that. One way to avoid that is to ask yourself, what is one thing that I am enjoying right now, that comes from the presence of this person? Then, we're really asking ourselves to understand ourselves, our own feelings, rather than pass judgment on someone else. I did that in expressing my enjoyment of Sarah's smile, above.

Don't let that little word "one," that I've used here, slip by unnoticed. That's such a helpful little word in making possible the expression of warm genuine appreciation. It can be used in saying "One thing I like about you is..." Think back on those phrases I just listed to help people get in touch with honest self-appreciation. Each one was bringing the person down to specific events and feelings and trying to focus the person on one of them. That not only avoids the pitfall of finding yourself feeling a judgment giver, it brings back feelings of the moment.

For example, during "news and goods" (see above) I often help a person who is reporting a kind of unfeeling account, by asking some specific highly focusing questions that deal with one aspect of the enjoyable situation. "Where were you standing when your father told you that the family was going to Fort Ticonderoga this weekend just as you wanted? Where were the chairs? Any pictures on the wall? Where was your father standing? Often this helps a person bring up the feelings of the moment because feelings that a person can bring back clearly are most easily associated with specific things and are hard, on the other hand, to associate with broad generalizations - the levels of abstraction where the fearful "I'm not all right" images seem to play around. For example a person might say, in "news and good" time, "I enjoyed myself this Christmas vacation." I might then help by saying, "Like the time...?"

Now, let's shift to another way that you can help the person who's receiving the expression of warmth, to deal with it. Notice that after you have expressed warm specific appreciation to another, there is a kind of awkward pause. You've said your bit. Then, according to the rules of conversation, it's his or her turn, but it's hard to take his or her turn right away. Some sort of conflict is going on in that person at that moment - conflict between the "I'm OKness" that you have stimulated in the person and the "I'm not adequate" kinds of images and other habitual self-depreciations that have deep roots below the level of consciousness. Be prepared for this, in the person to whom you have expressed this honest warm appreciation. Be prepared for her or him not to be able to pick up the conversation with anything but an awkward silence, a self put-down, some unnecessary self-analysis that neutralizes what you want to express ("I've gotten so that I don't mind smiling since my braces are off") or some flip attempt at humor that will make the thing you just said diminish into triviality ("I guess it's that new kind of toothpaste I've been using.")

What do I mean by "be prepared?" For one thing, be prepared to pick up the conversation yourself. Don't wait. You might just be prepared to manage the conversation for a few moments with a smile that says "You don't have to reply to that."

One of the pitfalls, that often catches the person being appreciated, is that she or he suddenly feels that it's necessary to give an appreciation in return. That turns out to be a way that people effectively neutralize the warmth

of the original appreciative remark because the return appreciation has a kind
of duty-given flavor. "I like your smile too." That makes the appreciative
interchange move over toward a sense of being a feelingless convention like
"How are you?" Again, the way to help the person being appreciated, at that
moment, is to just manage the conversation yourself. You might choose, for
example, to say something as simple as, "So. How are things for you this morning?"

The way that I find is the best to help children learn how to accept honest
appreciation is to have them see the way that I do it. When I feel embarrassment
or some kind of mild fear come up, when a child gives me an honest appreciation,
I let it out. Mixed with my smile and enjoyment comes some laughing - self-
consciousness. I try to be prepared to handle the hazard of the awkward pause
when someone expresses appreciation to me. Often I just say, "Thank you," or
sometimes I'll find myself saying, "Hey, that makes me feel good." Then sometimes I pause and let myself savor it. Often I find myself looking into a person's eyes with a smile at this time, expressing my upsurgence of warmth that
way.

Usually, what happens is that I have to take care of the person who has
just given me some honest appreciation. That moment after the appreciation, is
when that person is very vulnerable. He or she has broken a rule of society.
If it is a small child, society seems to be patient and tolerant of such "mistakes;" the non-written rule is that it's not so bad, but as the child moves
toward adulthood the tighter and tighter the rules that seem to be in the air,
become. One of the most important things is to make the person feel that you
feel that she or he is "OK" after the person has honestly appreciated you.
(The enjoyment that you show, even though it's mixed with honest self-consciousness
can go a long way here.) Then watch yourself that you don't use one of the many
ways that people use to negate appreciation or to neutralize it - the ways I've
explained above. I'll just run over these here as a summary to this section:

-Be prepared to handle the awkward pause.

-Be careful that you don't put yourself down to negate the
 appreciation ("I think my smile's kind of toothy.")

-Watch that you don't unconsciously exploit the vulnerable
 state of the person who's just appreciated you openly and
 honestly. (For example, don't stare at the person a bit
 with the kind of look that suggests that you are reflecting
 on whether this person is soft-soaping you or not.)

-Don't do an analysis thing on yourself or the appreciator.
 ("Yes, I know people in this world are really afraid to
 smile at each other. Why just the other day...")

I'll leave all this by coming to my final point, which is implicit in all
this discussion. YOU HAVE TO TAKE CARE OF THE PERSON WHO GIVES WARM APPRECIATION
TO YOU. Help the person so that she or he will be inclined to do it again and
not find herself feeling so awkward or full of crummy-like feelings that she
won't do it nearly as easily the next time.

That's perhaps a funny twist on which to end this chapter - your helping
children and others who express warm appreciation to you, when there is such
a conflict within yourself when the appreciation is really felt. You need the
help at that moment, yourself. I see this as being the underlying theme of
this whole chapter on handling the fear that comes from challenging the defenses
we have that protect the behavior patterns we've set up to live with our "I'm

not measuring up" anxiety. The most important way that the teacher or the parent can teach the child to handle this kind of fear is for the adult to show how it's done while she or he's trying it for himself. That makes all of this both a bit scary and adventurous at the same time, and, then, too, what a nice result... Then being a teacher of children or a parent, results in such important personal growth for you.

CHAPTER 8

COMING CLOSE TO THE ESSENCE IN EACH CHILD

How to use the intervue in reaching and listening to the real-from-birth person in each child (and yourself) with specific help and suggestions.

The beginning of an intervue is a time to switch gears. It is a time to deal with any light distress and preoccupation that either the child or you might bring that could get in the way of your both clearly feeling and enjoying special aspects of each other's real selves - which is the goal of the intervue. The beginning is a time to make sure that the child and you feel safe and comfortable. It is a time to set the tone of self appreciation and open sharing of feelings.

I usually come to the intervue with a mixture of feelings. Almost always, basically, I am in touch with my neat real self and it doesn't take much to heighten this awareness. But it often does take some attention to myself to cut through the preoccupations and uneasiness that have come up during the day for me.

Often this switching gears just happens without my having to work at it. Sometimes, for me, this happens on our way over to the restaurant where we have most of our intervues. Remember how Marian (Chapter I) observed that the sign on the door told you to "Use Other Door" of the two doors at the church's exit - but the door to which the sign directed you was always locked? Often children like Marian take me from the frustrations of the world to the clear-thinking logic with which we were born. Often children easily and naturally express to me how they like being with me - how they are looking forward to this special time. It might come to me through my pleasant awareness of the child's hand in mine as we walk along. It might be something that he or she says as we cross the street that reminds me how much the child trusts me. The child knows some-how that we'll touch the just-fine essence in both of us before we've finished with our intervue.

The word must get around that when you go for an intervue with Mr. Newman it's a comfortable be-yourself time. I say this because that's the way things start so often: in an easy natural way. Some of this has to do with the way I feel too. I try to intervue with children when I have plenty of energy. This is a time when I want to listen - to focus my sensitivities and fascination on our so enjoyable real selves - when I don't do much idle chatting or other things that might get us off into the world of the conversational facade which seals off real feelings.

This is a special time for me. It is special because this is a time when I want to get in touch with the lovely real-from-birth me - a treat that I miss as I fit in with relationship patterns during the day that often seem to me to be set up to protect people from getting too close to self appreciation. For example, when I answer intervue questions about ways that I appreciate myself I answer each question with a fresh response - another way that I enjoy one of the likeable aspects of me that has grown from my birth, that I've never expressed before.

I want to get right to the dimension of enjoying the real self in the child I am with. I want to enjoy his warmth, her spontaneous humor, proudness, courage, inventiveness, sensitive empathy - aspects of that child which were part of the just-fine person who was born all right and still is, under whatever real-self defeating protective behavior patterns the child has learned.

And because it is such a special time I find myself not settling for those usual conversational routines that steer us deftly around sensitive expression of our just-fine self, around self appreciation. Particularly in the beginning, I find myself managing the intervue - in the best sense of the meaning of the word "manage."

First I find myself taking care of myself so that I can make the intervue come out right. I help myself by sometimes starting our intervue with the first question for me - something I like about myself, perhaps. This helps me switch gears to being myself as opposed to being "conversational;" this models for the child, the real-self dimension tone that I want to set for our intervue.

Second, I manage the intervue by taking responsibility for helping the child feel safe. An example is my recent intervue with Steve, a boy who was new to our school. For one thing I didn't ask him to come for an intervue until I felt that he knew me. Near the beginning of the intervue I found myself telling Steve something about him that I liked. Like me, he needed to feel his or her just-fine self. Perhaps he needed, also, an antidote to the uneasy fear that might be coming up - fear that this intervue might find him lacking in my eyes - that I'd "find out."

Often helping a child feel safe involves allowing the child some "space" at the beginning of the intervue. At the restaurant this was accomplished for Steve while we waited to order and while we talked about what they had to eat.

It seems to help many children feel safe if they realize that this is a kind of simple and used-before routine for me - something that all the kids and I do. For example I usually get out my note-pad right away, put the date on the top, write the child's name there, ask the child where he or she was born and write that in, ask the child some other warm-up question or two and then, somehow, we both seem to feel easy.

I find myself getting across to the child that this is a time when we don't have to answer the other's questions if we don't want to. This is a part of the "permission to be yourself" that I find myself expressing in so many ways.

I always tell the child what I am going to do with my notes - how I shall share them with the teachers but not with any other children. Then I tell them that we might decide to share them with their parents but I will read the transcript of the intervue to the child first for his or her permission.* In Steve's case I told him about this when we first set a date for our lunch-intervue. (Most teachers, after they learn how to intervue, just keep a few sketchy notes which they jot down when they are with the child. These notes serve to refresh their memories, later, but are not complete enough to serve as records or show to parents.)

Early in the intervue I also try to get across the idea that this is going to be an intervue of me as well as of her or him. Sometimes we begin by our taking turns asking each other questions.

I hope that all of this talk doesn't make you, the reader, think that beginning an intervue is so full of do's and don'ts that a teacher won't be able to relax. As I write this, I find myself thinking back over some of the intervues I've had, analyzing and trying to distill out some guidelines - important experience to pass along to help teachers. I'm trying to bring all of this to you, item by item; but almost always the intervue itself just seems to "flow." If it begins right it usually goes right. After the first few times I find teachers beginning their intervues easily, doing the kinds of things

---

*Because of the legal requirements of the Freedom of Information Act it is necessary to clear this procedure with the parents first. I explain this in a newsletter to parents early in the school year.

I'm talking about here. These things just make sense to teachers as they make this a time when the child and the teacher can get close to the real-from-birth selves in each other.

Perhaps the best way to illustrate what I've been saying will be to pause now and look again at the beginning of that intervue I had a short time ago with Steve, who was eight-years-old then. We had just arrived at the restaurant for lunch on a cold wet day. Steve and I went over to the chalkboard to look at the list of "Today's Specials."

REN:* These are the specials for today, Steve that aren't on the menu.

Steve: I can't read cursive.

REN: OK (and I read the "specials")

Steve: I'll take the hot meatball sandwich.

   (We sat down at the round table in front of the west window.)

   (To Carol, our waitress:) I'll have the hot meatball sandwich
   and ginger ale.

   (Steve was moving the tines of his fork like a tuning fork and
   listening to the sound of each tine.)

   Listen to this sound. (I listened and looked.)

REN: I'd like the turkey club sandwich on whole wheat, please. OK, I'll ask
   you the first question, Steve: Where were you born and how old are you?

Steve: Chicago, Illinois. I'm 8.

REN: All right, let's see. I guess I need to talk for a little so that I can
   sort of get into this intervue. I kind of need to gently move aside some
   of the things that are up front in my mind and be right here, thinking
   about what is going on here. I guess the thing that is most on my mind
   right now is a kind of worry about something that might or might not take
   place tomorrow. Tomorrow if everything goes well I'm going to buy an old
   1912 railroad caboose car. I'm nervous because maybe something will mess
   that up. (I had spent all my spare time during that week arranging for
   a track to keep it on so I could begin restoring it - a boyhood dream of
   mind that was almost to be realized - or would this fall through? Would
   the owner change his mind at the last minute? Would...?)

Steve: Like the engine stops in the middle of the track and the train with
   the caboose on it backs into the engine?

REN: No, the caboose is off the tracks now. It's part of a clothing store that
   went out of business a short time ago.

Steve: Nervous about it'll get stolen before you buy it?

REN: No.

---

*Robert E. Newman

Steve: Well, what are you worried about?

REN: I'm worried that maybe the owner will change his mind.

Steve: Won't let you buy the train? What makes you nervous about that? You just won't get the train.

REN: Well, it's that I really want it badly and I don't want to get disappointed.

Steve: (warm smile) I get it.

REN: You know, Steve, one thing I like about you is how you really seem to want to get to the bottom of things - like how you kept at it until you figured out what it was that was making me "nervous," as you put it.

Have you ever been "nervous" about anything?

Steve: Yes... I don't know if it was really nervous... When I was watching "Monster Matinee"... you know that guy on that show with all the jewelry on him? Well, when he spoke... it gets me all shivvery.

Oh jeepers... it's scary.

REN: Do you have a question for me or should I ask you the next question?

Steve: Did you ever feel bad 'cause you couldn't so something?

REN: Yes... The picture that comes into my mind is when Robin, my daughter, called me and told me that our little toy poddle Petey was hit and killed by a car. She told me that they had buried him in the backyard. I remember how she started off... "Dad... I've got some real bad news..." I remember one of my feelings was that I couldn't ever get to see Petey again.

Is that what you meant by your question?

Steve: Not exactly...like that. I meant like you couldn't swim or something like that.

REN: What about you answering your own question about a time when you couldn't do something?

Steve: No, not really.

REN: Shall I go on with the next question?

Steve: Yeah.

REN: OK... I feel like asking a question that I invented. I call it the Magic Shoes question. If you could tell these magic shoes to take you anyplace, with anyone, to do anything... but just for a half hour, what's the first thought that comes through your mind?

Steve: I'd take a quick view of Florida to see what it's like before I go there. I'm going there spring vacation. I'm going with my mother and father.

REN: OK, My next question I call the Giant Memory Machine question. If there were this big machine over there that would take all your good memories except those you told it not to take and described for it, what is one memory that comes to your mind that you would not tell the Giant Memory Machine to take? (It would give back the memories it took but there are some pleasant memories you probably wouldn't want to lose ever, even for a few minutes).

Steve: The time when I went fishing for trout in New Mexico.

REN: That feels so warm and lovely to me on this cold rainy day. I see the picture in my mind. What's the picture in your mind when you think of it?

Steve: My mother and grannie were lying down. I was fishing with my dad and grampa. It was a real big pond. (laugh) When grampa swung the line back the hook caught his pants.

REN: I liked to watch your face as you were telling that story. I saw the story's feeling appear on your face just before you said the words - saw the feelings on your face and then words came out of your mouth.

What's one thing you're proud of about yourself? I can answer that about myself first, if you want me to.

Steve: When I saw a frog near a brook. When I went to my last school we were on a field trip. The rest of the people were walking on ahead and then I saw this frog. I kept on saying "Come on back and see the frog."

REN: One thing I'm proud of about me? Let's see... I'm proud of how I thought of the need to clean the wheel bearings on that caboose before it's moved. I was talking to a railroad man a couple of nights ago and he made a point of telling me how I should check all the bearings in case someone had put sand in the oil boxes. He told me but I had thought of it before he said it.

Want to ask me the next question or should I ask you?

I hope that you are coming to understand how important it is to me, when I intervue with a child, to heighten my awareness of the all-right real-from-birth selves we both bring to this special occasion. I hope you see, too, how this has an especially high priority for me at the beginning of an intervue. Other than trying to make sure that the child feels safe and comfortable, I've found that often I need to do more for me than for the child.

In the beginning of our intervue I got across to Steve that I had some needs to switch gears. He seemed to pick this up easily. He helped me, bringing to bear his wanting-to-know logic as he asked me to elaborate on why I was so worried about whether I would get this old caboose.

This happens often - children help me center down to my real-just-fine self at the beginning of an intervue. So often the children seem happy to help me switch gears and don't seem to need much of this for themselves as long as I help them feel safe and appreciated.

I almost always find that just being with me and beginning an intervue seems to be satisfying at the moment, for the children. This is the kind of shared listening-to-the-other-person that is often in short supply for each child. In Steve's case not only did appreciation for Steve come from the fact of this special time with him; I expressed to him some of the things I liked about him as we talked - like his way of getting through to what I was saying so that I felt he was taking me seriously and like the way his face was so expressive as he talked about the time his grandfather caught the hook on his pants.

Steve's questions helped me to center down to my real just-fine self. So what if I didn't get to buy the old caboose? My life would go on after this disappointment.* He seemed to sense right away that I was trying to move aside what this had stirred up in me - being "nervous" as he put it.

Often, then, just sharing "what's up" feelings with a child is important for me at the beginning of an intervue. The word "feelings" is important here. At the beginning of an intervue I'm modelling for the child the tone of our inter-change. If I start with reporting events without much involvement of my feelings that's the tone of the intervue that the child will pick up.

When I help teachers intervue with children I find I often need to stress how they should take care of themselves as well as the child at the beginning of the intervue. They need to deal with feelings of "what's up?" for them that might interfere with focusing their awareness on the enjoyable realness in themselves and the child who is with them. They need to set the tone of self appreciation, open sharing of feelings.

In the classes I teach for teachers who want to learn about using the intervue, we usually start off our training sessions with "News and Goods." (See Chapter VII). This seems to bring us to the feeling dimension and usually helps us set aside nagging uneasiness as we feel the countervailing little instances of enjoyment, wonder, and human warmth that are all around. I find that these teachers usually find that they exchange "News and Goods" to start their intervues with children. "News and Goods" is a good way to switch gears and begin the intervue on the dimension of specific feelings.

Teachers in these training classes tape record their intervues with children, then transcribe and duplicate them. Class members read copies of a teacher's writeup and then we each express one thing that we like about the teacher's intervue. What we want in an intervue soon becomes obvious from one illustration after another. At the same time we support each other by calling attention to what we like, as opposed to "tearing apart" what we have done.

For example, right away teachers seem to see how important it is to stress specific detailed descriptions of feelings, as opposed to generalized reports. The specific instances are usually close to where the feelings are. Consider this example:

Johanna: The trip to the farm last week was fun.

Teacher: What's one thing you liked about the farm trip?

Johanna: I know one thing... Finding a bird's nest with light blue eggshells in it. All the kids and I went on the hike.

Teacher: Just kids?

Johanna: No, Joyce and Betsy, David and Eileen were with us too.

Teacher: Were you in little groups or what? Anyone else see it?

---

*P.S. I did get it and am now well into the restoration work, having a very satisfying summer.

Johanna: No we were in a kind of long line on this trail at the time I found the nest. The people ahead of me just passed right by the nest and didn't see it. It was behind some leaves in this tree that bent right over the trail. I gave all the shells ('cept one) to Betsy. So now she has 'em. When we were leaving the farm Betsy whispered to me that she put the shells next to her bed in the barn. (Betsy lived on the farm)

As we read each other's first intervues, teachers usually see how few times other teachers in our class express self appreciation. As teachers become more experienced and learn more, we see increasingly, in their intervue writeups, teachers' sharing with a child "one thing I like about myself" or some similar affirmation. All of this both encourages teachers in our group to take the risk of saying to the child some specific thing they enjoy about themselves and at the same time supports each teacher with the knowledge that others, too, find this awkward at first. (Remember the discussion about these feelings of awkwardness? Chapter VII.)

I try to stress how teachers might handle awkward feelings by asking the child if he or she wants "me to go first to show you what I mean?" I also model this for teachers in our individual one-to-one intervues.

Early in our course I intervue with teachers individually in private and also in a group, with the class members listening and taking turns responding to my questions. During these sessions I use with teachers many of the starter questions that I have found are good.

As you have been reading some of my intervues in this book you probably have noticed that some starter questions come up repeatedly in my intervue. These favorites first came out spontaneously in one intervue and I liked what happened; so I found myself using them again and pretty soon I had a repertoire of tested intervue questions that fitted me well. I encourage teachers to do this.

Starter questions move us to where the real-from-birth feelings are and bring out people, events, things that have been or are part of the child's real-ness. Perhaps you have noticed in my intervues, that I only find myself using three or four starter questions in any one session - the intervue usually flows from the "place" where the starter questions take us. As we share our real selves, I find myself listening carefully to everything that a child says. If there is something that she or he says that I don't understand I almost always ask about it. So often another door to a fascinating part of the child's real life is just a word - something that catches my interest as I listen.

My favorite starter question? It is the Giant Memory Machine question. You might recall that it goes something like this:

REN: Pretend that over there on the wall is the front of a big machine. It looks sort of like some of those giant computer walls that you see on TV. There are lights that flash red, yellow, green... Dials that move. Rows upon rows of switches, tape reels that move with jerky circular motion and wires coming out of one end. Those wires go all through this room and into our chairs. The machine will take all of our pleasant memories for a bit unless we tell it about this or that certain memory that we don't want it to take. So... What is one of your memories that you don't want the mach-ine to take even for a bit? ...your first thought?

Often children tell me how much fun it is to tell about their pleasant memories. They say that they almost never are asked to do that. Usually the memories that children tell involve another person - often a favorite adult like a grandparent or parent or me. Consider this example from my intervue

with Eric. Eric was six-years-old. We had been intervueing for about fifteen
minutes, at this point:

REN: OK, here's my next question for you: I call this one the Giant Memory
Machine Question. Pretend that there is a giant machine over there that
will take all your pleasant memories for a bit (then it will give them
back to you) except those memories that you tell it not to take even for
a few minutes. What is one of those memories you don't want it to take?

Eric: Don't take away the memory of being here with you.

REN: That makes me feel good...

Did you know that you had a sunburst of brown inside your eye -
right around the black center?

Eric: Yes and the outside is really hazel.

REN: Who's one other person, other than me, who likes you?

Eric: My mother.

REN: What's one thing you like about her?

Eric: That she is so lovely. (He deliberately dictated the word "lovely.")

REN: What a beautiful word the way that you use it. Can you think of a time,
right off hand, when her loveliness came out?

Eric: This morning when she made me breakfast. She makes good eggs.

REN: What's one reason, do you think, that your mother likes you?

Eric: That I love her.

REN: Yeah...

Eric: I know she loves me. That's why she likes me.

REN: Who asks the next question?

I pause as I am sitting here remembering my intervue with Eric. So many
warm special memories come back to me of that time. (I would have a whole string
of memories to tell the Giant Memory Machine not to take!) I remember how easy
it was for us to center down on things that we liked about ourselves and each
other. Six-year-old Eric has not yet learned that most people feel "funny" if
they openly affirm another person or themselves. He seems clearly to feel the
glow from inside as he easily takes in honest appreciation from me.
So often the Giant Memory Machine question brings us to express our open
warmth toward another whom we feel enjoys us for what we are. Usually, I find
children telling about an adult from whom they feel this unconditional positive
regard. Often I ask the child to tell more than one memory that he or she
wouldn't want the machine to take away even for a few minutes - until I find
the child telling about a person with whom he or she seems to have an easy warm
relationship. Then I usually ask the child to tell me something he or she enjoys

about that person. We move on to something that the child feels the person might like in him or her. This brings us to appreciating ourselves in relationships, which is such a special part of the real person in each of us.

I never ask a child to talk about why he or she enjoys and is enjoyed by a playmate (especially a brother or sister), unless I sense that they have a peer relationship - one where each person has an equal standing with the other. So often children seem to be in relationships where one takes an unduely dependent role and the other is dominant to the point of diminishing the dependent one. Overtones of one "using" the other so often seem to be in their friendships - aspects of relationships that the children have learned as they have been manipulated by others and felt diminished.* These relationships are not manifestations of the lovely open no-strings-attached warmth that we see so easily in babies.

But when I do sense that two children have a peer relationship I find myself often asking the child I'm intervueing to tell me a way he appreciates the other person and is enjoyed by that person. To illustrate, here again, is another part of my intervue with Steve after we had been asking each other questions for about ten minutes:

REN: I see... You really feel good about your friendship with John.

Steve: Yeah.

REN: What's one thing you like about John?

Steve: He's fun. Like sometimes we play our version of Witch Hunt. We didn't know the story so we just make it all up. We do things like that. Witch Hunt is a movie.

REN: What's one reason you feel that John probably likes you?

Steve: I don't give up on him.

REN: You don't give up on him?

Steve: Some person might say, "You don't want to play with that dummy" or something like that, I don't give up on him. I don't go away.

"I don't give up on him..." I remember how this sunk way down in me as I was sitting there. What a bit of distilled loveliness-from-birth that shone clearly out of Steve. People aren't born afraid of relationships. People are born wanting, needing, and able to come close to those others in their lives with whom they share affection. Steve's tenacity in hanging on to that human essence is something that he needs to enjoy in himself as well as something others can enjoy in him. I felt that he left our intervue consciously valuing this "hanging-in" quality in himself where before he seemed to take it for granted. Me? What a lift for the rest of my afternoon. What a perfect reminder to me that in all of us their remains this human essence. Yes, I felt it's worth "working" at my relationships with people with whom I share a special affection.

Sometimes a child either doesn't speak of warm easy relationships in his memories or seems to talk about relationships apparently without much enjoyment

---

*See Chapter VI for a discussion of the ways children are so often controlled by manipulation of their fears of not measuring up.

of the affection received or given. I don't probe at these times. The intervue isn't a time for me to push a child to talk about relationships unless they
are affirmations of his or her just-fine, warm, self. But I find myself taking
note of what to me seems an absence of this warmth or an apparent uneasiness
when we get into this area. Perhaps one thing that this child needs from our
school is a chance to experience unconditional (no-strings-attached) positive
regard between people? ...just plain enjoyment of one another. I hope that our
intervue is a good start in that direction.

Perhaps some of this apparent uneasiness comes from the contradiction that
the appreciative tone of the intervue presents for the child. I remember the
time I intervued with Molly and how this twelve-year-old girl handled what seemed
to me to be, in her, a contradiction down below the level of verbal consciousness.
From the intervue Molly seemed to be receiving strong feelings that basically
she was just-fine. From the recordings down deep inside her she apparently was
receiving the message that she was not quite measuring up or was feeling other
self-doubting "music." The result: uneasiness.

This was our second intervue. (We had had one a year before.) We were
having lunch in my office after going to a fast-food restaurant to pick up ham-
burgers. I experienced the time as easy, light - a lovely sharing of our real
selves. There was a lull in the intervue near the end. Molly said to me,

Molly: Is it my turn to ask you a question?

REN: OK

Molly: This might sound sort of funny but it would make me feel better if I
    asked it. What's one thing you like about me and one thing you don't like
    about me?

REN: OK. Well one thing I like about you...? Can it be a little thing?

Molly: Yeah.

REN: My first thought is how I enjoy your eyes, but I've told you that before
    and I want this to be new stuff. I like your smile - but I've told you
    that before too - like that "bloop" right at the corner of your mouth as
    you smile. Makes me feel good, warm...

    OK, here's something I haven't told you: A few minutes ago, when you got
    up and started to walk around and look out the window, put away the paper
    wrappings from our lunch and all that... you were so natural. You just
    did what seemed sensible and in a way that it was so easy for me to relax
    with.

Molly: Because I didn't touch this and that?

REN: No, because I didn't have to make sure you were feeling all right. I
    knew, for example, that if you felt uneasy about something that I should
    know about, you'd bring it up. You took care of yourself so I could take
    care of myself. So I felt good.

Molly: One thing you <u>don't</u> like about me?

REN: OK, (My feeling was that I wanted to try hard to think of something that
    I "don't like" about Molly as this seemed important to her - perhaps

important in helping her accept the things I did like?

...perhaps important in allowing her to square my perceptions with the sense of herself-esteem balance that she had inside? ...perhaps to make my affirmations of her be ultra honest in her eyes and therefore specially real and specially nifty...?)

Let's see. I think of a time when I was at your house - like at that meeting that night. All I can think of was how you sort of made me relax and made it easy for me to talk easily to all those strangers there. Nothing I didn't like there...

Molly: Could you think of... Could be a time when I did something that wasn't so hot...?

REN: You know, Molly, I've been going over lots of pictures in my mind and I just can't <u>feel</u> any feelings or remember any time that you did something that irritated me or whatever. Can <u>you</u> think of a time when you irritated someone?

Molly: I asked my mother, this one time - because I knew something was wrong - and my mother said that I didn't listen to her (this one time). I went out and played and didn't do what she said. I do that sometime - you know, daydream after someone tells me something. ...sort of don't hear them.

REN: I don't mean, by the way, that I feel you're all perfect. For example your fingernail polish is cracked and not perfect. But you make me feel good inside - so I probably don't notice the imperfect things.

Molly: <u>One</u> of my fingernails isn't cracked - see, here (an impish smile).

REN: Well, then 10% of you is PERFECT (smile).

That was the last question exchange in our intervue. As we were going back to school I remember enjoying how well Molly was helping herself so that our specific affirmations could get through to her. Also I enjoyed the sensitivity she seemed to have to her own feelings.

The Magic Shoes starter question also often leads us to children's feelings about relationships. Consider this exchange with ten-year-old Beverly. We were just beginning our intervue:

REN: Shall we start with my usual intervue questions?

Bev: Yeah.

REN: Just look out the window at this beautiful sunshiny morning at 9:30. What would you tell your sandals if they were magic and could take you anywhere, be with anyone you wanted to be with, be able to do anything you'd like to do, be ahead in time (like out in space on a starship) or behind in time (like coming over with Columbus)...? ...but just for a half-hour. Then you'd be right back where you were when your half-hour started. You wouldn't have to explain to people why you were gone, by the way. This would be an extra half-hour in your life. It would be just a moment in theirs. It would be your secret to keep to tell people if you wanted to. So, what's the first thought that comes to your mind that you'd tell the magic shoes?

Bev: Take me to my cousin's house and have me in a magic show with her. She wrote that she's the leader of a magic show - tricks and all that sort of thing. She lives in Dubuque. We're really close. We're so much alike. We like the same things. We love swimming, going to the woods, lying down in the middle of nowhere, looking up at the sky, talking about what's happening.

REN: If you could say something to her right now, what might you say to her that would make you feel good?

Bev: If I could say something to her right now? Well, it would be "Hey, I want you to come back to Syracuse with me."

Remember that starter questions, like the Magic Shoes Question, are not intended to be used one after another. They are starters - to begin a line of questioning that one can find oneself caught up in and which are close to the child's feelings. I felt like pursuing this starter with Beverly. Here's how it went:

REN: Let's pretend that I'm a Big Magic Shoes Shot (smile) and I can arrange that anything I want to happen will happen. I've just decided that your cousin should be here in Syracuse - and she is. OK, now you go on.

Bev: I'd show her the school and my friends. I'd introduce her to Bill, maybe Pauline and Sonia. I'd say, "Yes, Jackie (that's her name) this is my school."

REN: What's one thing more that you like about Jackie? Just a little thing, perhaps - like how I like the way that you seem to take me seriously. I mean like the time I shared with your group at school, my problem of how to show the movie I made to the children without the teachers knowing until I surprised them with it. I felt that you were "right there" and listening and thinking with me. That helped me think and focus on my problem.

Bev: Like when I was out in Dubuque with Jackie. She had one day of her school left. I want with her to school. I was kind of shy. But she paid attention to me. She didn't leave me in the dust. She didn't go off with her friends.

REN: What's one thing that Jackie probably likes about you?

Bev: The way that a... That I don't let other people down. Like when she was here last summer. We were playing in the park near my house. Annie came up and told her (told Jackie) that I was supposed to play with her (Annie) and not Jackie because Annie was going away in a couple of days. I told her that, like, Jackie was my cousin and Annie didn't have a right to tell me not to play with her.

At that point I found myself having enough of what was developing into a replay of light distress between the girls. I felt too, that Bev would be quite happy to shift to another topic so I asked another question.

Sometimes in an intervue children aren't as easily verbal as was Beverly. Often when I intervue with a five-year-old, for instance, I ask the child to draw a story-picture to express her or his feelings. The story-pictures are almost always close to the child's feelings and often seem to be nearer to those deeper primitive feelings than the feelings that come out in intervue dialogue with more verbal children.

Consider this segment of an intervue with five-year-old Kate:

REN: I brought this pack of magic marker pens, Kate. For the next part of our intervue I'd like you to choose one color and draw a picture that tells a story.

Kate: OK, I choose blue.

I'm going to draw you a story about a rabbit, Rabbity, and cat named Catty. Well, see, here is Rabbity walking around in her yard and a cat came along and said, "Do you want to play ball?" (She drew in the cat.) "Not right now" Rabbity said,"'cause I have to eat dinner."
Next morning the Ribbit woke up and the cat came along again and said again, "Do you want to play ball?" ...just like here in the picture from yesterday. Rabbity said, "Yes, 'cept in half an hour I have to go inside." The cat felt kind of relaxed and wanted to play with somebody like Rabbity.

REN: So that's the end of the story?

Kate: No. Then Rabbity had to go in and when the rabbit went in, the cat cried. She liked the rabbit. The rabbit had to go in to eat her lunch at 12:00. If the rabbit would have stayed out, her mother would have found out and she would have been sent to her bedroom. She might have snuck in her closet and painted. She would have to stay there for ten minutes. Yes. She'd feel that's all right of punishment. Like she thinks it's appropriate.

REN: Appropriate?

Kate: Well, "appropriate" means it's kind of a good punishment and stuff like that.

Mr. Newman, I want to ask you a "knock knock" joke. It's like this: Knock Knock.

REN: Who's there?

Kate: I don't know.

REN: I don't know who?

Kate: I guess you don't know but I knew.

I wrote the following in my writeup of this intervue with Kate:

Kind of interesting that the Knock Knock joke came right after the rabbit story which was, I suspect, Kate, the Rabbit. Assuming that the subconscious makes perfect sense if one can just listen to it, Kate was telling us about herself and then the last line of the "joke" just fits: "I guess you don't know but I know" who's there. Yes, Kate we know...Kate, alias Rabbity.

I found myself marvelling at Kate's fine-tuned sense of expression.
...that Knock Knock "joke." What a perfect and poetic way to cap her story.
The surface lightness of the "joke" seem to contrast with the sadness of the
rabbit story in such a natural balance. I enjoyed too, how, in Kate's spontaneous honest way, she was able to get out some of the apparent burden that
perhaps she was carrying much of the time. ...the burden of fitting into her
family's strict routines and structured lifestyle. Needless to say what Kate
had to say was something that I'd raise in our child-study meeting with her
teachers.

I need to pause here for a moment to talk about light distress and children's worries, fears and self-doubting that spontaneously come up - often
"between the lines" - as we just read in Molly and Kate's intervue writeups.
I expect this. When we really feel the self-appreciative tone of the intervue
we jar loose those old deep self-images that so often remind us that somehow
we are lacking. Then, too, when a child feels safe in the intervue situation
he or she often spontaneously lets out cares and concerns. This "letting out"
is good for the child and helps me to learn some of the burdens that she or he
is carrying. But the purpose of our intervue is not therapy in the sense of
going into fears and worries. The purpose of our intervue is to experience
our real-from-birth selves with heightened consciousness. That real self is
just fine. It was born that way and still is that way even though, in some
children's cases, it has almost been crowded out as the determiner of day to
day behavior.

So, as in the intervue with Beverly, when I sense that we've had enough of
the light distress, I switch the intervue - usually by asking another starter
question. Because I have established that I am the one managing the intervue,
this is almost always accepted easily by the child. In fact I sense that one
reason children tend to feel so safe in our intervues is that they sense that
I won't let this be a time when we dwell on the fearful things in their lives.

Another way I help children move from the pockets of uneasiness in their
lives is to nudge them gently away from any self-putdowns that come up when
they feel honestly-given, specific self-affirmation in the intervue. Often
the way that I move away from children's self-putdowns is simply to accept what
the child says but not pick up on it in my line of questioning. Sometimes,
however, I make this a time when I "stick up" for the real self as I did with
Rob Cohen. Remember when I asked thirteen-year-old Rob the Magic Shoes Question and he responded (Chapter V):

Rob: My answer is going to sound really weird. I'd like to extend (those
     magic shoes) to size 19. I always wanted to hold a record. A guy in
     the army has size 18.

REN: Why do you want to hold a record?

Rob: When I went to camp, at Jamesville, I was unofficially the world's record
     holder for getting the most 10-leaf clovers in anyone's life. I guess I
     want to hold a record because I'll be known publically as the world record
     holder.

REN: Yes, but like if you have size 19 shoes, won't people also laugh at you?

Rob: Yes, but just as long as I'd be recognized - that's the point.

REN: But, how could you be recognized for what you've really got going for
     you right now?

Rob: Don't know.

REN: I mean the headlines would read something like "Weather predictor at 13 beats the multimillion dollar weather bureaucracy" or "13-year-old stock market whiz never fails"

Rob: How about "13-year-old in County League hits record field goal in big game."

REN: But my headlines were real possibilities, your headline was fiction.

One reason I am using this illustration from my intervue with Rob is that I assume that you know quite a bit about Rob's and my relationship as I described it in Chapter Five. As I said above, usually I don't argue with a child when he or she indulges in self-putdowns in an intervue. I just use my prerogative as the intervue manager to shift us away from the putdown. In Rob's case over the months, we had come to the point where we could talk about not putting oneself down. In our intervue I modelled for Rob what later he came to do more and more for himself: stopping his old behavior pattern of resorting to humorous self-putdowns and instead taking the risk of expressing bits of self-appreciation until this, too, became a way of behaving that was comfortable.

Along with switching my line of questioning because I want to nudge the child away from mild distress or self-putdowns, I often switch my questioning line because I feel that we are missing some of the particularly enjoyable aspects of the child's real self. I frequently find myself pausing, inside, and running over the real-self areas that I so often enjoy in people and in myself. This leads me to my next starter question. Let me list for you here the real-self areas that I have found I often want to move into in my intervues:

The courageous me... "Think of a time when you were a bit afraid to do something but did it anyway - and were proud of yourself?" This starter question, usually needs to be modelled by the teacher. I think, for instance of how I modelled an answer by saying to Steve, "At first I was reluctant even to think seriously about buying that old caboose - part of me seemed to be saying, 'Bob this isn't a practical thing to do with your savings,' and things like that. I had always easily done special things for others but almost never for myself. But after I wrote the letter bidding on it and had my bid accepted I was so proud that I had the courage to do it."

The warm loving and lovable me... Much of my intervues with Beverly, Sonia, Steve, and Eric found us in this area. "...and what's one reason she liked you, probably?" is a starter question that opens the door to children's feelings of lovableness as they remember special times with people who liked them for what they were; ..."and one thing you like about her?" helps children experience again their loving feelings.

The capable me... "I'm proud of the time I..." models for children an example of something about the teacher that is an expression of his or her capable self. Remember how I told Steve that I was proud that I had thought of the importance of cleaning out those caboose wheel bearings before the railroad man told me to do it? Sometimes the starter, "What's one time that you felt proud of yourself?" brings us into another real-self area at the same time:

The just-fine me... Here the child and I enjoy our essential all-right humanness. We accept honest appreciation from the other and from ourselves. Often, as was the case with Rob, this is the least exercised aspect of one's real self in the daily life routines - which are governed by rules against open expression of appreciation or allow, at best, the "fun? putdown" (Chapter VII). As I mentioned before, teachers seem to have more trouble modelling self-appreciation, in intervues, than any other aspect of their real-from-birth selves.

    <u>The keenly enjoying me...</u> Remember, in my intervue with Eric (Chapter VIII) how I enjoyed his expression of appreciation of me and our intervue, as he told of a memory he didn't want the Giant Memory Machine to take away?

Eric: Don't take away the memory of being here with you.

REN: That makes me feel good...

    Did you know that you had a sunburst of brown inside your eye - right around the black center.

Eric: Yes, and the outside is really hazel.

    As I felt a glow of self-appreciation I found myself noticing the beauty around the center of his eyes. So often in intervues, when we feel our just-fine selves we find ourselves noticing the intricate wonder in all of life. To put it in other words, when you feel the good about yourself you notice the goodness all around. You notice and enjoy your and others' subtle sense of humor, quirky playful selves, the whiff of early-morning mist hanging in the air...

    The intervue seems to be a time when children and I find ourselves enjoying so much that was right there all the time but we just didn't notice it before. And we notice it, during this time of heightened awareness, with the expanded sensitivity that we find so often in babies as they delight in the way our shirt collar feels to the touch, the way that...

    In the intervue we are going in the opposite direction from the need to have increasingly rich and elaborate things like loud stereomusic and expensive cars. We are moving into the wonder of the commonplace - the delightful ways that the corner of Molly's mouth "bloops" when she just begins to smile; the fleeting memory of that morning driving through Nevada that comes up in me when I first smelled the morning air today; the loveliness of the lone flower growing along the chemical soaked railroad right-of-way; the...

    This kind of a reaction from heightened consciousness comes spontaneously so often after we have been appreciating what we are - which is the overall tone of the intervue. But sometimes starter questions which point our attention to special things we take for granted, help. One that I like to use goes, "What is one special thing that one or more of your fingers did for you once? (and my modelling answer might be:) Like the time just this morning when my fingers helped me typewrite how to intervue with children. I'm writing a book about intervueing and things that go along with it. My fingers on the typewriter get down my words almost as fast as I can think of them. My thoughts just flowed this morning. Wow... Hey fingers, thanks! Now, what is one special thing that one or more of your fingers did for you, once?"

    Another line of question that almost always brings out the "keenly enjoying me" is "Tell me the first pleasant memory about..." Here's how this interchange might go.

REN: Tell me the first pleasant memory about something lightly moving.

Karen: The water on the lake one morning last summer at camp. That morning I went down along the lake on the way to breakfast just by myself. Such a neat feeling that... Well, it was just a neat-all-over feeling.

REN: ...wind against your face?

Karen: My first thought isn't about me it's about Sam, our dog, and how his
        ears fly out backward as he keeps his head out of the car moving along.

        <u>The inventive, problem-solving me...</u> I like old Charlie Chan movies. It's
so enjoyable to see how this low-key detective sensitively absorbs the elements
in a complex situation, turns them over and over in his mind and finally comes
up with a tentative solution.
        One of the fascinating human essences is our ability to put known elements
together in unique ways. This kind of creative adaptation is peculiar to human
beings. Animals and plants seem to have a set repertoire of solutions to their
problems. When a new situation presents itself for which the plant or animal
has no solution in stock, it perishes. (Remember the dinosaurs?) Another way
to say this is that human beings are uniquely adaptive to new situations. This
aspect of the real-from-birth person can be enjoyed in all sorts of contexts
- from creative expression in art, food preparation, writing, mechanical inventiveness, fun, fantasy...
        Usually, I find, children have to be helped to think of themselves as in-
ventive. It's just such an everyday thing that they haven't stopped to enjoy
it before. I do this, again, often by answering the question first, myself.
Consider this example from an interview with eight-year-old Richard - who liked
complex games and gadgets:

REN: Richard, I'll ask myself the next question and then ask it to you. It's
      "What's one time you remember when you were inventive?"

      OK, I'll answer it first. Let's see... Oh sure - a while ago I invented
      an answer to a question someone asked me about my Giant Memory Machine.
      I really had fun doing it. The person asked me: "Where do you keep your
      Giant Memory Machine when you don't use it in intervues?"

      So I said, "I keep it in four packing cases. There are casters on each of
      them and they hook together too. There is a fifth case that's the electric
      generator and gasoline tank to power it. The Giant Memory Machine is there-
      fore completely portable. I keep it under my apartment. There's a secret
      door there opening to the outside - on the west side of the building. It
      just fits in my Giant Memory Machinemobile. My faithful valet (smile) Kato
      takes care of it...

Rich: (smile) yeah... just like in Batman.

REN: Yes, I did pick up some ideas for my invention from Batman (smile).
      Now, Rich, what comes to you about a time when you were inventive?

Rich: The time I made up this war game that my friend Paul and I played a lot
       last summer.

REN: ...war game?

Rich: Yeah. I got a big sheet of brown paper that nearly filled the place
       next to my bed in my room. It came around a giant piece of glass that
       my dad put in our front window. When I saw that big piece of paper the
       game just came into my head. I drew these islands with cities on them,
       harbors and all that. Then I used bottle tops as ships - the Coke fleet
       and the Pepsi fleet were my two countries. Then each time you threw the
       dice you could take that many inches to move your ships. When a ship was

132

hit you'd turn over the bottle cap.

REN: Like you moved just one ship for the full number of inches?

Rich: No, you could move three ships two inches apiece or one ship six inches.
       By the time Paul saw the game I had rules made up about how to sink the
       other ships and all. Later we added aircraft carriers and planes and a
       lot of stuff.

   The spontaneous playful quirky me... As Rich described, the inventive
idea often first comes out spontaneously or in a playful or quirky way - as an
abrupt twist to the routine. "The spur of the moment" starter questions sometimes brings these special times out. Here's a bit from my intervue with nine-
year-old Steve:

REN: What's some little thing you did on the spur of the moment that made you
      feel good?

Steve: "Spur of the moment?"

REN: Yes, like the time I... Let's see, I remember, when I was writing my
      letter telling the caboose owner why I wanted the caboose. I found myself
      saying how I wanted to restore it carefully, like it was in the old days.
      That just popped into my head as I was writing that letter. That turned
      out to be one of the reasons he sold it to me. Actually, someone else
      offered him more money than I did.

Steve: You never thought of restoring it and all that, before?

REN: No not exactly. I had been interested in another old railroad car I had
      seen and how it was so beautifully restored but I really hadn't been
      thinking of doing all that careful work myself until I was in the middle
      of that letter.

      Now what about you, Steve, ...something that you did on the spur of the
      moment that turned out well?

Steve: Oh, I do things on the spur of the moment all the time.

REN: What's the first picture that comes into your head?

Steve: Well... Well the picture is of the time I met this old man down the
        street. I just was walking along and saw him with his dog. I said, "Hi."
        He said, "Hi." and I sort of just stood there. He said, "Princess likes
        to be petted," so I came in the yard and petted her.

REN: And this made you feel good...?

Steve: Yeah, his name is Mr. Selzi. We're good friends now. He has this neat
        shop in his basement. I go there a lot - just hang around. I built a
        Star Wars control panel there awhile ago. He had some old dials and stuff
        from a broken machine that he's got there.

REN: How did you get the dials on your machine?

Steve: Cut holes with Mr. Selzi's saber saw. You just drill a hole in the board first and then stick the saber saw blade through the hole and saw the big hole for the dial.

REN: How did you learn to use the saber saw?

Steve: He showed me. I can only use the fine-toothed blades though. The blades with the big teeth are too dangerous.

"Well the picture is of..." I've found that a good way to help children, like Steve, answer a question is to say, "Tell me about the first picture that comes into your head." This starts children's thinking with the specific and avoids the problem of unconsciously getting mired down in pre-articulation organizing steps. Before children can express something with specific feeling, often they need to "get the picture," and sort it out. This logjam of thoughts and jumble of feeling prevents easy and clear expression. So often, then, children tend just not to say anything, or move away from the spontaneous clear expression of their feelings.

If I can help children begin with disjointed parts of the "picture" as it flits around in their minds I find that they stay at the level of spontaneous feeling; they seem easily to get to their point, too, because they sort it all out as they talk about the picture. I can help them do that as I listen, question, and support them in getting it all out. Here's an excerpt from my intervue with six-year-old Connie who needed, I felt, more than my question to help her express feelings of self appreciation. I modelled a response for her to teach her the "What's the picture?" way to begin expressing feelings of self appreciation. We were about the middle of our intervue and I asked Connie:

REN: Connie, what's one thing that you like about yourself?

Connie: Don't know.

REN: OK, I'll go first. When I answer this kind of question, I first try to tell about the picture I get in my mind when I think of something that I like about myself. If the picture isn't about something that I like about myself I wait until the next picture comes as I keep repeating the question, "...one thing I like about myself...?"

Let's see... One thing I like about myself...? Oh yes, I'm getting a picture. I was in my car this morning coming down here to the school. As I drove along on the way I found myself thanking a lot of people I saw. Just felt like doing that. ...well, about five people I guess. I just thanked them for the beautiful things about them that I saw.

Connie: Were they people that you knew?

REN: No, I was in my car and they didn't hear me. I remember one woman who had such beautiful hair. Another person looked so natural - like the sunshine and freshness. Another person was smiling and it made me smile. I sort of thanked them for bringing their beauty into my sight, I guess.

...yes... I guess what I like about myself is... I know what it is - that I don't miss a lot of the beauty in the world that is all around me. Sometimes I do miss a lot but usually I don't.

OK, Connie, what's the first picture that comes into your mind when you ask yourself, "Something I like about myself?"

Connie: Well, it's about this ring here on my finger. I was at a birthday party really really near Easter. We were going around collecting eggs and the eggs had prizes in them. And I found the one with the plastic ring in it. But one day that ring broke. And I was very very sad. I went to the craft store one day with my mother. We found a lady selling rings. My mommy put my hand on the big thing she was selling them on - the table. My mommy said, "Are there any rings that would fit one of these fingers?" And the lady put on the smallest ring on my little finger. It fit and that's how I had my ring.

REN: If you wanted to tell your mommy how you feel about all that, now, but you couldn't just say "Thanks," what's one thing that comes to your mind that you'd like to say to her?

Connie: I love the ring (smile).

REN: So one thing you like about yourself is...?

Connie: How I remember the times that I loved my mommy special.

The question, "What's the first picture that comes into your mind...?" has helped so many children say one thing that they appreciate about themselves as they deal with the pre-articulation logjam - the logjam that often seems so blocking as they try to override the old self-doubting recordings which lead us to withdraw from self-affirmation.

"Like the time...?" is another phrase I use a lot to help children get into their answers to intervue questions. This, again, helps the child get away from the tendency to organize his or her answer before speaking. It helps the child move right into a picture that is in her or his mind. It takes away the "big deal" aspect of it all - I just want the child to tell me about the time...

"What's one thing that..." is another helpful phrase. Again, I can't emphasize enough how important it is to help the child to answer a question by just thinking of <u>one</u> thing and not necessarily the most important or best thing. Almost always when I ask the child a self-appreciative question I preface it with "What is one..." I might ask: "What's one thing about you, you like? Doesn't have to be the most important - just one...?

Another phrase that I find myself using often, in this case at the end of our intervue is, "So what's one thing that you're looking forward to?" This helps us carry over our sense of well-being and raised consciousness - carry it over to the prospect of leaving and dealing with the routines and cares of the day. When I model the response to this question I try to pick a little thing to look forward to - something that will remind the child of the nifty little things that are ahead for her or him.

Here's the ending of an intervue with Cal, age eight-years. I had just modelled my response to the "one thing you're looking forward to" question.

REN: So, Cal, we'll have to go back to school now. But before we do, tell me something that you're looking forward to - something that you feel sure will happen.

Cal: (Quickly) -(no hesitation.) My father's birthday tommorow.

REN: One reason you're looking forward to that?

Cal: We always have chocolate crumbles birthday cake.

    All of these phrases and starter questions have one thing in common: They help children get right to their feelings. They are at the other extreme from leading children or yourself to self-analysis or detached description.
    To avoid moving away from feelings I remember one teacher's note pasted on her tape recorder:

NO ANALYSIS PLEASE

This teacher saw from her transcribed intervues, that she was spending time leading children away from their feelings by such questions as "How do you think that you learned to 'hang in' with friends?" or "Why did you decide to go to the Hidden Valley Camp?" This teacher quickly learned that the intervue was not a time to inquire into why you behave as you do; it was not a time to burden the teacher with listening to lengthy descriptions; it was a time to enjoy, appreciate and feel the real-from-birth self in each child, in yourself.
    Now I feel that you have in hand the best from my experience to guide you if you want to begin intervuing with children. Most of the teachers I train in intervuing, tape record each of their intervues and then type the ones they like for us to go over in our training class. Try that. And don't think that each intervue has to be a gem. I hope that you won't expect your intervues to turn out like the examples in this book, right away. I've been intervuing for years. I have taught myself; I hope you will take the time to do that for yourself. One of the best ways I have learned is to transcribe some of my intervues and share them with other teachers. I have found, also, that when I type the intervues (transcribed from notes or a tape recording) I go back over the scene - with much more perspective. I often find myself reflecting on and enjoying aspects of the child (and myself) that I wasn't consciously aware of during our intervue. Transcribing the intervue gives me "space" to turn over in my mind thoughts and feelings that don't have time to assert themselves clearly during the intervue when my attention is on the immediate scene and the child.
    It's so important for me, during the intervue, to be keenly attentive to the child - each word he or she says, gestures, squirming in the chair... Once I've switched gears into involvement with the child and our intervue I try to keep the attention on the child unless I'm modelling a question. For example when the child is sharing a feeling I usually accept and enjoy what the child has to say without bending the light of attention back to me with something like, "Yes, I'm that way too. Why just this week..."
    And what do I do when the intervue just isn't working? I stop. Quite often I tell a child that this is the end of part one in our intervue. Then we pick it up on another day. Sometimes this is just what the child needs as then at the second intervue he or she knows what to expect and can relax and get into it better. Quite often this is better for me too. Tomorrow I won't be feeling some of the uneasiness from my old recordings that I might be feeling today.
    So... Pick up your tape recorder or your notepad and begin.

CHAPTER 9

WE PARENTS

How we might share with our children the adventure of growing
from our real selves.

As I have been writing this book I have been sharing manuscript drafts
with some of my students - elementary teachers who enroll in courses with titles
like "Listening to Children." Many of these teachers look at this book and our
discussions both as teachers and as parents. Some of the teachers are just
beginning to raise their own children.

We often choose to exchange journals about our own children as being parents is such an important part of ourselves. In this chapter I've brought together thoughts which I've written in several of these journals. I call it my
journal to a young teacher named Tracey. Here is the journal:*

SCHOOL OF EDUCATION - SYRACUSE UNIVERSITY

MEMORANDUM

TO: Tracey   DATE: 11/25/78
SUBJECT: FROM: REN

I got your journal last night when I got home.
It's now 6:30 in the morning. I have a few minutes before I pick up Robin
for breakfast. We go out to breakfast a couple of times or more most of the
weeks. She has to be back for her ride to high school at about 7:30 so we like
to get going by 7:00.
It's dark outside. My typewriter is facing the window so I can see myself
in the glass. The light is on the left side of my face.
I think of sitting here at this same electric typewriter thirteen years
ago with my three-year-old Dusty on my lap. She would tell me what to type and
I'd type it - letters to so many of our relatives. Never have done so much
corresponding before or after that nifty time. Some of the evenings I'd be
tired and I could feel the tension of the day registering in the muscles on my
calves, my eyes. But that time with Dusty was still a delight. Oh yes, I was
interested in teaching children to read and write and it interested me how fast
she was learning this way. (She learned to read in a few months and soon she
was typing many of the words that we were using.) But... Yes, (I see myself
smiling in the mirror-window in front of me) it was that neat feeling I always
got - how Dusty looked forward to coming up and "writing" with me on my lap.
I'm smiling now. It's always felt so neat to hug Dusty, to feel the affirmation
of our... Well, to express to her what words just couldn't; how my old recordings
just were standing still; how I was loving the way she just seemed to be so
satisfied there on my lap. Both of us were there in present-time, savoring every
minute of it in a matter-of-fact-way.
It's a quarter to seven. Have to be off to pick up Robin. I'll go on with
this later.

---

*I like to write on memo blanks as this tends to get away from the "Dear Tracey"
personal letter format. This way we avoid much of the put-it-off-until-tomorrow
uneasiness associated with letter writing.

It's now Wednesday morning, the day after I wrote the above to you. It's 7:05 on the clock. Rained last night, but just a bit. There is a still fall feeling around even though most of the leaves are on the ground. The tree just outside my window has a leaf or two on most of its twigs - waiting for the next strong wind to blow them off. ...no wind that I can sense so far this morning. ...a few puddles around - just enough to mirror some of the lines from the tree branches overhead. A bird just flew into the tree. As she came at the tree she spread her wings wide and flat toward the tree, stopping most of her forward motion. Then bloop - up she lifted herself against the resistance of the air and dropped onto that branch. She's gone now. Left while I was typing this.

As I worked yesterday, I found myself thinking of writing this note to you. Your question "What are a few things you might say to this new parent so that the grass of Tim's real self won't be confined to the cracks...?" came in and out of my head. As I was driving along yesterday morning I got the idea that this is something I might like to share with others, too, and perhaps write as part of a last chapter for parents in God Bless the Grass. We'll see what comes out of this journal but my thought now is to give your question top priority for the next few days during this special time in the morning when I can sit here and think, feel, and write.

Just stopped and went into the kitchen to clean my glasses. Saw a spot on one lens as I was looking at the page here in the typewriter. When I wrote about giving top priority to your question and writing it for others, I found that I noticed the spot. Felt a distraction from the clarity I felt before. Guess I suddenly got cold feet - some fear came up... Don't think the fear was around the question of "Will I have something to say?" because I feel that I have plenty to say. It's more that it was triggered because I wonder if I can express the fullness... I don't want to express what I feel just half-way. It's too important; too special for me; I want to do this just right. I guess too, that I don't want to propose some new theory of parenting or something like that. I'm more interested in what makes sense to me rather than what doesn't make sense to me in others' views. I want to talk about what I have learned - what has been such a meaningful part of my life. I want to talk with parents about our experiences and our emotions as parents. I want this to grow out of their reading my book, from the case studies, from my own autobiographical material, and from my conclusions after I have worked with so many children and parents. By first thinking about these issues in the school setting, parents can approach the tough questions, the self-doubting areas of parenting more clearly. That won't be so close to home. Thus we can talk in the last chapter, for a bit, about our own parenting.

Now that I've expressed that, I feel in touch with the real me again - in present time and not cloudy-headed from the closing-me-down uneasiness that came up just a few minutes ago. It's neat how what I just did can bring me into present-time and away from the chilling old "music" from the recordings which were laid in so long ago. It feels good not to be all that afraid to be afraid.

Well, let's see... What has this talk about fearfulness to do with your helping Tim grow up in touch with his real-from-birth self? What strikes me is that the fear of being afraid, in this deep sense, is the single most important reason that people adapt to manipulation by the approval-givers. Later this often leads to real-self-defeating behavior as we've seen in so many of my examples in God Bless the Grass. The fear of coming close to the self-doubting uneasiness of those old recordings is chilling; elaborate subtle "rules" have evolved to keep us from getting close to that fear, such as the rule that we must try not to experience the fear feelings. These rules make it seem that the well adjusted, "have-it-all-together" ones don't have this fear. Tim needs to see that you feel fear but you can deal with it - you can stay open and sensitive to all the feelings around and in you, including the uneasy fearful ones. He needs to see you "letting it out" - all the ways that you, too, can express your spontaneous warmth and love; your tears when they well up; your laughter that just happens; your sensitive noting of detail in the reflection from a rain puddle; the meaning-to-the-person in the ever-so-slight quiver of her eyelid when she speaks... And, he needs to feel needed... ...needed because you can learn from him - the fresh young person who hasn't been conditioned by years of "the rules," as you have. He can experience your delight in how easy it is for him to draw from his real self - "be" with open warmth, pride, feelings of capability, letting the hurt out with crying, trembling, with...

He is going to need your model of staying open and sensitive in spite of the fear feelings; he's going to need his feeling of being needed as inspiration and example to you of being in touch with one's real self. He's going to need that support in his life because it will be just a matter of a few months until he begins to pick up the dominant cultural message: <u>Be Cool. Don't show that you feel afraid. Don't be weak and experience fear</u>. "Oh no," you might say, "he won't pick that up because he's <u>my</u> child;" but he'll get it. He'll get it from such little things as a fond well-meaning grandparent's picking him up when he cries with the "Now now, don't cry" message given with full love and beautiful comfort when he needs it, but passing on at the same time, the cultural dictum that it's not OK to let out an expression of fear; you're not strong when you do. The message from our way-of-life adds up to this: "Close down your sensitivity when you experience fear." I think of the aperature of a camera which lets in less and less light as you close it down in its place over the lens.

Let Tim help you with this. As I said before, he needs to know that you treasure his being in touch with his feelings, his real self. Watch him experience the full range of feelings. Watch him laugh, cry, shake, be wide-eyed in wonder, chuckle with you as you share with him the little things all around, as you sense how he needs you and how you need him. When you are with Tim, allow his presence to support you in drawing from your real-from-birth self. Share with him your delight in the morning sunshine as it inches across the lawn, pushing back the shadow and changing the frosty silver to rich green. Allow yourself to let out your warmth and loving. ...that hug, that ride for Tim on your shoulders, touching and holding him when he seems to be afraid and vulnerable, those special minutes when he's cuddled next to you as you read one of your favorite picture books to him. Let Tim help you experience your real self. He's tuned into the essential humanness simply because it's not blunted yet; it's not set aside in his need to protect himself against uneasiness - the uneasiness that seems so chilling partly because he'll receive the message not to confront that fear, not to let it out, not to experience it. It <u>must</u> be terrible if you aren't allowed to go near it.

As you and Tim continue to grow, make special times so that the two of you can delight regularly in your real selves. For me, those special times were on Saturday mornings and into the afternoons when the girls and I went off to the library, to our favorite junk shop and to all sorts of adventures. These were days when I allowed the quirky, fun-loving, warm "where are you at?" and "this is the way I feel" real me to come out. Pretty soon little rituals set in, too, like one of the girls walking on the two-foot-high wall next to the sidewalk on the way to the library while I held her hand as we skipped along; she feeling almost as tall as I was. Then, as I mentioned above, the nightly story-reading time would be a special time for us - when we experienced so much beauty with artists like Robert McCloskey in his book <u>Time of Wonder</u>. Yes, Tracey, spend some time in that special island of feelings and close sharing called the children's room of the public library.

As the girls have grown and as times have changed, we've kept our special times when we might share our real selves. The girls are fourteen and sixteen now. Rather than being with both girls at the same time I usually find I like to spend special times first with one girl and then with the other. I've found that breakfasts are particularly special - when we are closer to our real selves; when the needs and pressures of the day haven't stepped up the recordings' volume. But lunches and dinners can be special, too, as times when we find it easy to share who we really are. How much I enjoyed feeling the courage to fight-against-the-tide that was coming through to me from one of the girls as we were sitting in a sandwich shop at a shopping mall not so long ago. When she needed to be assertive with her friends she was finding plenty of strength even though it didn't feel very comfortable to her much of the time.

One of the reasons I enjoy intervuing with school children so much is that I can enter into the reality of sharing our essential humanness. I need that. Children help me and I help them. The children want more intervues than I can take time to do. They need them too.

In our intervues we express appreciation of ourselves and of the other person. This need of mine and of the children can be an important part of your relationship with Tim. I've said a lot about expressing appreciation, affirming, in the book. I won't repeat myself here except to hope that you delight, with Tim, in some of those specific times when you can feel proud of yourself. What about YOUR saying in so many ways, "Hey, Tim, look what I can do!"? I know that you'll find it easy to share in his proudness when he says that to you about himself. I find myself sharing, with my girls, spontaneous proud feelings when they come up - and they do often. I find that both of the girls help me - remind me often of how I must be proud of such and such. Then, too, within the context of our self-appreciation it's easier for us to let out spontaneously the times when we're "stuck," when something seems to be in the way of our doing what we want to do; when we're tired and for the moment feeling easily discouraged, perhaps close to the old recordings' self-doubting aura.

This brings up another thing in my mind - what about when you or Tim feel angry feelings toward the other person? Yes, what about that? You're hurting when you feel those angry feelings. Your hurt is further intensified because of the conflict between the love that you feel and, at the same time the angry thoughts you have about the other person. I think of the times I have had strong angry feelings toward one or both of my children. I think of that winter day when I had been having a nagging achy cold for three weeks. I drove over to pick up the girls at a ski hill about a mile from here. Can't remember the particulars but the feeling as I got out of the car was that I was alone, no one cared a damn about me... On the way back to my apartment maybe the girls were bickering between themselves, I don't remember. Anyway I found myself just yelling out "Stop it! Just STOP it! I've just had enough!" There was silence, then one of the girls got mad at me - started to argue with something like, "What have I done?" in what came across to me as a pouting "You're so unfair." Well, we drove on and I just felt yukky and lousy - and more alone - and more mad. I remember stopping the car in front of the apartment and telling the girls to stay seated for a few minutes. I remember stopping, asking myself how I really felt and then found myself blurting out something about feeling this feeling of "nobody gives a damn about me." I remember tears coming to my eyes. I remember the silence in the car. ... I remember saying something about how I knew it really wasn't that way but that's the way it felt right then.

After that I found myself talking with the girls, later in the day, about how a lot of uneasiness came flooding up out there in that parking lot at the ski slope. Can't remember all the details of what we said. But I remember the picture - of our talking in front of the fireplace where I had built a glowing fire.

I don't want to leave this scene before I say something about what it illustrates. I think it illustrates what I meant by saying that under anger there always is hurting. It really helps me to know that and to act on that. I think that Robin and Dusty were able to sense my hurting, grounded as they were in their love for me. That was what REALLY was going on. Sure, I was being "unfair" probably, in the heat of my anger, but that wasn't really what was at issue for us, as it worked out, when they sensed how I was hurting.

It so often happens that when the angry person gets a chance to express how she or he is hurting then the other person can help by just recognizing how it hurts, at least. For my children and for me this expression of hurting often comes out without words - through tears. Sometimes they don't gush out because all of us have been subjected to the "you're weak if you cry" conditioning. But often tears well up. Our eyes are damp.

I'm saying, Tracey, how important it is to help Tim (and you) let out this deep hurting under the anger - not just the surface accusations and hostility. I have found that I can let out a lot of the deep hurting in my weekly co-counselling (as I've described in the book) and that this lessens, so much, my needs to let it out with my children. But there are times when the strong hurting feelings come up under a froth of anger toward one or both of my children - times when I need to deal with that hurting then and there.

How can we help make our home a safe place where we all feel safe enough with each other to let out our hurting - safe enough from the old recordings' "I'm not measuring up" self-doubting; safe enough to follow the fascination of our quirky real selves spontaneously; safe enough to risk crying when we need to, asking for help when we hurt; safe enough to take the delightful risks of expressing love and support in full measure for each other, for ourselves; safe enough to delight openly in our proud little moments?

One key way I can help us feel this safety is to minimize the stinging feeling of put-downs. I found myself realizing in the early years of my parenting that it hurt me immensely when I experienced one of my girls bringing up hurting in the other through put-downs. I found myself so sensitive to each of my girls, as I delighted in their real-person loveliness, that probably I was more aware of the hurting within one or the other of the girls than she was. "Hey, you guys, I really don't know the ins and outs of this exchange between you - don't know who's the bad guy and all that - but I do know how it hurts in me as I take it in. I don't even know how much it hurts you guys... What you do on your own is your business but when you're with me, putting the other guy down is something that I have real trouble with. Please stop it."

And I didn't leave it all up to them. I did (and do) all that I can to soothe the kind of hurting that one girl might be feeling that results in put-downs coming across to the other. I remember one night we were out shopping. I was with one girl while the other was in the store trying on things. I found myself sensing the "down" hurting feelings in the girl I was with. I steered her into the little earring shop sandwiched in between two bigger stores because "I think this is one of those nights that you need something special - just for you. Let's see if we can find a pair of earrings that go with your neat smile that I enjoy so much."

I think I'll stop now Tracey. Have to make it to a 10:30 meeting. See you in class on Tuesday.

So, dear reader of this book, where does all this leave us? It certainly suggests to you, most probably, that for me being a parent and being a teacher are all part of just "being" in the sense of taking guidance from one's real

141

self and being helped to do that by my children while I help them.

As I was sitting here mulling over the journal to Tracey, I thought how inescapably I find myself living in two worlds while at the same time living in the world where they merge. Take the question of put-downs, for example: My daughters are teenagers. As I see it, the teenage world that they find at junior and senior high school is saturated with the put-down; at best people use the "fun? put-down" that I talked about in Chapter VII but often I hear what I just thought of calling "chain put-downs." (Like chain smoking) I don't feel moved, here, to talk about how bad this is, but I am struck by how different it is from the neat times when I'm just with Dusty and Robin or with one of them.

I find myself sharing with them (as I find myself sharing with the children I teach at school) how the way we are relating IS different, quite different, from the ways we usually express appreciation to others, to ourselves, at school, or on the job and other places where people play roles and wear facades that hide their real selves, where judging is in the air and where people are kept in line by the approval-givers. These are places where the "I'm not quite measuring up" fear tones from the old recordings are fanned.

I find that many of the people, caught up in settings which repress honest expression of appreciation, enjoy very much even brief times when they can be close to their real-from-birth selves, when they can relate to this lovely humanness in another. I'm saying that I don't find people fighting me and arguing that what I want is wrong. Most of them are quick to show by their actions that they want it too. (It feels good, for example, when someone helps me remember some of the times when I've been proud of myself as a parent.) But what I find is these people saying skeptically "Sure, all that is fine but that's not the way things are."

But they are wrong when they say "That's not the way things are" if they are implying that the grass isn't growing through the cracks. It isn't hard at all, for example, in an intervue with an elementary schooler, a teenager, or a college sophomore, to enjoy our proud feelings openly. Just think of the intervues in this book. Sure, it's important to know how to do it - how to help yourself and the child feel safe enough to follow these different "rules," but I teach that to people all the time and they learn quickly, too. It's not all that hard to make safe-to-be-one's-real self "inside centers" in the middle of a school or in the hurly burly life of a parent.

I learned early in my life, when I began teaching, that I could have an "inside" way of living with children in our classroom. Then, when my own children came into my life I found myself having "inside centers" in my parenting relationships with my own children, as I have been recalling on these pages. Then when I moved to found our own elementary school I expanded those "inside centers" that at first were just inside one classroom and in home relationships to a whole school full of opportunities for people to draw from their real selves. In all those settings I felt aware - quite aware - of the "outside centers" in our lives (like the local playground, the neighborhood culture, the wider friendship patterns of the children, the varied home scenes in childrens' lives).

Relating with Tim at home can be one of those "inside centers" where you express your appreciation, your hurting when it inescapabily bubbles up and interferes with what you want in your relationship with Tim. You can delight in your own neat quirky spontaneous humor, his courage in asking for help at one of those times when it's hard to do so. You can enjoy.

As Tim grows up you will probably see him involved in things like put-down games with his junior high school friends. There will be plenty of times when you have to "bear it" as you transport a carload of young teens to the movies. That's part of one of the "outside" centers that Tim will be involved in.

There will be many times when you want to step in and help Tim as you sense his feeling hurt and his not knowing that he is hurting. He might feel "down," angry, or tend to "turn off" his feelings. This might happen a lot in the swirl of playing with his friends.

These are times when he is hurting but is only in touch with his reactions to his pain (the anger, the withdrawal, the need for approval from his friends at almost any cost.) One way that you can help Tim at times like these is not to be judgmental - not to give way to the anger that you might feel about the pressing demands from this outside center in his life; anger against his being pushed so hard to deny the voice of his real self. One way that I find to keep from being judgmental is to let out a lot of my own frustrations and feelings of powerless hurting in sessions with my co-counselor or with a safe-for-me-feeling friend. It also helps me to understand where it all comes from - what brings out children's apparent self-protective insensitivity, the awkward acceptance of the deny-your-real-self rules I experience in children's outside centers. It comes from the old recordings "Am I measuring up?" fearful music in each of the children. It is heightened by the conflict children feel at different times and with differing degrees of conscious awareness - conflict between the open warmth, pride, and sense of wonder from their real selves and the "be cool," "appear to have it have it all together" coverup demanded by their peer culture apeing the adult culture; conflict between hurt and anger from being manipulated by approval-givers and then turning around to judge their own worth by how good they are at doing that to others - how good they are at feeling power through giving and withholding approval; conflict between knowing the beautiful warmth of hugging and touching those they are close to and the chilling cultural message that this isn't quite right except with one's close opposite-sex partner; conflict from...

I find, however, that fortunately, I'm not expected to enter the swirl of children's banter which comes from and seeks to protect young people from this conflict. I can drive the car or appear to be following my own thoughts in other settings, seemingly apart from what's going on around me. Most of the children prefer it that way.

Lecturing the children, setting rules in your car about "no put-downs" or getting across, in some other way, your disapproval of their behavior just won't help Tim at all. I've tried that and found that what came across to most of the children was that "Mr. Newman doesn't like us."

But, as I've said above, you can have a sharing-of-our-real-selves kind of atmosphere in the "inside centers" you have set up in your life, perhaps around the family dinner table. What Tim can be learning is what it's like in both his "inside" and "outside centers." Then he will, in effect, be able to choose how to make sense of it all by himself in his choice of friends, in his moving into a "crowd" or perhaps in his learning how to have "inside centers" in a definitely "outside" setting like the typical high school. Then, perhaps, he won't feel that he has to be in such-and-such a crowd and shun other friends. Much of Tim's strengths will come from his deep sureness that he's OK - that he has the root feeling of "measuring up" and is comfortable with himself. Much of this you can give him when he's a pre-schooler. Much of this you can help him experience as he feels openly his fun quirky self, his warm loving self, his keen sensitivity to wondrous little things all around, his... ...as he feels your enjoyment of his real self.

You and Tim's teachers can help him experience the real self which is his birthright. You can do it at home and the teachers can do it at school. Both you and his teachers can let Tim help you feel your own pride, your own loving warmth, your wonderment with the stillness at dawn, your fascination with the intuitiveness of a master cabinetmaker at work.

Rest assured that this birthright is as tough and strong as it is gentle and easily bent. It's down there, pushing to get out in more places than just the "cracks." Tim can help us, we can help Tim let this strength prevail in our lives and in the lives of those we touch.